The Sovereignty and Goodness of God, Together with the Faithfulness of His Promises Displayed

Being a Narrative of the Captivity
and Restoration of Mrs. Mary Rowlandson
and Related Documents

Related Titles in
THE BEDFORD SERIES IN HISTORY AND CULTURE
Advisory Editors: Natalie Zemon Davis, Princeton University
Ernest R. May, Harvard University
Lynn Hunt, University of California
at Los Angeles
David W. Blight, Amherst College

The Sovereignty and Goodness of God, Together with the Faithfulness of His Promises Displayed

Being a Narrative of the Captivity
and Restoration of Mrs. Mary Rowlandson
and Related Documents

Edited with an Introduction by

Neal Salisbury

Smith College

BEDFORD/ST. MARTIN'S   Boston   ♦   New York

For Bedford/St. Martin's
President and Publisher: Charles H. Christensen
General Manager and Associate Publisher: Joan E. Feinberg
History Editor: Katherine E. Kurzman
Developmental Editor: Kate Sheehan Roach
Managing Editor: Elizabeth M. Schaaf
Production Editor: Stasia Zomkowski
Copyeditor: Carolyn Ingalls
Indexer: Steve Csipke
Text Design: Claire Seng-Niemoeller
Cover Design: Richard Emery Design, Inc.
Cover Art: Courtesy of the Trustees of the Boston Public Library, Boston.

Library of Congress Catalog Card Number: 96–86785

Copyright © 1997 by Bedford Books

Manufactured in the United States of America.

5

n   m   l

For information, write: Bedford/St. Martin's, 75 Arlington Street, Boston, MA 02116 (617-399-4000)

ISBN: 0–312–11151–7   (paperback)

Acknowledgments

Figure 1. Sourcemap: *Handbook of North Americans* (gen. ed., William C. Sturtevant), vol. 15: *The Northeast,* ed. Bruce G. Trigger (Washington: Smithsonian Institution, 1978), p. 161.

Figure 2. Courtesy of Chapin Library of Rare Books, Williams College, Williamstown, Massachusetts.

Figure 3. Courtesy of the American Antiquarian Society, Worcester, Massachusetts.

Figure 4. Courtesy of Strawberry Banke, Portsmouth, New Hampshire.

Figure 5. Photo by Walter Doyle, Clinton, Massachusetts. Courtesy of the Lancaster Public Library, Lancaster Massachusetts.

Figure 6. Courtesy of Museum of Art, Rhode Island School of Design, Providence, Rhode Island. Gift of Mr. Robert Winthrop.

Figure 7. Courtesy of the American Antiquarian Society, Worcester, Massachusetts.

Figure 8. Courtesy of the American Antiquarian Society, Worcester, Massachusetts.

Figure 9. Courtesy of the American Antiquarian Society, Worcester, Massachusetts.

Figure 10. Courtesy of the American Antiquarian Society, Worcester, Massachusetts.

Figure 11. Courtesy of the Trustees of the Boston Public Library, Boston.

Figure 12. Sourcemap: Henry S. Nourse, ed., *The Narrative of the Captivity and Restoration of Mrs. Mary Rowlandson* (Lancaster, Mass., 1903), facing p. 76.

Figure 13. Courtesy of Plimoth Plantation, Inc., Plymouth, Massachusetts.

Figure 14. Courtesy of the American Antiquarian Society, Worcester, Massachusetts.

Figure 15. Courtesy of the Trustees of the Boston Public Library, Boston.

Foreword

The Bedford Series in History and Culture is designed so that readers can study the past as historians do.

The historian's first task is finding the evidence. Documents, letters, memoirs, interviews, pictures, movies, novels, or poems can provide facts and clues. Then the historian questions and compares the sources. There is more to do than in a courtroom, for hearsay evidence is welcome, and the historian is usually looking for answers beyond act and motive. Different views of an event may be as important as a single verdict. How a story is told may yield as much information as what it says.

Along the way the historian seeks help from other historians and perhaps from specialists in other disciplines. Finally, it is time to write, to decide on an interpretation and how to arrange the evidence for readers.

Each book in this series contains an important historical document or group of documents, each document a witness from the past and open to interpretation in different ways. The documents are combined with some element of historical narrative — an introduction or a biographical essay, for example — that provides students with an analysis of the primary source material and important background information about the world in which it was produced.

Each book in the series focuses on a specific topic within a specific historical period. Each provides a basis for lively thought and discussion about several aspects of the topic and the historian's role. Each is short enough (and inexpensive enough) to be a reasonable one-week assignment in a college course. Whether as classroom or personal reading, each book in the series provides firsthand experience of the challenge — and fun — of discovering, recreating, and interpreting the past.

Natalie Zemon Davis
Ernest R. May
Lynn Hunt
David W. Blight

Preface

Mary Rowlandson's *The Sovereignty and Goodness of God,* first published in 1682, is an English Puritan woman's account of her captivity among Indians during Metacom's War (1675–76) in southeastern New England. Although Metacom's War was well documented, most written descriptions of it were provided by clergymen and other English leaders. Their accounts help us understand the chronology of events and illustrate what might be called the "official," or at least the elite, English viewpoints. But those accounts tell us little about the experiences and perspectives of ordinary colonists and even less about how Native Americans perceived the conflict.

Rowlandson's narrative is quite unlike the others. Often termed the first "Indian captivity narrative," *Sovereignty* is far more complex than the kind of formulaic popular literature characterizing most works in that genre. It is a powerful rendering of a cross-cultural encounter under the most trying and extreme of circumstances, in which the protagonist/author finds the very boundaries of her cultural identity being tested. The outcome of that test, as Rowlandson relates it, graphically reveals just what the limits of toleration of different peoples and cultures actually were for many, probably most, colonists. In this respect, her narrative by itself offers little direct insight into Native American perspectives on the conflict. Nevertheless, it does offer one person's perspective and, upon our careful scrutiny, tells us more about cultural identities and boundaries in colonial New England than what a casual glance would reveal. The fact that *Sovereignty* is also the first North American publication by a living woman makes it still more interesting, especially because the issue of gender roles and identity lies just beneath its surface. And finally, because Mary Rowlandson came from one of many English towns located adjacent to a Native American community, her narrative reflects the breakdown of what had once been neighborly ties between the two peoples.

Scholars studying Rowlandson's text have been limited by having read it either in relation to other Puritan writings, to later captivity narratives, or to other writers who were women. This edition seeks to present *Sovereignty* in relation to Rowlandson's life and to the world in which she lived and wrote and in which her narrative was first read. The text follows that of the earliest surviving edition of *Sovereignty,* the second edition, or "addition," as the title page terms it, published in Cambridge, Massachusetts, in 1682. All but four pages of the first edition, published earlier the same year in Boston, have been lost. Other recent editors have elected either to publish the fourth edition (London, 1682), which was the earliest attempt to "modernize" Rowlandson's remarkable prose, or have modernized her still further in hopes of making her more accessible to modern readers. The Bedford Books edition proceeds on the assumption that the closest possible approximation to Rowlandson's original text will give readers a feeling for the power and rhythm that imbued it and made it so appealing to contemporaries.

To introduce readers more fully to Rowlandson's world, her narrative is supplemented by seventeen related documents. One document is her husband Joseph's final sermon, which accompanied the narrative in its earliest editions, and another is an account of a later captivity that intersected with Rowlandson's in an interesting way. The remainder concern Metacom's War, and most relate in one way or another to Native American experiences during that war. Several are written by native people themselves; and some of the others, though recorded by non-Indians, attempt to represent native voices. These documents introduce a wide range of perspectives on the war and on Anglo-Indian relations in late seventeenth-century New England. At the same time, they introduce some kinds of documents that are little known to students and indeed to many scholars. As I have done on occasion in Rowlandson's narrative, I have altered spelling and punctuation in some of the documents in order to render them readable and relatively clear as to their meaning.

The introductory essay is intended to provide background on the historical contexts within which Rowlandson experienced her captivity and later wrote and published. The essay presents her life in connection with the emigration of English Puritans to America, with early relations between natives and colonizers, and with the subsequent transformation of those relations in ways that culminated in all-out war in 1675. Indeed, the essay situates both her writing and the publishing of her narrative in the context of postwar New England and the struggle over how the war would be remembered by colonists. Above all, the introduction tries to suggest the complexity of issues surrounding Rowlandson's experience as they relate to cross-cultural dynamics in seventeenth-century New England.

ACKNOWLEDGMENTS

Many people have helped make this edition a reality. From Bedford Books, I received enormous support, helpful suggestions, and practical advice from Chuck Christensen, Sabra Scribner, Neils Aaboe, Kate Sheehan Roach, Katherine Kurzman, Elizabeth Schaaf, and Stasia Zomkowski. My research tasks were eased by the resourceful assistance of Ann Lattinville and Allison Wenger, whose work was generously supported by the Smith College Committee on Faculty Compensation and Development, and by the staffs of the Smith College Interlibrary Loan Service and the incomparable American Antiquarian Society. Most of the research and writing was completed at the Society while I held a National Endowment for the Humanities Fellowship there during a sabbatical leave from Smith College. Although this edition of Rowlandson's narrative is based directly on the second edition (Cambridge, 1682), it owes much to the labors of previous Rowlandson editors, especially Henry S. Nourse, Charles H. Lincoln, and Robert K. Diebold. My knowledge of and thinking about Rowlandson's and related histories have been nourished over the years through exchanges with John Demos, Thomas Doughton, Mary Maples Dunn, Evan Haefli, Deborah Madsen, June Namias, Alice Nash, Barry O'Connell, Ann Marie Plane, David Stewart-Smith, Polly Strong, Kevin Sweeney, Teresa Toulouse, Laurel Thatcher Ulrich, and many of my students at Smith, as well as by the honors thesis defense of Nadene Joy Tabari, Mt. Holyoke College '94, for which I was a reader and examiner along with Don Weber and Amy Kaplan. I am also grateful to Donna Keith Baron, Thomas Doughton, Ed Hood, Holly Izard, Jill Lepre, Maryanne MacLeod, Jenny Lee Pulsipher, and Nadene Tabari for sharing their unpublished writings with me. Finally, the manuscript benefited from the many encouraging comments and constructive criticisms of Janet Coryell, Susan Curtis, Thomas Doughton, James Merrell, Barry O'Connell, and Dana Salisbury.

Neal Salisbury

Contents

Illustrations

The Sovereignty and Goodness of God, Together with the Faithfulness of His Promises Displayed

Being a Narrative of the Captivity
and Restoration of Mrs. Mary Rowlandson
and Related Documents

PART ONE

Introduction: Mary Rowlandson and Her Removes

THE SETTING: METACOM'S WAR (1675–1676)

In proportion to total population, the bloodiest and most destructive war in American history was neither the Civil War, World War II, nor the Vietnam War. It was, rather, a conflict known as Metacom's (or King Philip's) War, for the Wampanoag Indian leader usually seen, somewhat misleadingly, as its instigator. Though confined to a corner of New England and lasting little more than a year, Metacom's War took the lives of about five thousand of the Indians and about two thousand five hundred of the English, roughly 40 and 5 percent, respectively, of the two peoples' populations. Many more on both sides were left seriously wounded, homeless, impoverished, orphaned, widowed, and in the case of the natives, exiled as slaves and refugees. The best known of the war's many captives was Mary Rowlandson, captured in February 1676 when Nipmuc, Narragansett, and Wampanoag Indians attacked the English town of Lancaster, Massachusetts. Rowlandson published an account of her captivity that provides unique and valuable perspectives on a war that stunted colonial New England's territorial expansion and economic growth for a generation and ended the legal and political autonomy of the region's Native Americans.[1]

We tend to think of the many "Indian wars" that punctuate American history as pitting tradition-bound natives against hardy white pioneers, newly arrived from some distant eastern locale in search of new lands. In such scenarios, the two peoples are so set in their predetermined ways that they have little understanding of, or interest in, each other's language and customs. Metacom's War defied that stereotype in several respects. Although the first colonists had moved from England in the east to New England in the west, they had done so more than thirty years before the war broke out. And those early immigrants were now outnumbered by settlers who had been born in New England itself. In fact, Metacom's War was not a war between strangers but rather one between neighbors. For half a century both the Indians and the English had learned much about each other in the course of trading, working, negotiating, socializing, suing, complaining to their leaders about one another, occasionally fighting, and—in a few cases—attending school and church and even living together. So strong were these bonds that when Metacom's War broke out, some Indians fought for the English against other Indians, even against friends and relatives, while others sought to remain neutral.

How could people so familiar with one another have engaged in so wantonly destructive a conflict? Like the Civil War, Metacom's War was one in which peoples who had long coexisted rather abruptly concluded that they could no longer do so peacefully. The English population and its agricultural ways reached a point during the 1660s when continued expansion could come only at the expense of Indians who had already suffered considerable losses of population, primarily from diseases brought by Europeans, and of land. The English were pressuring natives to give up yet more land as well as control over their own communities. These pressures drove many Indians to equate English encroachment on their land with the death of their culture. Other Indians thought that siding with the English was the only realistic means of ensuring their own survival. The war also brought to the surface deepseated resentments by some people on each side toward all those on the other. Some colonists, in particular, translated their hatred into violence against pro-English Indians, resulting in the death and suffering of a considerable number of these Indians and leading many to switch to the anti-English side during the conflict. These developments raised the standing in native eyes of leaders such as Metacom (called "King Philip" by the English) of the Wampanoags and Shoshanim of the Nipmucs, who had long maintained that the English were the inveterate enemies of their people.

We can see how much more deeply rooted the English antagonism toward the Indians was than the reverse when we look at the ways the two peoples accommodated each other during their half-century of coexistence. Although the colonists had adopted corn cultivation and other native practices to facilitate their subsistence, it was the Indians who had done most of the adjusting. While most Indians spoke at least a little English and some even read and wrote it, only a few colonists had mastered Massachusett, Narragansett, or one of the other native tongues of southern New England. English merchants marketed furs procured by Indians and sold the Indians large quantities of English cloth, tools, and other goods. And many English households used Indians as servants, slaves, and wage laborers. The colonists, on the other hand, purchased few native-produced commodities for use in their daily lives and there is no evidence that any English ever put themselves in the position of working for any Indian. Although between one thousand and two thousand Indians converted to Christianity, any colonist engaging in native religious practices would have been regarded by Puritans as devil-worshippers. As such they would could have been punished with death, as were many colonists accused of witchcraft. While Indians were subject to colonial laws and governments in their dealings with non-Indians, the colonies would allow no English person under any circumstances to be bound over to any native community for justice. Moreover, colonial governments strictly enforced the segregation of Indian and English communities.

Underlying these policies and practices was a European belief that human beings were divided into "civilized" and "savage" peoples. European Christians were "civilized" by virtue of their religious, political, and cultural institutions and practices, and stood in sharp contrast to Native Americans and other "savages" who were considered to be religiously superstitious and lacked European hallmarks of "civilization" such as the nation-state and private property. The New England colonists were divided as to whether Indian "savages" were capable of becoming "civilized," and many feared that close and sustained contact between the two peoples could threaten the "civilized" veneer of the English. But all the colonists agreed on the clear superiority of their own culture to that of the natives. In short, the colonists never considered Indians their equals and never relinquished any of the authority by which they claimed to rule their respective territories and the native inhabitants within them.

At the human level, then, Metacom's War was a complicated event, characterized at once by the antagonists' familiarity with one another, the English feeling of superiority to Native Americans, and by a deep

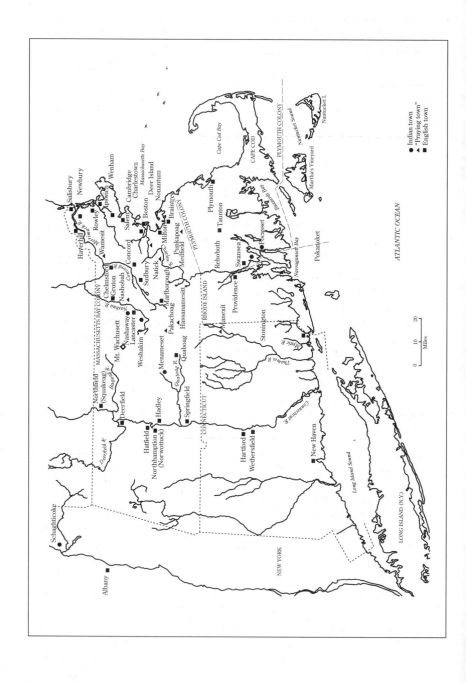

Indian town ●
"Praying town" ▲
English town ■

ATLANTIC OCEAN

PLYMOUTH COLONY

Nantucket Sound

Nantucket I.

Martha's Vineyard

CAPE COD

Cape Cod Bay

Buzzards Bay

Pocasset

Pokanoket

Narragansett Bay

Plymouth

Taunton

Rehoboth

Swansea

Providence

Manexit

Stonington

Mystic R.

Thames R.

New Haven

Wethersfield

Hartford

Connecticut R.

CONNECTICUT

RHODE ISLAND

PLYMOUTH COLONY

Hassanamesitt

Quabaog

Pakachoag

Menameset

Weshakim

Lancaster

Mt. Wachusett

Nashaway

Weston

Northfield
(Squakeag)

Deerfield

Hatfield

Northhampton
(Norwottuck)

Hadley

Springfield

Quaboag R.

Deerfield R.

MASSACHUSETTS BAY COLONY

Schaghticoke

Albany

NEW YORK

LONG ISLAND (N.Y.)

Long Island Sound

Salisbury

Newbury

Wenham

Ipswich

Rowley

Haverhill

Wamesit

Chelmsford

Groton

Nashobah

Concord

Sudbury

Marlborough

Natick

Nashua R.

Concord R.

Merrimac R.

Punkapoag

Medfield

Milton

Braintree

Nonantum

Deer Island

Boston

Charlestown

Cambridge

Salem

Massachusetts Bay

0   10   20
Miles

mutual contempt. While hardly the cause of the war or an adequate explanation of its intensity, people on each side felt that those on the other had betrayed them by violating the unwritten terms of their earlier coexistence. Such feelings undoubtedly heightened the animosity and cruelty that they visited on one another.

MARY ROWLANDSON AND HER NARRATIVE

Of the several dozen contemporary accounts of Metacom's War, the one offering the deepest insights into the war as a human experience is Mary Rowlandson's *The Sovereignty and Goodness of God* (1682). Mary Rowlandson was little known outside the small town of Lancaster, Massachusetts, until the day in February 1676 during the war when a party of Indians attacked the town, seizing her, her three children, and nineteen of their neighbors. For the next three months, she lived as a captive among Nipmucs, Narragansetts, and Wampanoags as they fought the colonists. She witnessed the violent deaths of her daughter, relatives, neighbors, and other English colonists. In order to survive, she had not simply to live with her Indian captors but to become part of their society. Finally, as the war was winding down in the colonists' favor, she was ransomed and reunited with her family. Six years later, she published her now-famous account of her captivity and her understanding of its meaning.

For most readers over the past three centuries, the distinctive quality of Rowlandson's narrative lies in the combination of her unique experience and her powerful depiction of that experience. In the book Rowlandson portrays herself as a devout Puritan (as the English Protestant followers of the Swiss theologian John Calvin were called) confronting the hellish terror of life among so-called savages. Stripped of family, home, and all the other forms of comfort and security to which she was accustomed, she wandered frequently to the edge of temptation and despair. But in the end, she always recalled that God, far from abandoning her, was testing her and, through the medium of the destructive war with Indians, her fellow colonists. Her redemption and her return to English society, as well as the colonists' victory in the war, proved to her that omnipotent God can bestow justice and mercy on both individuals and whole societies. She drew on the Bible to supply not only particular passages pertaining to particular events but also an

Figure 1 *(left).* **Southern New England, 1675**

overarching framework for her to understand her experience of suffering and redemption. (Unlike Anne Bradstreet, the only North American woman author to have published before her, Rowlandson does not draw on the Greek and Roman classics or any other literature outside the Puritan tradition.) Taken at face value, the narrative vividly dramatizes the Puritans' belief in the inherently sinful nature of human beings, even the relatively few whom God had chosen to save from hell. And more specifically, in her warnings to Puritans about taking God for granted as their lives become more comfortable, the author articulates a theme sounded repeatedly by New England ministers in the late seventeenth century.

Yet the very qualities that have earned Rowlandson a firm place in American literary and cultural history have also raised questions for some readers from her time to ours. In proclaiming the distinctiveness of her experience, was she also claiming to be elevated spiritually above those Puritans who did not share her experience of captivity? It would have been troubling for anyone to make such a claim, particularly if that person were not a minister, and above all if that person were female. Rowlandson's gender has raised other questions about the narrative as well. To what extent did she, as opposed to the clergymen who encouraged and sponsored her narrative's publication, shape its contents? Is there within the text a distinctively female voice, independent of other voices, or do Rowlandson's male sponsors speak for her? And what about her relations with her captors? Could any woman in her situation have withstood such an experience with her sexual and spiritual virtues intact? Despite her strident denunciations of the Indians as devilish savages, some scholars have seen her intimate moments with individual Indians and her maneuvering through the natives' social world as signs that her Anglo-Puritan allegiance weakened during her captivity.

Beyond the meanings of her captivity for Rowlandson and her seventeenth-century readers, the narrative raises questions about the Native Americans who predominate there. Who were these people, and what were they fighting for? And why did they capture people like Mary Rowlandson? Who were the "praying Indians" against whom Rowlandson rails throughout her narrative, and who were the noncombatant Indians who assisted in obtaining her release? Rowlandson herself provides no direct answers to these questions; indeed, her blatant biases render her suspect as an authority on any factual information relating to native people. Nevertheless, the narrative provides a valuable window overlooking the cross-cultural tensions that exploded in war in 1675. In order to appreciate fully her narrative's value in this respect, we must read it as historians read all documents, that is, critically and in conjunction with other evidence from the period.

Rowlandson divided her narrative into twenty "removes," by which she identified the twenty occasions when she and her captors broke camp and traveled elsewhere. But like most other New England colonists, her entire life was punctuated by removes from one place to another. By examining her life through the places she lived and the removes between them, we can begin to understand why her narrative took the form that it did and how it illuminates the world in which she lived.

THE GREAT MIGRATION

Although Mary Rowlandson's narrative is autobiographical, in that it is a first-person account of a life, it is not an autobiography as such, which would recount the events of an entire life up to the time of its writing. Rather, it focuses exclusively on the three months of her captivity, when Rowlandson was about thirty-nine years of age. As a result, the details of her life before and after that three months are almost completely unknown. Of Rowlandson's origins, we can be certain only that she was born into a farming family somewhere in Somerset county in the south of England about 1637. Her father, John White, and her mother, whose maiden name was Joan West, had been married in 1627. Mary was the fifth of eight children born to John and Joan White.[2]

Although Mary White's personal life in England is largely hidden from us, we know a great deal about the world into which she was born. England in the 1630s was being swept by economic, social, and religious upheavals. A shift toward specialized, commercial agriculture led many wealthy landowners to "enclose" tracts customarily cultivated by the rural poor, forcing the latter to move from one locale to another in search of work and food. Many "middling" (neither rich nor poor) landowners also tried to profit from raising crops or livestock; while some succeeded, others faltered because their holdings were too small. Like their poorer counterparts, many of the "middling sort" moved elsewhere within England in order to improve their prospects. Prior to and apart from its North American colonies, then, England was a country where people commonly moved from one place to another.

England's "middling sort" placed a high premium on achieving and maintaining their personal independence. Perceiving both the rich and the poor as "idle" and, therefore, morally corrupt, many of them were drawn to Puritanism. John Calvin, the Puritans' principal source of inspiration, rejected both the Roman Catholic tenet that God granted salvation to those people who performed "good works" while on earth and Martin Luther's contention that "faith alone" would carry them to heaven. Both were wrong, Calvin argued, because they maintained that an individual's destiny was in his or her hands rather than in the hands of God. For Calvin, it was human beings' sinful nature and the wiles of Satan that repeatedly misled them into thinking they could control their own lives. Only in order to show the power of his grace did God from time to time "elect" a few "saints" for salvation. Defying the orthodoxy of the established Church of England, which followed Catholic teachings on salvation, many found in Puritanism a measure of assurance that their experience of divine grace might mean that they were among the few who would be saved. At the same time, their beliefs provided a code of conduct that enabled them to substitute a stern piety and self-discipline, in both religious and secular matters, for blind obedience to established authorities. Puritanism enabled them to see "godly" people as morally if not politically superior to the ungodly.

In the fellowship of others who had experienced God's grace and whose conversions had been validated by learned and committed ministers, English Puritans forged a powerful movement that addressed a range of economic and political as well as religious issues in early seventeenth-century England. Fearful that the Puritans threatened religious and political order, most English leaders, including King Charles I, supported the Church of England's efforts to root out dissenters from the ranks of its clergy. As a result many Puritans developed a heightened alienation toward their homeland. Joan White, Mary's mother, would later tell her fellow church members in Wenham, Massachusetts, that she "was brought up in a poor, ignorant place."[3] While most Puritans remained in England in hopes of reforming their native land, a sizable minority crossed the Atlantic in what became known as the "Great Migration." Altogether about twenty thousand English, mostly Puritans and Puritan sympathizers, moved to Massachusetts Bay and the neighboring colonies of Connecticut, Rhode Island, New Haven, and the older colony of Plymouth between 1629 and 1642, when the outbreak of civil war in England largely halted emigration. Joan White would later say that "her heart was drawn to New England because good people [meaning Puritans] came hither."[4]

Arriving in Salem, Essex County, Massachusetts, in 1639, Mary White and her family found themselves in a society that was young but already heavily populated. By then newcomers to the crowded maritime port and farming community were being granted land far from the town center. John White received a sixty-acre tract located about six miles outside of town. While the tract was sufficient to feed his immediate family, White knew—possibly from personal experience—how England's acute shortage of land often deprived the sons of hardworking families of a decent inheritance. Like other New Englanders, he sought to ensure that his progeny and those who came after would be amply provided for. Over the ensuing years, White acquired several additional tracts north of Salem, including one tract on a brook that he leased to the operator of a saw and grist mill. By enabling White and his neighbors to obtain such basic necessities as wood and flour without going to Salem, the mill reinforced their effort to form the separate town of Wenham.[5]

Joan White played an equally critical role in forming the new town by helping establish its church in 1644. When standing before the congregation to give evidence of the workings of God's grace in her, a requirement for membership, she told how she was "for a long space of time living in the far woods" and could only occasionally attend church in Salem or in Ipswich to the north. Like other successful applicants, she cited numerous passages in the Bible that constituted landmarks on her way to the experience of grace, and then answered questions put to her by the minister, John Fiske.[6]

In publicly relating her conversion experience, White acted in a capacity permitted few New England women in the 1640s. Since 1637, when New England's magistrates and ministers had banished a radical Puritan named Anne Hutchinson, along with her followers, most churches had ceased allowing women to speak publicly in any capacity. Hutchinson had boldly challenged the authority of New England ministers by claiming that all but two of them adhered to a "covenant of works." By this she meant that in judging the validity of prospective church members' experiences of grace, the ministers veered dangerously close to the Catholic doctrine of salvation by means of good works. Moreover, she proclaimed her views at meetings that had become popular with a large segment of the Boston congregation, both male and female. Brought to trial and pressed on her views, Hutchinson declared that she was assured of her own salvation because of a direct revelation from God. In other words, the individual was the only human able to judge whether or not he or she was saved, and the clergy had no special power or ability to bring to bear on such authorities. Such a view of grace was far too radical for most Puritans, including Hutchinson's more moderate followers. The fact that she was a woman declaring her spiritual authority in a public setting made her even more dangerous in the eyes of Massachusetts authorities. She and her closest adherents were banished from the colony, with most, including Hutchinson herself, moving to the more tolerant Rhode Island.[7]

By the time the Wenham congregation was convened in 1644, then, it was one of the few in which women still related their conversion experiences in public and spoke regularly in church meetings. Among the most articulate of these women was Joan White. White is also noteworthy because her husband, like several other Wenham men, was not a church member.[8] The Whites were not unusual in this respect. As in most societies throughout history, New England had a preponderance of women in its churches. Whereas men represented their families regularly in economic and political affairs outside the home, the church was the one public arena in which women had a role, however limited. John White's failure to join did not mean that he was unsympathetic to Puritan views. For example, like all Puritans, he passionately supported the cause of Parliament against the royalty during England's civil war (1642–48). While less fervent in his devotion, White apparently respected his wife's capabilities, for he not only attended a church in which she enjoyed privileges not available to him but also left her in charge of the household for two years (1648–50) while he returned to England to settle some financial affairs.[9]

When her father returned from England, Mary White was about thirteen years old. Born in England, she had crossed the Atlantic as a child and grown up in a small, isolated community. Her family's material conditions had steadily improved as a result of hard work and John White's shrewd investments. But as a young girl, and given her father's long absence, she was almost certainly closer to her mother, from whom she was acquiring the combination of boldness, independence, and piety that would one day be revealed in her narrative.

THE ANGLO-INDIAN FRONTIER

In 1653, fourteen years after arriving in Massachusetts Bay, Mary White and her family moved again. Although the Whites had accumulated a considerable amount of land in Wenham, John White apparently thought it insufficient to ensure the continued prosperity of his family line. Leaving Mary's twenty-year-old brother, Thomas, in charge of the Wenham holdings, the Whites moved fifty miles west to another new town, Lancaster. Lancaster was a study in contrasts to Wenham. Besides being known for its disreputable inhabitants, the town's nearest neighbors were Native Americans.

At the dawn of the seventeenth century, the native peoples of southern New England (the area of the present states of Massachusetts, Connecticut, and Rhode Island) probably numbered more than one hundred thousand. But first visiting explorers and then colonists soon brought devastating epidemics of smallpox and other diseases to which Indians lacked sufficient immunity, reducing the population in some areas by as much as 90 percent. Hardest hit were the Indians of the eastern coast, where communities formerly numbering in the hundreds now held only a few dozen.[10] One English visitor, arriving in 1622, remarked that the "bones and skulls" of the unburied dead "made such a spectacle . . . it seemed to me a new found Golgatha."[11] While living in Wenham, Mary White might have seen an Indian or two from time to time along a road or in the larger towns of Salem or Ipswich. Lancaster was another story. The neighboring Nipmuc people of Nashaway had helped the town get started and continued to contribute to its economic well-being.

The following discussion of the Nipmucs and other native peoples of southeastern New England and of the early developments in Lancaster as they relate to the process of colonial expansion will provide a background for the rest of Mary Rowlandson's story.

Two Towns Called Nashaway

Long before the first Europeans arrived on New England's shores in the sixteenth century, native communities were connected with one another through elaborate ties of exchange. The trading of goods, accompanied by ceremonies, was not simply a means by which Indians obtained items of practical value. Many of the objects exchanged were valued primarily for their spiritual powers—certain minerals like quartz, for example, and sea shells such as the quahog, which was used to make sacred wampum beads. Power rested in those communities and their political leaders, known as *sachems,* whose location and strength enabled them to provide their neighbors with trade privileges and (if necessary) military protection in exchange for tribute in the form of valued goods.

When French, Dutch, and English traders began frequenting New England's coast, they sought pelts of beaver and other animals so they could cash in on a European craze for fur hats, while natives were just as eager for the visitors' metal, cloth, and glass wares.[12] As a result of this new trade earlier patterns of exchange shifted so as to favor those Indian communities with the most direct access to European traders, sometimes inducing rivalries over such access. One such conflict fused with English expansionism to produce southern New England's first major war, known as the Pequot War (1637). The other Indians in the region that soon became Connecticut were alienated by the efforts of the powerful Pequots to control trade between themselves and the Dutch. Seeking to colonize Connecticut, the English organized a powerful anti-Pequot coalition of Mohegan and Narragansett Indians that eventually crushed the Pequots.[13]

The Pequot War and the colonization of Connecticut changed the balance of power in southeastern New England. Now each of the powerful Indian confederacies or alliances was closely tied economically to an English center of power—the Wampanoags to Plymouth, the Narragansetts to Rhode Island, the Mohegans to Connecticut, and the Indians of the Connecticut River valley to a powerful Springfield-based trader, William Pynchon. In each of these instances, Indians and English had sufficient need of each other that, for the time being, they treated one another as equals. In eastern Massachusetts, however, the combination of Indian depopulation from epidemics and the massive Great Migration from England had left Indian communities greatly reduced in size and separated from one another by new English settlements.

The power vacuum in eastern Massachusetts was filled in 1644 by a treaty in which Massachusetts Bay formally extended its authority over the Indian communities located nearest its settlements. The sachems of these communities promised not only to obey all laws pertaining to them but also to direct their political loyalties to the colony. In return, the colony promised to protect the Indians from outside attacks and encroachments on their lands. To seal the agreement in a manner familiar to the natives, the sachems presented the colony's legislature, known as the General Court, with a quantity of wampum (valued by colonists as a substitute for scarce English currency), and the court responded by presenting each sachem with a red coat and, for them to share, "a potful of wine."[14] In effect, Massachusetts Bay had become the new tribute-collecting power in eastern New England. Besides the coastal Pawtucket and Massachusett Indians, the colony's new tributaries included the Nipmucs of Nashaway.

The inclusion of Nashaway among Massachusetts Bay's subject Indians reflected the fact that the village was no longer remote from English settlement. In 1641 the General Court had authorized a group of investors to seek out potential mines in order to enhance the colony's economic self-sufficiency and "to purchase the interest of any Indians in such lands where such mines shall be found." When the investors reported a year later that they had found an iron mine near the Nipmuc village of Nash-

Figure 2 *(right).*   **English Map of Southeastern New England, 1634**

The South part of New-England, as it is Planted this yeare, 1634.

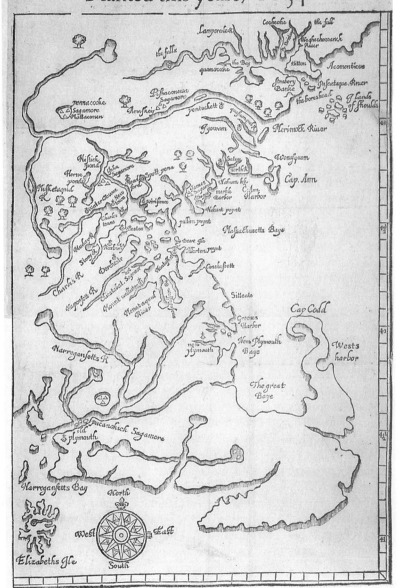

away, the Court authorized them to develop the mine and establish an English town at the site. In 1643, several prospective miners, fur traders, and farmers moved to the new town, which they likewise called Nashaway. In 1645, after Indian Nashaway had submitted to Massachusetts Bay's authority, its sachem, Showanon, deeded an eighty-square-mile tract to his new neighbors and trading partners with the proviso that they not disturb the natives in their hunting, fishing, and farming.[15]

English Nashaway's beginnings were anything but promising. Although Indian trails connected the town to the outside world, it lacked a road over which wagons and carts could be hauled. Newcomers arrived so slowly, complained Governor John Winthrop, "that in two years they had not three built houses there," causing its minister to leave in disgust. For Winthrop, the problem was not simply the town's isolation but also the quality of its inhabitants, most of whom "were poor men, and some of them corrupt in judgment, and others profane."[16] He was referring to people such as Thomas King, who was charged with "having defiled his wife before their marriage"; Stephen Day, who had been accused of fraud; and Robert Child, a Puritan dissenter who advocated religious toleration and admission to the colony's congregations of any members of the Church of England who applied.[17] As we saw earlier, the Puritans had fled England in part because the Church of England insisted on imposing its views on Puritans and persecuted ministers who preached Puritan views. If implemented, Child's proposal would have opened Puritan church membership to those who opposed Calvinist principles. And because in Massachusetts voting rights were restricted to male church members, the measure would have threatened Puritan control of the colony.

Child, along with most others in Nashaway, soon left the isolated little town. By November 1647, a majority of the town's landowners petitioned the Court to rescind the grant so they could leave, but the Court refused, saying that it "does not think fit to destroy the said plantation, but rather to encourage it."[18] As late as 1651, the town was again the subject of scandal when Elizabeth Hall, whose husband was in England at the time, allegedly greeted a male visitor by stating that all property, including "men's wives," should be held in common "as in the apostles' time." Although Hall sued her accuser for slander, her husband summoned her to England before the case went to what would surely have been a sensational trial.[19]

The struggle between Puritan and alternative views of morality was not confined to English Nashaway, for a comparable conflict was raging among its Indian neighbors. When submitting to the colony government in 1644, the sachems pledged not only to be loyal and obedient but also "to be willing from time to time to be instructed in the knowledge and worship of God."[20] This aspect of the agreement proved to be the opening move in what became an ambitious effort, led by Puritan minister John Eliot, to convert the colony's Indians to Christianity. But Eliot focused thereafter on the coastal Massachusett communities, where he organized seven all-Christian Indian "praying towns," largely ignoring Nashaway. Although he had little time to nurture the Indians' piety, Eliot did intervene in Nashaway politics, at the behest of the General Court, when the Christian sachem Showanon died in 1654. The sachemship in southern New England generally remained within the same families, but members of the community often selected from several candidates when there was no obvious successor. Two of Showanon's relatives were candidates to succeed him; one was a devout Christian named Matthew and the other, said by the English to be a "debauched and drunken fellow," was named Shoshanim. With Eliot and another minister making the colony's preference known and undoubtedly distributing the gifts that were customary on such occasions, a majority of the Nashaway Nipmucs proclaimed their preference for Matthew.[21]

Although Indian Nashaway's commitment to Christianity was apparently less than unanimous, its loyalty to the colony was never in doubt during the 1640s and 1650s. Its people had welcomed the English not only by selling them part of their land but also by regularly trading them furs for manufactured goods and, most likely, by many other casual acts that went unrecorded. Nashaway's evident security began to attract families who sought the comforts found in older English settlements. Perhaps to make that security even more evident, the inhabitants renamed the town in 1653, first calling it Prescott and then West Towne before finally agreeing on Lancaster, the name of an English county that carried no association with their Indian neighbors. By then the town was also emerging from its isolation by becoming a link on a road connecting eastern Massachusetts to Connecticut.[22]

Lancaster and the Rowlandsons

Arriving in the year of the name change, the Whites were among a large number of new families moving to Lancaster as its prospects seemed to be improving. After a decade in which the number of families was never more than about a dozen, it suddenly boasted thirty-five households by 1654. For John White, the motive of acquiring additional land was once again uppermost; within a year of his arrival, he was the largest landowner in town. How Joan White felt about leaving Wenham is less clear, but she may already have known that Lancaster had finally recruited a minister, Joseph Rowlandson, whom she surely had met when attending church in Ipswich. Whether Joan, who was the White family's spiritual mentor, helped incline Mary toward the clergyman is uncertain. In any case, Mary White and Joseph Rowlandson were married in about 1656.

Like his new wife, Joseph Rowlandson was born in England, accompanied his family in the Great Migration to New England, and settled in Essex County before moving to Lancaster. But while the Whites were pillars of the community in Wenham, the Rowlandsons were near the bottom of Ipswich society in wealth, social status, and reputation. Rowlandson's father appeared frequently in court, most often for failing to pay assessments, and his brother became an object of public derision after his wife won a divorce, charging he was impotent.[23] Though studying for the ministry, Joseph had his own brush with the law. In 1651 he posted on the door of the Ipswich meetinghouse—the town's bulletin board—an anonymous broadside ridiculing New England as a region where envy had triumphed over truth in the administration of justice. Specific references in the text indicate that he was lashing out at those who had harassed his family by collecting fines and initiating lawsuits. His identity was quickly discovered and Joseph Rowlandson was charged with "scandelous lybell," for which he was fined and forced to make an abject, lengthy apology. Nevertheless, he went on to graduate from Harvard College in 1652 and, after waiting more than a year, accepted an invitation from Lancaster to become its first minister.[24]

Whereas John White had left a son in Wenham to manage the family's holdings there, Rowlandson brought his destitute parents with him to Lancaster. Whereas all the Whites knew how to read and write, only Joseph among the Rowlandsons could sign his name.[25] Nevertheless, as a minister, Rowlandson made up for his family's deficiencies not only because he was entitled to a generous allotment of land but because he had earned the right to be addressed as "mister." In status-conscious England and its colonies, "mister" was reserved for men of authority and learning, such as ministers, magistrates, and military officers, and was also applied to very wealthy merchants. But landowners who lacked the inherited status of either aristocrats or gentry, no matter how large their holdings, were addressed simply as "goodman." Through maintaining diligence in his studies and by overcoming considerable social and legal obstacles, Joseph Rowlandson enjoyed a privilege denied John White and every other man in Lancaster. Because the status of wives in English society followed that of their husbands, Mary Rowlandson became the only woman in town to be addressed as "mistress"; had she married anyone else, she would have been known, like all the other women, as "goodwife." Besides satisfying both families' ambitions, the marriage of the once penniless and despised minister to the daughter of the largest landowner made them by far the most prominent couple among the town's generation of younger adults.[26]

The White-Rowlandson marriage ought to have brought Lancaster the respectability in the eyes of eastern colonists that kept eluding the town. But the combination of Lancaster and Joseph Rowlandson, with their respective histories of contentiousness, proved too explosive. At around the time the Rowlandsons were married, a female church member, Mary Gates, was charged with "making bold and unbeseeming speeches in the public assembly on the Lord's day" against the minister. Apparently Rowlandson had disputed Gates's mother's contention that she had given him satisfaction for some grievance, the nature of which has not been preserved in the town records.[27] While it may be tempting to think of Mary Gates as another Anne Hutchinson, the feud appears to have been a more personal one of the sort that Rowlandson was embroiled in with other Lancaster residents. Most of the disputes arose when townspeople questioned the extent of Rowlandson's landholdings and the validity of his titles to some of them. In addition, many disliked the minister's threat to accept an offer from a church in Billerica, Massachusetts, unless Lancaster enhanced his income. Meanwhile, the General Court responded to the renewed feuding by appointing a three-man commission to monitor the town. Partial to Rowlandson, the commission in 1657 ordered the selectment to build a meetinghouse and raise his salary, which they grudgingly did.[28]

The surviving records are fragmentary, but something of a pattern emerges in these disputes. On one side were the town's early settlers, the wealthiest of whom traded regularly with the Nipmucs of Nashaway and all of whom chafed under efforts by the General Court to regulate their affairs. Pitted against them were newer arrivals, some of whom, like the Rowlandsons and Whites, owned more land than any of the old-timers and who readily looked to the Court for support. Unlike their rivals, the newcomers had no economic stake in relations with Indians. Whereas trader Stephen Day could tell the General Court he had entertained "both English and Indians at my house from day to day for some years together," Joseph Rowlandson appears to have contributed nothing to the lagging missionary effort at Nashaway except by taking a Christian Indian youth into his home as a servant.[29] The fault line running through frontier Lancaster had economic and even cultural dimensions.

In the end, however, the fault line proved transitory. By the early 1660s, as the townspeople fought yet another battle over Rowlandson's landholdings, relations between Lancaster and Nashaway were beginning to change. While Indians had once hunted beaver and other fur-bearing animals solely to satisfy their own needs, the onset earlier in the century of the English demand for furs and the Indian demand for European goods had led native hunters to procure as many pelts as they could. As a result, beaver, otter, marten, mink, and other fur-bearing mammals had become virtually extinct in southern New England. But English traders at Lancaster and elsewhere customarily provided their native clients with trade goods in advance of each hunting season, with the understanding that the Indians would satisfy their debt with furs. The sudden decline in furs left many Indians indebted to the traders. Therefore, some Lancaster traders pressured their Nashaway creditors to satisfy their debts with land in lieu of furs.[30] Thus Stephen Day obtained 150 acres of upland from the Nashaway sachem, Matthew, while John Prescott obtained a tract from another Nashaway Christian, James Quanapohit.[31] Other traders, like John Tinker, sold their interest to Simon Willard, the wealthiest trader in central and eastern Massachusetts, and moved elsewhere.[32] By the end of the 1660s, the end of the fur trade and the transformation of the remaining traders into major landowners had closed the social and factional divide in Lancaster.

By the early 1670s, Lancaster was finally acquiring respectability in English eyes. A sure sign of the change came in 1672 when Joseph Rowlandson, once known for precipitating conflicts, was called to Boston's bitterly divided First Church to help resolve a conflict.[33] In the following year, three decades after the establishment of English Nashaway, the General Court's special commission submitted its final report. It found that the people of Lancaster were now living in harmony and capable of handling their own affairs. Accepting this judgment, the Court at long last granted the town its full autonomy.[34]

But the very changes that had brought stability to Lancaster undermined its ties with its Nashaway neighbors. Indeed, the early 1670s brought a deterioration in Indian-English relations throughout the colonies. The decline of the fur trade was only a part of a larger process by which the Indians' lives were being transformed. Throughout the nearly half century of English colonization, the native population continued to decrease from the effects of European-derived diseases, while the newcomers were multiplying more rapidly than almost any other group of people in the world at the time. Compared to Lancaster with its thirty-five households in 1654, Nashaway numbered only fifteen or sixteen twenty years later. Not only traders but also colonial authorities were now pressuring Indians to sell land in order to make room for the younger generation of colonists coming of age.[35] Even on the land remaining, life was becoming more constricted. English livestock invaded Indians' cornfields and, along with English plows, devoured the grasses that attracted deer and other animals on which the natives depended for meat.[36] As a result, Indians throughout the region were reassessing their relationship with the colonies. Some turned to Christianity, others turned away from it, and still others were so confused by the rapid changes that they could not make up their minds. For some of these, the wares of another kind of English trader—the liquor dealer—became an illusory source of respite. Tensions were compounded in Nashaway when the Christian sachem, Matthew, died and was succeeded by Shoshanim, the "debauched and drunken fellow" who had been passed over in 1658. His rise to power makes clear the transformation occurring among Lancaster's once-friendly neighbors.

The deterioration of Indian-English relations at Nashaway and Lancaster was but a variation on a theme being played out in much of southern New England. An Indian perspective on these changes was provided by the Wampanoag sachem, Metacom, in June 1675. He told Rhode Island Governor John Eaton how English cheating, discrimination, and pressures to sell land, submit to Plymouth colony's authority, convert to Christianity, and consume alcohol had undermined a half-century of friendship and driven the Wampanoags of Pokanoket to the point of war (see Document 1). Natives in the Massachusetts portion of the Connecticut River valley and among the Narragansetts and Niantics in Rhode Island and eastern Connecticut were also expressing anti-English sentiments.[37]

Of special concern to the English as tensions mounted were the Nipmucs, who occupied the southern New England heartland linking the colonies' potential Indian enemies. Anxious to ensure their loyalty, Daniel Gookin, Massachusetts Bay's superintendent of Christian Indians, toured the Nipmucs' villages in July 1673. As missionary John Eliot had done three decades earlier among the Massachusett Indians to the east, Gookin hastily sought to organize the Nipmuc villages into Christian communities, called "praying towns," by appointing "praying Indians" as ministers and magistrates to govern them. At Nashaway, he introduced Jethro, a Christian Nipmuc from another town, as its new minister and exhorted Shoshanim and his people to "abstain from drunkenness, whoredom, and powwowing [traditional religious ceremonies and healing practices], and all other evils" in order to be assured of "eternal and temporal happiness." But whereas Gookin's seven other stops resulted in the establishment of new praying towns, neither Nashaway

Figure 3. Massachusetts Bay Colony Seal
The seal advertised the colony's missionary intentions by depicting an Indian saying, "come over and help us."

nor Weshakim, a smaller village nearby, were recognized as such.[38] Having experienced English meddling in their politics as well as the other kinds of transformation listed by Metacom, the people of Nashaway had learned to distrust the intentions of the English, particularly their missionaries.

A WORLD UPENDED

The event that finally triggered open war was the death of another native who had struggled to reconcile the growing chasm between the Indians and the English. John Sassamon was a Christian Massachusett Indian who had lived in John Eliot's first praying town of Natick, where he had learned to read and write English. He went on to attend Harvard College, but at some point he left his life among the English to become an interpreter, English-language scribe, and counselor for the Pokanoket Wampanoags and their sachem, Metacom, or "King Philip." Sassamon served Metacom for more than a decade, even as Plymouth-Wampanoag relations grew increasingly bitter. But in March 1675, with tensions at fever pitch, Sassamon informed Governor Josiah Winslow that Metacom was conspiring with other Indians to launch an all-out war against the English. Whether Sassamon was telling the truth or had invented his tale in order to ingratiate himself once again with the English was never determined, for a week later he was dead. Three associates of Metacom were accused by a Christian Indian who testified that he had seen them beat Sassamon to death and throw his body in a pond. Plymouth selected a jury of twelve Englishmen plus six Christian Indians, especially appointed to give the trial an appearance of evenhandedness. The jury found the three guilty and, on June 8, 1675, they were hanged. Having already expressed his distrust of the English system of justice as it concerned Indians, Metacom and his followers were mobilizing for war even as the trial progressed. Fighting broke out later that month when Pokanokets began attacking colonists in the Plymouth town of Swansea.[39]

Metacom's War

Metacom's War began disastrously for the English. First, English soldiers in Plymouth proved powerless to halt the Pokanokets' attacks and prevent the "squaw sachem," Weetamoo, and her followers from Pocasset from joining their fellow Wampanoags.[40] Then in July, those Nipmucs who had decided to fight the English began attacking towns and troops at will in central Massachusetts.[41] One such attack was staged by Nashaway Nipmucs against their Lancaster neighbors in August 1675. Led by one Monoco, known to the English as "One-eyed John," the attack resulted in the deaths of seven inhabitants.[42] The incident prompted Lancaster to designate several large houses, including the Rowlandsons', as garrison houses, in which all the inhabitants gathered to better defend themselves against future attacks. The war spread farther westward in

September when Indians in the Connecticut River valley launched a series of surprise attacks on nearby English towns. Finally, in December 1675, the English attempted to take the initiative by moving against the hitherto neutral Narragansetts, hoping to cripple them before they entered the war with their own offensive. Attacking the Great Swamp Fort, which held several hundred Narragansett women and children as well as fighting men, the English burned the fort and most of those inside. Although they devastated the Narragansetts, their own losses were so great that it took them three months to recover militarily. Long before then, surviving Narragansetts and Wampanoags fled their coastal homelands, where relatively small forces of English troops might have trapped them, and joined the Nipmucs at several sites in central Massachusetts.[43]

Why had the English, with their far greater numbers and their seemingly superior organization and technology, fared so badly? To a significant degree, the answer lies in the differential effects of Anglo-Indian contact on the two peoples' ways of waging war. Having defeated the Pequots handily in 1637 and having intimidated Native Americans with threats and shows of force on numerous other occasions, the colonists saw little reason to doubt their military superiority to people whom they deemed "savages." Following European military conventions, colonial troops marched in tight columns, expecting to meet their foes on an open field or to besiege them in a fortress. Most soldiers were armed with a type of musket known as a matchlock, a heavy, cumbersome weapon whose firing mechanism had to be carefully ignited and whose barrel had to be placed on a forked stake known as a "rest" before each shot was fired. Approaching to within fifty yards of their enemies, European armies customarily fired simultaneous volleys straight ahead, placing little emphasis on accuracy. New England Native Americans, on the other hand, recognized almost immediately that the flintlock, a far lighter musket with a self-igniting mechanism, was more compatible with their emphasis, both in hunting and warfare, on mobility and long-distance accuracy. By 1675, most Native American fighting men carried flintlocks as well as bows and knew, either in their own communities or nearby, an Indian blacksmith who repaired guns.[44]

The natives had also learned a new form of warfare from the English. Precolonial conflicts among natives were small-scale affairs, usually between families rather than whole communities, and occurred only when the norms of reciprocal exchange had broken down. Casualties were few and victory brought at best some additional tribute as a means of restoring balance. During the Pequot War (1637), an English officer complained of his Indian allies that "they might fight seven years and not kill seven men. . . . This fight is more for pastime than to conquer and subdue enemies."[45] But the Mohegan and Narragansett Indians knew that annihilating a foe would mean losing a trade partner or source of tribute. The decisive moment in the English defeat of the Pequots had come when colonial troops attacked and burned a Pequot village on the Mystic River in Connecticut, killing several hundred inhabitants, most of them women, children, and other noncombatants. (The December 1675 attack on the Narragansetts was similar in intent and result.) The harshest criticism of the English destruction of the Pequot village had come from the then-allied Narragansetts, who complained that English warfare "was too furious and slays too many men." Given the memory of the Pequot War and the evident willingness of the English to attack, capture, and slay noncombatants, Indians in 1675 recognized the need to be equally ruthless.[46]

Also working against the English were many colonists' generalized fear and hatred of all Indians. When war first broke out, pro-English natives volunteered their services in all the colonies, where they proved effective not only as warriors but also as scouts, advisers, and spies. But authorities in Massachusetts and Plymouth encountered such formidable popular hostility toward the native allies that they finally discharged this most valuable asset to their cause. Unlike in Connecticut and Rhode Island, nearly all pro-English Indians in Massachusetts and Plymouth were Christians. Upon learning that some anti-English Nipmucs were converts, many colonists immediately concluded that all Native Americans were traitors and that praying Indians were the most deceitful and treacherous of all. Praying Indians were frequently harassed and, in several notorious instances, killed by vigilantes. When missionaries and others, such as Eliot and Gookin, sought to defend the natives, their lives too were threatened. Indeed the issue of whether to consider praying Indians friends or foes precipitated a political crisis in Massachusetts that for a time threatened to erupt into civil war, like Bacon's Rebellion, which was raging at that very moment in Virginia. To avert that outcome in their own colony, Massachusetts authorities rounded up loyal Massachusett and Nipmuc families and moved them to Deer Island in Boston harbor. While safely separated from hostile colonists and from anti-English Indians, who might either attack or try to recruit them, the imprisoned Indians lacked means of obtaining adequate food and shelter. Meanwhile, without Indian assistance, Massachusetts troops proved utterly unable to locate their enemies and prevent the ambushes and surprise attacks that devastated the colony from the fall of 1675 to the following spring.[47]

Meanwhile, the anti-English Wampanoags, Narragansetts, and Nipmucs contemplated their next moves from their camps in central Massachusetts. Whereas southern New England Native Americans customarily broke up into small groups during winter, these Indians were amassed in large concentrations that could obtain sufficient food only by pilfering the abandoned English towns in their vicinity. At the same time, Metacom sought to broaden the natives' base of support still further. Early in January he traveled west to Hoosic, on the Massachusetts–New York frontier, apparently seeking the support of both the Mohawks of the Five Nations Iroquois and of their antagonists, the Algonquian-speaking natives of the Hudson Valley and Abenakis of northern New England and New France. He even hoped for direct French support. But the gathering was attacked and broken up by a contingent of Mohawks, armed and encouraged by New York's colonial government. Not only had Metacom and his accomplices been routed, but also there was every indication that the Mohawks would now play an active role in the war in New England, constituting a powerful force in the west to supplement the concentration of English settlers to the east.[48]

With the Mohawks looming to the west and the English still trying to regroup to the east, the Indians recognized the need for some decisive blows against the latter. Undoubtedly they understood that the colonists' vulnerability would prove short-lived. Accordingly in January 1676 they planned a series of attacks against five exposed frontier towns, beginning with Lancaster. We know about these plans because of the testimony of two Christian Nipmucs, who at extraordinary personal risk, quietly agreed with a few English officials to live among the Indians for a few weeks as spies while pretending to share their hostility to the colonists. One of them, James Quanapohit of Nashaway, who had earlier fought alongside Monoco against the Mohawks, learned from his old comrade-in-arms of the plans to attack Lancaster (see Document 2). On January 24, he arrived with the news at Gookin's home in Cambridge after a difficult journey through the snow. However, in the absence of an attack since the Narragansetts' defeat in December, and with some English mistrusting Quanapohit because he was Indian, colonial officials did nothing toward augmenting the fourteen soldiers already stationed there. But fears and rumors abounded at Lancaster itself, leading the town to dispatch several men, including Joseph Rowlandson, to Boston to plead for troops to defend the town. The Lancaster men were still in Boston when on the evening of February 9, the second Nipmuc spy, Job Kattananit, arrived at Gookin's house to report that four hundred Indians would attack Lancaster the following morning. Gookin immediately sent word to troops stationed near Lancaster to fly to the town's rescue. When the first soldiers arrived, they found the Rowlandsons' garrison house in flames and at least fourteen of the town's inhabitants dead and twenty-three captured.[49]

Although the troops' timely arrival forced the Indians to withdraw, limiting most of the damage and casualties to the Rowlandson garrison, Lancaster was fatally damaged. Even with troops guarding the town, the inhabitants remained vulnerable to attack while their food supplies ran dangerously low. Two weeks after Rowlandson's capture, a scouting party reported to the governor that at Lancaster they "found several houses [outside the Rowlandson garrison] deserted, having corn and cattle about them."[50] In a petition sent to the General Court on March 11 (see Document 3), the remaining residents asked for carts sufficient to transport them and their possessions to safety, referring to Lancaster as "this prison."[51] By the end of March, all inhabitants of the recently prosperous town had been evacuated.[52] For his part, Joseph Rowlandson remained in Boston, appearing frequently as a guest preacher in area churches. Less than two weeks after his family's capture, he told worshipers at Boston's Old South Church that "god is true to himselfe and to all that put their trust in him . . . god is too wise to be deceived by any and too faithfull to deceive any that trust in him."[53] These thoughts were undoubtedly a powerful consolation for Rowlandson as he pondered his family's fate. At about the same time, he declined an offer from the colony of a position as army chaplain, presumably so he could devote his time to securing his family's release.[54]

Captives and Captors

While the preface to Mary Rowlandson's narrative states that the attackers were Narragansett, the narrative itself makes clear that the attackers also included Nipmucs and Wampanoags.[55] These Indians were part of a larger intertribal encampment at the Nipmuc town of Menameset (which Rowlandson calls "Wenimesset"), about twenty-five miles southwest of Lancaster. It was here that Rowlandson was taken on the day after her capture and, over the next two weeks, transformed from English mother and wife to Indian captive. During that time, her daughter Sarah died in her arms; she encountered but could not remain with her two other children, Mary and Joseph, Jr.; and she was sold by her Narragansett captor to his sachem, Quinnapin. Quinnapin became her "master" and his three wives her "mistresses."[56]

Quinnapin came from a distinguished Narragansett family. His great-uncle, Canonicus, and uncle, Miantonomi, had been Narragansett sachems who had befriended the dissenter Roger Williams after he had been driven from Massachusetts in 1636. Their act enabled Williams to found a new, religiously tolerant colony on the shores of Narragansett Bay that was later called Rhode Island. Williams secured Narragansett support of the English cause in the Pequot War, but thereafter English-Narragansett tensions increased. Their mutual antagonism was sealed in 1643 when Massachusetts Bay, Connecticut, Plymouth, and New Haven formed a loose confederacy called the United Colonies of New England, from which Rhode Island was pointedly excluded.[57] By the 1660s, the Narragansetts were forming an alliance with their former rivals, the Wampanoags of Plymouth. Quinnapin contributed to the strengthening of that bond in at least two of his three marriages. One of his wives, whose name is not known, was a sister of Metacom's wife, and another wife was Weetamoo (whom Rowlandson refers to as "Wettimore"), "squaw sachem" of the Pocasset Wampanoags.[58]

Like many other southern New England sachems, Quinnapin had several spouses, both to connect him by kinship to other powerful families and to assist in providing the extraordinary hospitality expected of native political leaders.[59] What was unusual in his case was that one of his wives, Weetamoo, was even more politically powerful than he. For her part, Weetamoo had likewise used marriage to enhance her political position. Her first husband had been Wamsutta, older brother of Metacom and the latter's predecessor as sachem of the Pokanoket Wampanoags. Their marriage had united the two most powerful Wampanoag communities— Pocasset and Pokanoket. In 1662 Wamsutta died of mysterious causes after leaving a conference with Plymouth officials, an event that led Weetamoo, Metacom, and other Wampanoags to accuse the English of poisoning Wamsutta. A second marriage to the sachem of a smaller Wampanoag community became a casualty of the split among Wampanoags as Metacom's War erupted in 1675. Her second husband cast his lot with Plymouth, while Weetamoo fled to the still-neutral Narragansetts, where, soon after, she married Quinnapin.[60] When the Narragansetts and Pocassets entered the war, Weetamoo became, from the English perspective, a formidable foe. One author at the time wrote that "she is as potent a prince as any round about her, and has as much corn, land, and men [as Metacom] at her command," and another claimed that she was "next unto Philip in respect of the mischief she hath done."[61] It was Weetamoo who would emerge as the most important of Rowlandson's "mistresses" and her greatest nemesis.

Rowlandson's experience as a captive was shaped by the tensions between her identity as Mistress Mary Rowlandson, English wife of the

Puritan minister of Lancaster, and her status as the non-Indian female "servant" of a Narragansett "master" and of a Pocasset Wampanoag "mistress." While her narrative was definitively shaped by how she remembered and chose to represent her experience *as she was writing it later* (to be discussed more fully later), it also provides some evidence of these tensions as she experienced them during her captivity. The very shock of the attack and her capture, the death of one child and her separation from the rest of her family, and her entry into a mobile, generally hungry society of Native Americans at war combined to cut Rowlandson off from nearly all the worldly associations that, without her giving it a thought, had constantly reminded her of who she was and where she belonged in the world.

Of course Rowlandson was more than a wife and mother; she was a Puritan saint who recognized in her experience a testimony to her utter dependence on God's grace for salvation in the afterlife and on his providence for her fate while still on earth. It was divine providence, she believed, that spared her life and took the lives of her friends and kin, allowed the escaping Indians to cross the Baquag River (now called Miller's River) while halting the pursuing English troops at its banks, and caused an Indian who participated in an attack on Medfield to bring her a Bible from the ashes of that town. It is divine providence and the Bible that supplied her with a framework for interpreting her entire experience and the events bearing on it.

Beyond being a woman and a saint, Rowlandson was English and European, a facet of her identity that had undoubtedly assumed special importance after her move to Lancaster, with its proximity to Nashaway, and loomed even larger when she found herself a member of a subordinated minority group among Nipmucs, Narragansetts, and Wampanoags. In European parlance, she belonged to that portion of humanity deemed "civilized," whereas the natives were mere "savages." As such she saw and characterized them in terms such as "black creatures," "hell-hounds," and "wild beasts of the forest," while portraying the English as motivated by only the purest impulses. The attempt to "civilize savages" by converting them to Christianity had produced only the treachery of the praying Indians against which she railed repeatedly.

Yet alongside the stridently ideological tone of much of Rowlandson's narrative are passages that suggest other perspectives on her experience. Especially as it moves forward in time, the text frequently undermines the impenetrable social and cultural barrier posited in the civilized/savage dichotomy. That Rowlandson could communicate with her captors in English, that flintlock-armed native warriors were so effective against her people, that she encountered anti-English Indians who professed Christianity—all testified to the ambiguities that had complicated cultural boundaries at Nashaway, Lancaster, and elsewhere in southern New England during the preceding half-century. These ambiguities enabled Rowlandson to discover dimensions of Indians' existence that belied the category "savage," as when some Indians offered her sustenance and comfort even while others scorned her, when her and her son's masters facilitated visits by their captives with one another, and when Quinnapin and Metacom himself treated her with respect and compassion. Even when ascribing such acts to divine providence (which she did not in every instance do), Rowlandson undermined her blanket condemnations of Native Americans as inherently "savage," by carefully differentiating among them as individuals. (For example, of the many English accounts of Metacom's War, Rowlandson's is the only one, besides that of John Easton [see Document 1], to portray Metacom with any degree of sympathy.) Rowlandson personally breeched the cultural divide as she maneuvered through the mobile, intertribal society of her captors, exchanging her knitted goods and cultivating the favor of powerful men such as Quinnapin and Metacom.

Besides her formal identity and beliefs, what factors in Rowlandson's background shaped her response to captivity? And how did these factors serve her during her ordeal? As a relatively prosperous, married, English Puritan woman, Rowlandson was accustomed to managing a household of a husband and three children, plus servants and visitors whose numbers undoubtedly fluctuated over time. She was intimately familiar with the preparation of food, the sewing and mending of clothing, the bearing, nurturing, and religious education of children, and many other domestic tasks performed by white New England women. She was also the most prominent member of a community of women that conducted neighborly exchanges of goods and labor, oversaw childbirths, offered charity to the needy, and enforced community mores. In addition, as the minister's wife, she was one of God's "saints" and a leading member of her Lancaster congregation, a role that gave her additional social power.[62] However, except as church members, women in colonial New England derived their identity and whatever power they exercised from the male head of their household, be he father, husband, or, in the case of servants, master. Thus, while Rowlandson during her captivity considered herself still married to her husband, she represented herself in her narrative as a "servant" in Quinnapin's household.

Native women's roles were roughly comparable to what Rowlandson knew in the sense that they too revolved around marriage, motherhood, and domesticity. But cultural differences meant that, in practice, women in the two societies shared few experiences. Premarital sex was common for both native women and men, notwithstanding the female "modesty" so frequently commented upon by English male authors. Divorce was likewise relatively easy to obtain and more frequent among Indians than among English. Unlike their English counterparts, Indian women gave birth alone, returning to their community after a day or so. Also, women isolated themselves from their families and communities during menstruation. Native societies were mobile, even in peacetime, and were attached to community homelands rather than to a fixed structure that could be called a "home" in the English sense. The added labor of moving one's household at seasonal intervals prepared Rowlandson's captors, female as well as male, better than her for the exigencies of wartime mobility. And native women not only cultivated crops of corn, beans, and squash but also gathered and prepared an astonishing variety of wild plants, nuts, berries, and shellfish as well as the meat and fish brought by the men. English women, on the other hand, relied almost entirely on a much narrower range of largely domesticated foods, so that Rowlandson was virtually unable to locate foods or otherwise survive in the wild, despite having lived her entire adult life in central New England. Moreover, as we have seen, women could rise to become sachems, although there is no record of a "squaw sachem" having more than one spouse at a time, as was common among their male counterparts.[63]

Aside from Indian familiarity with English ways and goods and her own extraordinary psychological and religious resources, Rowlandson the captive appears to have flourished, relatively speaking, because of her "pocket." As Laurel Thatcher Ulrich points out, a New England woman's pocket was not attached to her clothing but rather tied like an apron. In it she carried sewing materials that she might turn to should she have a few minutes of spare time, as well as any number of other objects connected with her range of responsibilities. During her captivity, Rowlandson's pocket contained her Bible, her morsels of food, her needles and yarn, and, most likely, other items which she could conceal or suddenly produce as a situation demanded. In this sense her pocket was both a tangible link to her earlier identity as well as a key to her survival and temporary self-fashioning as a captive.[64]

Rowlandson's adoption of the terminology of English servitude — "master," "mistress," and "servant" — to describe her position in Quinnapin's household is also instructive because, given her status and wealth, she almost certainly had experience with the institution as a mistress in Lancaster. Indeed, it is likely that the Christian Nipmuc who had lived with the

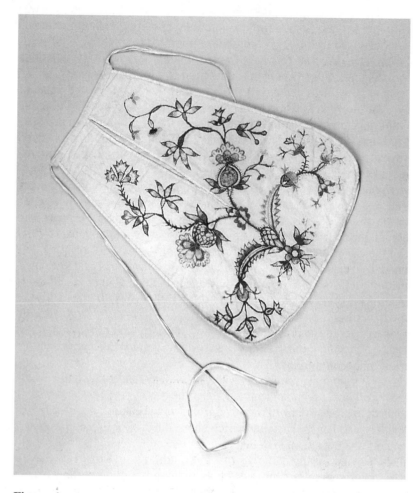

Figure 4.
This handmade pocket is similar to the one worn by Mary Rowlandson before and during her captivity.

Rowlandsons in Lancaster was, like many other native children placed in English households, a servant.[65] Yet in defying Weetamoo and in consorting with Metacom, Rowlandson broke the rules of her own society whereby servants obeyed their masters and mistresses and deferred to all others of superior status. But Rowlandson had no intention of remaining a lowly servant, especially to "savages." During the twelfth remove, after she had complained about the weight of her load and Weetamoo had slapped her, Rowlandson remarked on her captors' "insolency," as if they were defying her authority rather than the other way around. Indeed, it is the Indians' treatment of the English rather than the customs they observe themselves that Rowlandson finds so repulsive. She reports, for example, that Quinnapin had three wives in relatively matter-of-fact fashion, and even describes two ceremonial dances in a tone that is more condescending than contemptuous. For Rowlandson, it was the situation of her captivity rather than native culture as such that inverted the proper order of things.

In actuality Rowlandson was not a servant in the English sense but instead an adopted member of Quinnapin's household, whose status was highly ambiguous. Well before Europeans arrived, Indians in northeastern North America had been seizing prisoners of war for a variety of reasons. How such captives were treated depended on several factors: their usefulness, their comportment, and their captors' needs and dispositions. Captives might become full members of their adopted families, remain in subservient positions, be given or traded to other households, be held as hostages to be ransomed or exchanged for opponents' captives or gifts from opponents, be killed instantly, or—in relatively rare instances—be tortured and executed.[66] Rowlandson's narrative indicates that the Indians who captured English prisoners during Metacom's War tried to keep most of their captives alive, killing only those whose condition impeded their movements or who tried to escape. Quinnapin's and Metacom's kind treatment of Rowlandson undoubtedly arose in part from a recognition of her status in the English world and her value—political more than economic—as a hostage. For her part Rowlandson shrewdly seized on her status and reputation among the English to enhance her position in Indian society.

Rowlandson's consciousness of status and rank comes through most vividly in her depiction of Weetamoo. In her resentment of this "mistress," we can sense *Mistress* Rowlandson, the woman accustomed to deference from all the goodwives and other women of Lancaster. In her description, Rowlandson makes no allusion to Weetamoo's position as a powerful sachem in her own right. Instead we see a Weetamoo who is "severe and proud" and whose attention to her personal appearance seems merely vain and obsessive rather than the concern of one whose dress and body decoration mark her political position. Rowlandson further attempts to diminish Weetamoo's stature by stating that, after all her preparation, the Pocasset sachem went to "work," making "girdles of wampum and beads," as though Weetamoo herself were little more than a servant. But the labor of drilling wampum shells was performed by Indians near Long Island Sound, where the shells were found; the shells were strung into belts and worn only by those in positions of political or religious responsibility. (Weetamoo is undoubtedly making the ceremonial belts that she later dons for the dance described in the twentieth remove.) In her evident contempt, Rowlandson betrays her rivalry with the most prominent woman in her new community.

During her captivity, then, Rowlandson was neither the entirely unreconstructed English Puritan nor the "white Indian" who, like some later captives, completely forsook her original identity.[67] Not only did she learn how to function in Indian society, but she also learned to live as an Indian, subsisting on minuscule portions of ground nuts, horses' hooves, and other food that she would formerly have found inedible. (She acknowledges only indirectly that the Indians, traveling constantly in desperate straits as they were, would also have found such fare lacking under ordinary circumstances.) Yet however much she might have lived like an Indian, Rowlandson's sense of her own identity was either too secure or too rigid to permit her actually to become one. It is noteworthy that when her sense of who she was momentarily weakened, she became less like an actual Indian than like the "savages" she and other colonial writers constructed in their accounts of the war. Certainly Rowlandson's most remarkable lapse from "civilization" occurs during the eighteenth remove when, ravenous after eating her own measly portion of horse feet, she grabs another from the mouth of a starving child—not an Indian but an English child— and quickly devours it. More generally, Rowlandson depicts herself with none of the generosity she frequently ascribes to individual Indians.

Redemption

Rowlandson's most successful moments as a captive came when she was able to play on the ambiguities of her status and of the Anglo-Algonquian cultural divide as it had evolved over the preceding half-century. Nowhere is this ambiguity more apparent than during the events leading up to her release. During the two weeks after her capture, the Indians based at Menameset attacked the English town of Medfield. But with six hundred English troops approaching, the natives fled northward, eluding their pursuers by crossing the Baquag River. Late in February they joined about three thousand other Indians from throughout New England near the site of the former Abenaki village of Squakheag, more recently the English settlement of Northfield. From there, small war parties conducted raids on English towns. Except for the false start aborted by Weetamoo on the twelfth remove, Rowlandson herself remained north of the Baquag for about six weeks. In early April she and the others in her party returned to Menameset and then proceeded to Mt. Wachusett, near the abandoned towns of Nashaway and Lancaster. There she became aware of two sets of developments affecting her fate. One was the growing demoralization of the anti-English Indians after learning of the death of the leading Narragansett sachem, Canonchet, and following their heavy losses in the fight at Sudbury. The second was the beginning of negotiations between the Indians at Mt. Wachusett and the Massachusetts colony government, with Christian Nipmuc mediation, for the release of her and other English prisoners.[68]

From the beginning it was clear that pro-English Nipmucs held the key to the release of the English captives. It was they who had relatives and friends at Mt. Wachusett and other encampments in central Massachusetts and who, if anyone, could approach these encampments without being harmed. The obvious place to find someone to undertake such a mission was Deer Island where, as we have seen, the colony confined friendly Indians. By March 1676, about four hundred pro-English, Christian Massachusetts and Nipmucs struggled to survive there, prisoners of their supposed allies and coreligionists. On at least one occasion after Rowlandson's capture, Daniel Gookin had gone to the island at Joseph Rowlandson's behest to seek volunteers willing to carry a message to the enemy. It is hardly surprising that, given the colonists' treatment of them and the prospect of what might happen should they be seized while serving the English, no one stepped immediately forward. But in late March, Joseph Rowlandson persuaded John Hoar, a Concord lawyer and fearless advocate and protector of Christian Indians, to intervene for him. Hoar induced Tom Dublet, a Nipmuc otherwise known as Nepanet, to carry a message to Mt. Wachusett (see Document 6). At the insistence of Shoshanim and other Nipmuc sachems, Nepanet was joined for the second round of negotiations by another Nipmuc, Peter Conway, whose Indian name was Tatatiqunea (see Documents 7 and 8).[69]

Although the captives were held by Narragansetts, Wampanoags, and Nipmucs, it was the Nipmuc sachems who negotiated for all the captors. While the sachems could not write their own letters, they were able to call on Indians in their own ranks for this task. These scribes were Nipmucs who had become literate in English while attending mission schools in the praying towns. While embracing much in the religion and culture of the English, they joined the anti-English cause either when the war broke out or as an alternative to confinement at Deer Island. On the other side, several different Christian Nipmucs served as scribes for the anti-English Indians, among them Peter Jethro (see Document 8), whose father Gookin had urged Nashaway accept as its minister two years earlier; and James Printer (see Documents 9 and 10), surely one of the most extraordinary presences among the anti-English Indians. Printer, known among Indians as Wowaus, derived his English name from having been apprenticed to New England's leading printer for sixteen years, until returning to his home and family in the praying town of Hassanamesit at the outbreak of war. Among other works, he had printed numerous Puritan missionary tracts publicizing his and other Christian Indians' piety. Falsely accused along with ten other Christian Nipmucs of participating in the August 1675 raid on Lancaster, he narrowly escaped death at the hands of an English lynch mob. Three months later anti-English Indians attacked Hassanamesit and gave the outnumbered inhabitants the choice of accompanying the raiders to their encampment or remaining in their town and having their corn stores burned. Knowing that if they left their village in search of food, they would almost certainly be captured by the English and sent to Deer Island, Printer and the other Hassanamesit Nipmucs chose to join forces with their captors.[70]

Despite the Nipmucs' participation, negotiations proceeded slowly at first. In the sachems' first reply to the English, Peter Jethro addressed for them a reminder to the English of their many losses and the fact that the colonists now "on your backside stand" (see Document 7). Responding to this message, the English expressed particular interest in Mary Rowlandson. At this point the Indians insisted that Rowlandson set her own price. After some hesitation, she suggested twenty pounds. Writing for the sachems, James Printer demanded not only the ransom but also that Joseph Rowlandson come personally for his wife. The English instead dispatched Hoar, but the fact that any English person of note would deal directly with them apparently satisfied the Nipmuc sachems. Nevertheless, it took three often agonizing days, until May 2, 1676, for Rowlandson to be released in Hoar's care. Thereafter the release of captives held by the natives proceeded more swiftly, so that Rowlandson's two surviving children and most other English hostages were freed by the end of the month.[71]

The release of Rowlandson and other captives was closely connected to the declining fortunes of the anti-English cause. Rowlandson's narrative amply testifies to what is probably the single most compelling factor in this decline, the natives' severe shortage of food. As the growing season approached, the Indians had two choices. They could remain north of Baquag River, try to find enough arable land and seed corn to grow crops sufficient to sustain them, and hope that English troops would continue to regard the Baquag as a boundary they would not cross. Or they could return south, resume attacking English towns, and hope to pilfer enough to eat until they regained their homelands. Returning south would enable them to build on the demoralization they had already inflicted on the colonists' society. The Indians chose the latter course and, for a short time, appeared to have the advantage. But even before their victory at Sudbury, many natives had begun to recognize that the colonists would prevent them from resuming their normal lives in their homelands. For that reason Shoshanim and other sachems began to negotiate over the release of captives, while others, including (as Rowlandson indicates) Metacom, opposed them. Indeed the return of the English captives was part of a larger process whereby the Indian opponents of the English were scattering, with most heading for their homelands. By the end of summer, fighting in the southern New England colonies had ended.[72]

REORDERING AND REMEMBERING

After her release, Mary Rowlandson spent a night near abandoned Lancaster and on the following day joined her husband in Boston. The two surviving Rowlandson children were reunited with their parents by the end of June. After three months in the home of another minister and his family in nearby Charlestown, the Rowlandsons moved to a house in Boston that was rented for them by a local congregation. They finally ended their dependence on the charity of their fellow colonists in the spring of 1677 when Joseph accepted an offer to become the minister at Wethersfield, Connecticut. Capitalizing on Mary's fame, he was able to command a starting annual salary of one hundred pounds with annual twenty-pound increments over the ensuing five years, making him one of the highest paid clergymen in New England. When he died a year and a half later, his library of books—all of which would have to have been acquired after the destruction of his home in Lancaster—was worth eighty-two pounds.[73]

Postwar Consequences

Like the Rowlandsons, most other characters in the drama surrounding Mary's captivity did not return to their prewar homes. But unlike the Rowlandsons they found few comforts. Many did not survive and those who did dispersed in many directions, often far from southern New England.

The fates of many Native American protagonists were especially harsh because they were dictated by the victorious English. After returning to the vicinity of Pokanoket, Metacom was shot and killed by a pro-English Indian. Plymouth troops decapitated, drew, and quartered his body. After

Figure 5.
This cupboard, which was purchased by the Rowlandsons shortly after their move to Wethersfield, Connecticut, demonstrates the material comfort they enjoyed in their postwar home. The floral design and other features mark it as the work of Peter Blin, a French-born Huguenot (Calvinist) joiner who made furniture for wealthier Connecticut families in the late seventeenth century.

presenting Metacom's slayer with one of his hands, they carried his head to the colony capital where it remained on public display for several decades.[74] Weetamoo likewise returned to the Plymouth area where she drowned while trying to elude pursuing English troops. To the distress of some Indian prisoners, her body was decapitated and displayed without the head in nearby Taunton.[75] Quinnapin, Shoshanim, Monoco, Peter Jethro, and even the latter's father, Jethro, once designated by Gookin as Nashaway's preacher, were captured alive. Considered leaders of the uprising, they were publicly hanged with great fanfare.[76] James Printer, on the other hand, took advantage of a pardon extended briefly in July 1676 to any anti-English Indians not accused of murder and pledging loyalty to the colony. Within weeks, Printer returned to his employer and resumed printing books and tracts for the New England reading public.[77] The colonies sold most other Indian male captives to slave traders who took them to the West Indies, Bermuda, Virginia, the Iberian peninsula, and, in at least one instance, North Africa. There are no figures on the number of Indians shipped out as slaves except in tiny Plymouth colony where the official count was 188. The wives, children, and other family members of Native American captives were generally retained as slaves within the colonies (see Documents 13 and 14).[78]

As an apprenticed member of a Boston household, James Printer probably fared better than most Indians who had remained consistently loyal to the English. Even Job Kattananit and James Quanapohit, who had previously risked their lives on behalf of the colonists, were confined to Deer Island during the anti-Indian hysteria that gripped Massachusetts Bay. Given the colony's record during the war, there can be little doubt that an undetermined number of loyal Indians were among those enslaved thereafter. Whether or not they were Christians, most other natives were confined to Natick, Wamesit, Punkapoag, and Hassanamesit, the only praying towns of the original fourteen to be reopened. What had been voluntary religious communities prior to the war had become government reservations.[79] Nevertheless, many Indians did not give up on the prospects of returning to their homelands, and in later years asserted their ownership through lawsuits or simple reoccupation. Thus it was that Nipmucs and other native peoples persisted in eastern and central Massachusetts into the eighteenth and later centuries.[80]

Meanwhile other southern New England natives, particularly those who had opposed the English, fled the region and found refuge among Mahicans and other Algonquian-speaking Indians in the colony of New York or among Abenakis, both in upper New England and in Catholic praying towns established by French missionaries in Canada.[81] Although those in New York were prevented from taking up arms against the English, those who went north found opportunities to avenge the loss of lands and family members during Metacom's War. While attempting to cultivate friendship with both imperial powers, most Abenakis leaned toward the French as a result of English encroachments on their land and English efforts to subordinate them politically. When England and France went to war in 1689, the Abenakis, Nipmucs, and other Indians to the north found ample motivation to enlist in the French cause by raiding English villages to the south.[82]

Whereas the Rowlandsons were able to cut their ties to Lancaster and move to Wethersfield, most of their former neighbors lacked the options Joseph's occupation provided. Yet they had to wait three more years before a committee of overseers allowed them to resettle their lands. Thereafter the town struggled with poverty and, until 1689, with less than full autonomy. Its congregation did not regather and install a new minister until 1690.[83] Resembling the struggling backwater of earlier years more than the relatively prosperous town it had been on the eve of the war, postwar Lancaster differed strikingly from both images in one important respect: its relationship with Native Americans. When Massachusetts consolidated its Indian towns after the war, nearby Nashaway was not reoccupied, and the nearest Indians were at Hassanamesit, about twenty miles to the south.[84] But after the outbreak of King William's War in 1689, Lancaster relived the experience of Metacom's War on several occasions when attacking Nipmucs and other Indians killed and captured some of its inhabitants.[85]

Interpreting Captivity

The postwar order taking shape in New England, then, was one in which the disparities in numbers and power between natives and colonizers were even greater than before. It was in this setting that colonists engaged in a struggle among themselves over how they would publicly remember and interpret the recent war. By the end of 1677 — little more than a year after the war ended — more than a dozen accounts and explanations of the conflict had been published in Massachusetts and England, and several more were in preparation.[86] To a great extent this outpouring can be ascribed to authors' efforts to cash in on the tastes of a lucrative English (including colonial) literary market. But for several authors, the war raised issues that went directly to the heart of New England's collective identity. For Increase Mather, the ambitious young minister of Boston's North Church, the devastation inflicted by the Indians demonstrated God's anger with the colonists for abandoning the spiritual rigor and piety of New England's founding generation and lapsing into the pursuit of personal,

Figure 6.
Ninigret, Eastern Niantic sachem, ca. 1681 (unknown artist.) This oil painting is
the only known portrait of a New England Indian made during the subject's life-
time. Ninigret's clothing and accoutrements reflect his participation in an Anglo-
Indian material world.

material gratification. Only a thoroughgoing spiritual reformation in which the colonists collectively begged God for forgiveness and changed their ways would lift the threat of Indian attacks. For William Hubbard, the minister of Ipswich, on the other hand, the war was caused not by God but by Satan, who unleashed the barbaric "savages" resisting the expansion of "civilization" into the "wilderness." What New England needed, he believed, was not a return to a narrow biblicism but unity in the face of a threat by alien others to destroy a vibrant, godly society. Both men were responding to the region's growing absorption into a transatlantic commercial economy and the resulting influx of material goods and of non-Puritan people and ideas that did not fit comfortably within the Calvinist vision of the founders. Whereas Mather viewed this influx as a frightening development for Puritans, Hubbard saw it as a challenge.[87]

Meanwhile Daniel Gookin, the Massachusetts Bay superintendent of Christian Indians, had written a very different kind of history and sent it to London in hopes of having it published. Rather than presenting a comprehensive overview of the war, Gookin set out explicitly to vindicate the praying Indians' loyalty and conduct during the war and to demonstrate the extent to which these pious Christians had been persecuted because of an unyielding hatred of all Indians on the part of many colonists.[88] In these various interpretations of the recent past, the authors were endeavoring not simply to inform and entertain their readers but to influence current debates on what kind of society New England was and should be, who was part of it and who was not, and—by implication—to suggest where the locus of political and moral authority should lie.

Among those preparing an account of the war in this period was Mary Rowlandson. Although the circumstances under which Rowlandson began composing her narrative are not made explicit in any surviving evidence, there are good reasons for suspecting that she at least drafted it several years before it was published in 1682. If we look to the narrative itself for clues, we find that Rowlandson refers to her family's stay in Boston in the past tense, suggesting that it was written after about May 1677. And the narrative implies that Joseph Rowlandson is still living, which would place its composition before November 1678. While such implicit dating could well be an artifice deliberately constructed by Rowlandson to make it appear that the narrative was authored at this time, the power and immediacy with which she conveys her experiences suggest that they were still fresh in her mind when she wrote them down. Indeed one scholar, Kathryn Zabelle Derounian, has argued that Rowlandson penned her narrative soon after her release for therapeutic reasons, in order to gain the distance she needed to recover from her trauma and understand it in Puritan terms. Also, Mitchell Robert Breitwieser makes a powerful case for Rowlandson's writing in order to assuage her grief over the loss of her daughter (and, in the process, subverting Puritan norms relating to mourning).[89] In addition, there is the testimony of the preface, which states that Rowlandson composed her narrative as a "memorandum of Gods dealing with her, that she might never forget, but remember the same . . . all the days of her life," and the fact that the manuscript circulated for some time among private hands before Rowlandson was finally prevailed upon to publish it.

Despite the preface's protests on behalf of Rowlandson's modesty, it seems clear that she sought to participate in the debates among those who were interpreting the war's history in print. In understanding the war and her captivity as manifestations of divine providence, Rowlandson aligned herself with Mather's viewpoint as opposed to Hubbard's. In doing so, she not only derives numerous spiritual lessons for herself, she asserts that the English cause itself was dependent on God's favor. Thus of the five "remarkable passages of providence" she enumerates during the final remove, three were military failures by the English army. As with Mather, Rowlandson cites divine providence to explain the humanity showed her by Indians, and she shares Hubbard's deep-seated hostility toward Native Americans.[90]

Rowlandson parted company with Mather and Hubbard on one critical point: the treatment of praying Indians. Both men noted the loyalty and contributions to the English cause by the Christian Indians, and Mather even includes mistreatment of them as one of New England's sins. Rowlandson, on the other hand, reserves her greatest contempt for native converts to Christianity. For this reason it would seem that, of all contemporary historians, Gookin was Rowlandson's primary target. Whereas other authors note the contributions or suffering of praying Indians in passing, he wrote a book-length account that detailed the contributions of James Quanapohit, Job Kattananit, and other native Christians, as well as the sufferings and injustices they had suffered. The purpose and thrust of his book was to exonerate the praying Indians and to condemn his fellow English for punishing innocent people.[91] To counter Gookin, Rowlandson offers ample evidence of Christian Indians mocking, fighting against, and killing colonists—and in some cases going unpunished. She has seen one of her tormentors, she writes, "walking up and down Boston, under the appearance of a Friend-Indian, and severall others of the like cut." Moreover, she uncritically repeats fraudulent accounts of praying Indian behavior. At the end of the first remove, for example, she blames Printer and the other Christian Nipmucs accused in the earlier attack on Lancaster, ignoring the fact that they were exon-

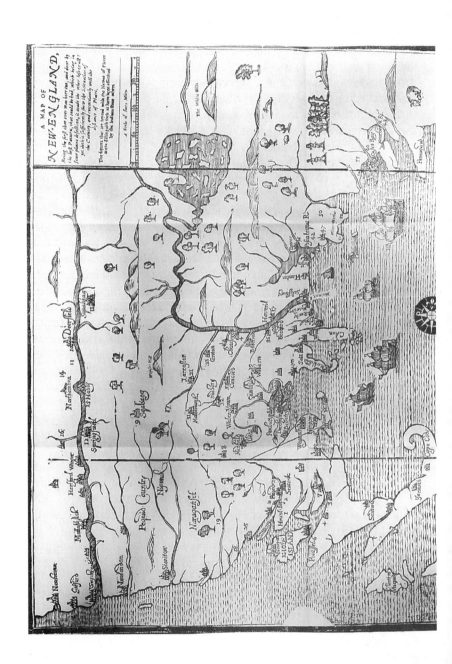

A MAP OF
NEW-ENGLAND,

Being the first that ever was here cut, and done by the best Pattern that could be had, which being in some places defective, it made the other less exact: yet doth it sufficiently show the Scituation of the Country, and conveniently well the distance of Places.

The figures that are joyned with the Names of Places are to distinguish such as have been assaulted by the Indians from others.

A Scale of Sorts Miles

erated in court.[92] Yet as with her other statements about Indians, she speaks in strikingly different tones when referring to individual Christian Indians whose actions benefited her. "Though they were Indians," she writes when Tom Dublet and Peter Conway arrived to effect her release, "I gat them by the hand, and burst out into tears; my heart was so full I could not [at first] speak to them; . . ."

There are suggestions in her narrative and elsewhere that Rowlandson also wrote in order to clear her name with respect to a number of rumors and innuendoes. Shortly after her capture, Nathaniel Saltonstall, a prolific chronicler of the war, took pains in one of his reports to dispel a rumor that Rowlandson had been forced to marry Monoco, the Nashaway Nipmuc known to the English as One-eyed John. In the preface to her narrative, the author implicitly repudiates any notion that Rowlandson's virtue had been violated, noting her "modesty" about publishing, the "coy phantasies" that some may entertain wrongly about her captivity, and the "anxieties and perplexities" attending her experience. Rowlandson herself remarks, during the ninth remove, that no Indian offered her "the least imaginable miscarriage," and notes, during the twentieth, that on the one occasion she saw an Indian drunk, it was her master, Quinnapin, who treated her properly even while chasing his wives. Apparently some colonists thought that Rowlandson was glorying too much in her victimhood, for near the conclusion of the narrative, she notes that "some are ready to say, I speak it [her experience] for my own credit; but I speak it in the presence of God, and to His glory." Although it was never expressed directly, there may also have been resentment over Rowlandson being elevated publicly above the other captives, especially near the end when she was the focus of English efforts at redemption and was in fact the first to be freed.

Mary Rowlandson's life took another abrupt, shocking turn when, in November 1678, her husband Joseph died suddenly at the age of forty-seven. Soon thereafter the Wethersfield town meeting voted that she should receive Joseph's current compensation of 120 pounds for the rest of that year and thereafter a stipend of 30 pounds annually "so long as she

---

Figure 7 *(left).* **Map of Southern New England, facing west, 1677**
Published shortly after the end of Metacom's War, this map accompanied William Hubbard's account of the conflict. When compared with the earlier English map (see Figure 2), it shows English towns dominating the landscape, with remaining Indians pushed to the periphery of English settlement. In denying the fact that native people persisted in the immediate vicinity of colonists, Hubbard joined the postwar trend among many English to pronounce them as having disappeared.

shall remain a widow among us."[93] Like most other widows in the English colonies, she did not remain one for long. Nine months later she married Samuel Talcott, also of Wethersfield, whose own wife had recently died. Talcott had attended Harvard but, unlike Joseph Rowlandson, did not enter the ministry. Instead, he became a wealthy landowner who represented Wethersfield in Connecticut's General Court and, during Metacom's War, sat on the colony's war council. But like Joseph Rowlandson, Samuel Talcott was addressed as "mister."[94] Thus before she published her narrative, Mistress Mary Rowlandson had become Mistress Mary Talcott.

Publicizing Captivity

How and why was Rowlandson's written, privately circulated manuscript transformed into a published work? (Since she published under the name Mary Rowlandson, this introduction will continue to refer to her that way.) There is substantial evidence indicating that Increase Mather played a central role in getting the manuscript published.[95] Mather and the Rowlandsons were old acquaintances, and Mather had gone to the Massachusetts Bay Council just a week after the Lancaster attack with Joseph's request for assistance in securing his family's release.[96] As part of his long project to demonstrate the role of divine providence in shaping human lives and events, Mather had begun as early as 1670 collecting evidence to support his thesis. The project culminated in 1684 with the publication of *An Essay for the Recording of Illustrious Providences,* which featured not only survivors of Indian captivity but survivors of other catastrophes, such as maritime accidents and severe storms, and evidence of God's working through ghosts and other supernatural phenomena.[97] By far the best-known evidence of providential deliverance in New England, Rowlandson's captivity and redemption were recounted in both Mather's history and most other histories of the war. Finally, it was Mather who was leading the way among New England ministers in using the press to publish his sermons and other writings, thereby spreading his fame far beyond the churchgoers who heard him on Sundays. In 1674 he had engineered the establishment of the first printer in Boston, breaking the long monopoly held by Cambridge across the river. His influence persisted after that printer died and was replaced by Samuel Green, Jr.[98] In 1681 Green published an edition of English author John Bunyan's *The Pilgrim's Progress,* a fictionalized account of one person's spiritual journey to piety. On the last page, Green advertised several forthcoming publications, including Rowlandson's narrative.[99]

Green's advertisement implied that Rowlandson's tract would appear by itself, but it actually arrived as part of a larger package. The packaging offers some important clues about the anxieties surrounding the publishing of a female author in colonial New England. For one thing, Rowlandson's tract was bound with the final sermon preached by Joseph Rowlandson before his death in 1678. To be sure, Joseph's sermon was thematically related to Mary's narrative. Entitled "The Possibility of God's Forsaking a People that have been Visibly Near and Dear to him, together with the Misery of a People thus Forsaken" (see Document 16), the sermon was a standard jeremiad[100] in which Rowlandson cited the Old Testament to show precedents for God's being angry with his chosen people. Like the ancient Israelites, he maintained, New Englanders were guilty of pride, ingratitude toward God, and a litany of other sins betraying their spiritual complacency. His final words echoed a theme that his wife's experience must have driven home with particular intensity: "Forsake your sins whereby you have forsaken him. . . . If there be any, Son or Daughter, that will not leave their sins for God, God will leave such."[101] In general, the sermon is a long theological footnote to the narrative, and it was undoubtedly regarded by Mather as a useful weapon in his war with those who opposed his efforts to instigate a spiritual reformation. But while it was not uncommon in New England for the last sermon of a well-known minister to be posthumously published, Joseph Rowlandson's fame derived largely from that of his wife and his sermon was hardly the main attraction in this package. Not only had Green not bothered to mention the sermon in his advance advertising, but also he had placed it after the narrative in the bound volume. There is little reason to suppose that anyone would have bothered to publish Joseph's sermon were it not for his wife and her narrative.

But if Joseph Rowlandson could not appear in print without Mary, neither could she stand alone without him and without the clergyman who authored her narrative's preface, presumably Increase Mather. The preface begins by situating the attack on Lancaster in the context of the war's military history and goes on to mention Joseph Rowlandson before referring in any way to Mary. And when Mary finally does become the center of discussion, the preface never directly names her but refers to her sometimes as Joseph's "precious yokefellow" and "dear consort," but mostly as "Gentlewoman." The author, whether Mather or another, seems to have hoped that an emphasis on Rowlandson's marital status and social rank and an avoidance of her individuality would in some measure obviate the fact of her gender. At the same time, the preface is at pains to assure readers that the "Narrative was penned by the Gentlewoman herself" and published in spite of her "modesty." In this way, it strives to overcome the doubts of those who believed a woman incapable of writing on her own, who feared that the act of writing would somehow detract from a woman's femininity, or who assumed that a woman could not have survived captivity without compromising her marital fidelity or her cultural identity. The author expresses the hope that "none will cast any reflection upon this Gentlewoman, on the score of this publication of her affliction and deliverance." She has a "dispensation of publick note, and universall concernment," he says, which is the stronger for her being married to a minister. She is fulfilling a vow to praise God publicly; "[e]xcuse her, then, if she comes thus into public, to pay those vows, Come and hear what she has to say."

The preface is an elaborate effort to legitimize Rowlandson's appearance not simply as a female author but also as a woman offering her direct, unique perspectives on the experience of God's grace in her own life. In a society that had not, after nearly half a century, forgotten the threat posed by Anne Hutchinson's claims to spiritual authority independent of the clergy, the preface's author understood the need to frame Rowlandson's narrative by pointing out that its author was a woman whose orthodoxy could not be challenged. Popular expectations surrounding her narrative, anticipated in Green's advertisement, made clear that Rowlandson was going to have a following no matter what form her narrative took. The goal of the preface was simultaneously to emphasize the narrative's theological significance and to reassure advocates of reform that Rowlandson was in agreement with them. The presence of Joseph Rowlandson's sermon—whether or not anyone read it—was a further attempt to signal that Mary's act of writing and publishing took place within and not outside conventional boundaries of theology and gender as established in the United Colonies of New England.

Rowlandson herself provides ample guidance for gleaning her narrative's theological message. The most obvious way she does this is through frequent citations of biblical passages as demonstrating the meaning of her experience or state of mind on a given occasion. Even before an Indian gives her a Bible plundered during the raid on Medfield, Rowlandson refers to or quotes verses that reassure her that such afflictions struck God's chosen people in ancient times and that he never forgets his promise to redeem those saints who do not forsake him. Some commentators have pointed to these references as evidence that the narrative was significantly shaped by clerical influence, either Mather, Joseph Rowlandson, or someone else among those who read it in manuscript. There is no reason to doubt the probability that others, including members of the clergy, read the manuscript and made suggestions to its author, as is the case with most published works. But it is clear that Rowlandson, as the daughter of a woman who converted to Puritanism independently of her husband and as the wife of a minister, was sufficiently steeped in the Bible and in Puritan interpretations of it to draw such conclusions on her own.

In fact Rowlandson does more than cite scripture to establish herself as an authority on spiritual matters. The entire narrative serves to remind her readers that, as indicated in the preface, she has experienced the extremes of terror and redemption as few other mortals have. She summarizes this experience and its meaning in an eloquent passage near the end of the narrative, after she and her family have found refuge and security in the Boston home of James Whitcomb:

> *I can remember the time, when I used to sleep quietly without workings in my thoughts, whole nights together, but now it is other wayes with me.* When all are fast about me, and no eye open, but his who ever waketh, my thoughts are upon things past, upon the awful dispensation of the Lord towards us; upon his wonderfull power and might, in carrying of us through so many difficulties, in returning us to safety, and suffering none to hurt us.

And further on:

> *Before I knew what affliction meant, I was ready sometimes to wish for it.* . . . But now I see the Lord had his time to scourge and chasten me. . . . Affliction I wanted, and affliction I had, full measure; . . . yet I see, when God calls a person to any thing, and through never so many difficulties, yet he is fully able to carry them through and make them see, and say they have been gainers thereby.

Neither here nor elsewhere in her narrative does Rowlandson refer to any mediating force in her relationship with God. While a man's testimony of such an experience might have escaped notice, a woman's was highly problematic. Recall that Rowlandson's mother, forty years earlier, was an exception among women who could voice such experiences even within the confines of her congregation. And it had been only four years since the first woman author—recently deceased poet Anne Bradstreet—had been published in New England (or, for that matter, in North America). All that stands between Rowlandson and the direct revelation from God that sealed Anne Hutchinson's fate is the mantle of clerical authority provided by her husband's sermon and the preface.[102]

Protected by that authority, Rowlandson goes beyond strictly reporting her private, spiritual experience into the all-male realm of public discourse. She joins Mather, Joseph Rowlandson, and other jeremiad preachers by castigating those who concern themselves with worldly goods and pleasures at the expense of concern over their and New England's spiritual fate. Rowlandson goes still further when she criticizes Massachusetts's conduct of the war. Although ascribing to God's providence such failures as the army's refusal to pursue her captors across the Baquag River, the very mention of these failures constituted a criticism of the army. In the narrative's larger context, she is criticizing colony leaders who neglected their responsibilities and put colonists in harm's way by failing to prosecute the war with sufficient vigor.

Even more bold is Rowlandson's condemnation of the praying Indians. Here she took on the entire missionary enterprise in New England and in so doing defied its chief source of support, consisting of virtually the entire clerical and political elite in New England, including Mather. Implicit in her indictment is a radical departure from Puritan orthodoxy, namely that some people, because of the circumstances of birth, have no potential for being saved, that in effect they lack the souls that distinguish God's human creatures from all others. In so suggesting, Rowlandson contributed to a nascent shift in the way Anglo-Americans distinguished Europeans from alien "others," from a basis in religion and culture to one in what would in the nineteenth century be called "race." In short, Rowlandson used her position as a clerically approved author to pronounce judgments on a wide range of political and intellectual questions, ranging well beyond where any other woman in the seventeenth-century colonies was able to go.

By asserting her authority so boldly, Rowlandson seemed to be trying to quash any lingering doubts among her readers—and perhaps in herself—that she had ever been attracted in any way to life among her captors. Yet while a claim to authority, the passage quoted before also suggests a persistent discomfort, as if what Rowlandson knew, what haunted her in the stillness of night, was the realization that her experience among Native Americans—and the native people themselves—could not be fully contained by her narrative, by Puritan theology, even by the Bible. Perhaps she had been touched in ways she could not fully fathom by her experience. Perhaps, after all, her experience *was* one that could not be fully communicated to and shared with her fellow colonists.

However it was understood by her readers, Rowlandson's published narrative proved to be an instant success. The first edition sold out so quickly that Green, having committed himself to several other projects, was unable to answer the demand. He therefore referred the narrative to his father, Samuel Green, Sr., a Cambridge printer, who published not only a second but also a third edition in 1682.[103] Apparently the three editions so saturated the New England market that another edition did not appear until 1720. The most authoritative study of American best-sellers, written before evidence of the Boston edition was discovered, calculates that the second and third editions alone sold more than one thousand copies, meaning that more than one percent of the New England population purchased the book. It is clear, not only from the evidence of sales but also from what is known about colonial New England readers, that many people read, or heard read aloud, each copy and that Rowlandson's audience included large numbers of ordinary colonists as well as ministers and other members of the region's elite.[104]

An irony connected with the second and third editions is that Green, Sr. now employed James Printer. Thus the text that made the strongest and most virulent case for praying Indian disloyalty was printed by the man who, by being not only pardoned for fighting the English but also getting his old job back, most directly defied the blanket categorization that divided New Englanders into "savage" Indians and "civilized" English. Printer also illustrates how, even after Metacom's War, the colonists still depended, in certain crucial ways, on Indians who embodied the cultural and political ambiguities prompting Rowlandson's hatred of Christian Indians. The irony is compounded by the fact that, with all but four pages from one copy of the Boston edition having disappeared, Printer's edition is the one closest to Rowlandson's own writing.[105]

Meanwhile one of Rowlandson's Boston printers sent a copy of the first edition to London, where a fourth edition appeared, also in 1682, but with a different title. The New England editions, aimed at a Puritan audience and intended to reinforce calls for spiritual reformation, appeared as *The Sovereignty and Goodness of God*. For England's more religiously diverse reading public, the publisher retitled the narrative as *A True History of the Captivity and Restoration of Mrs. Mary Rowlandson*.[106] In New England, where Rowlandson's sponsors sought in every way to downplay her personal role as both author and actor and were narrowly concerned with their own region, the subject was God; in England, where readers' interests were more secular and cosmopolitan, the title foregrounded Rowlandson and suggested an exotic adventure.

Mary Rowlandson's Legacy

Fifteen years after *The Sovereignty and Goodness of God* was published, another instance of captivity provided an added twist to the long history of Rowlandson's relations with Native Americans. Near the end of the conflict that is known in the colonies as King William's War and in Europe as the War of the League of Augsburg (1689–97), a party of French-allied Indians attacked the Massachusetts town of Haverhill and captured about forty inhabitants. The fleeing Indians then broke up into several smaller bands, one of which held an English woman named Hannah Dustin, her nurse, and seven children, including a twelve-year-old boy captured the year before at Worcester, Massachusetts. Unlike Rowlandson, Dustin concocted a plan to escape. One night she, the boy, and the nurse awoke, quietly and methodically killed and scalped ten of the natives (a woman and a small child escaped), and led their party to safety. A few weeks later, a scalp-bearing Dustin entered Boston to great acclaim and successfully petitioned the General Court for scalp bounties for herself, her nurse, and the boy. She received not only her allocation, but many gifts as well as literary immortality when Cotton Mather, son of Increase and by now a prominent minister in his own right, recorded her story (see Document 17). Dustin also visited another well-known colonist, Samuel Sewall, who, in recording the meeting in his famous diary, pointed out a connection between New England's two best-known captives. Dustin told him that "her Master, whom she killed, did formerly live with Mr. Rowlandson at Lancaster." In this brief statement lies the only recorded evidence of contact between Rowlandson and Native Americans before her capture. Sewall's entry goes on to say that the unnamed Indian told Dustin "that when he prayed the English way, he thought that was good; but now he found the French way was better."[107] Apparently the Rowlandsons, like a number of other English families during the middle decades of the seventeenth century, had taken a young Christian Indian as a servant into their home, thereby gaining some labor while promoting the "civilization" of a "savage."[108] More than likely, the boy was one of the Christian Nipmucs from nearby Nashaway. Whether or not he joined the fight against the English in Metacom's War—and perhaps the attack on Lancaster— thereby reinforcing Rowlandson's hostility toward Christian Indians, is not clear. In any case, he was one of many Indians who had fled north to begin a new life in Canada.

Although the name Mary Rowlandson was widely known in New England after *The Sovereignty and Goodness of God* was published, Mary Talcott of Wethersfield, Connecticut, lived out her days as Samuel Talcott's wife and, after he died in 1691, as his widow. Her one appearance in the historical record as Mary Talcott came late in her life and constituted a strange postscript to her captivity. In 1707 she posted bond following the arrest of her son, Joseph Rowlandson, Jr., the pious boy of the narrative who was now a prosperous Wethersfield landowner and merchant. A man claiming to be the long-vanished brother of Rowlandson, Jr.'s, wife suddenly appeared and charged that, five years earlier, Rowlandson and another brother-in-law had gotten him drunk and sold him as an indentured servant to a shipowner bound for Virginia. The court, apparently not trusting either party, postponed making its decision for thirteen years before finally ruling in favor of Rowlandson's accuser. By then the verdict was moot, for Rowlandson, Jr., and his accuser had both died. But the incident brought the theme of forced captivity back into the life of Mary Rowlandson when, as the widow Talcott, her former good name could not dispel the suspicions directed against her son. Like her son, she was spared the ignominy that would have followed the court's finding, having died in January 1711 at about seventy-three years of age.[109]

Rowlandson's fame grew in the years and centuries after her death. A fifth edition of her narrative was published in 1720, and it has been almost continually in print since 1770.[110] Through the mid-twentieth century, it was read primarily by those seeking religious or moral edification or simply a good adventure story. The fact that Rowlandson was female undoubtedly made it especially significant for female readers by implicitly expanding the perimeters of female identity. Although attracting scholarly interest during the mid-nineteenth century, Rowlandson has only recently become widely read by students of American history and literature.

Rowlandson's influence endures beyond the popularity of her narrative. While the earliest European account of captivity among North American Indians is in portions of the narrative of the shipwrecked Spanish explorer, Alvar Núñez Cabeza de Vaca, first published in 1542,[111] Rowlandson deserves credit for inventing the particular Anglo-American genre known as the captivity narrative. Her account gave rise to hundreds of imitators, first from New England, then from other colonial regions and, finally, from throughout the independent American republic. Most colonial narratives followed Rowlandson by opening with a dramatic, surprise Indian attack, narrating the captive's travels, and ending with her or his release. They usually stressed the religious and moral meanings of the captivity experience and reinforced constructions of the sharp divide separating "civilized" from "savage" peoples. Over time, variations on Rowlandson's formula developed. One was the advent of the third-person account, narrated by someone other than the captive, such as Cotton Mather's account of Hannah Dustin (see Document 17). Other narratives were related in the first person but betrayed the heavy hands of non-Indian editors, such as James Seaver in Mary Jemison's narrative. Some narratives, like Jemison's, told of captives who, instead of returning home at the end, chose to remain with their captors. Others intro-

Figure 8.

As the American colonists' showdown with England approached in the 1770s, the threat posed by Indians was equated in many colonists' minds with the threat posed by the British. Men, and even women such as Rowlandson, were touted as examples of patriotic resistance. This engraving first appeared in a children's adventure story, "The Life and Adventures of a Female Soldier," in 1762. When the printer decided to produce a new edition of Rowlandson's narrative, he reused the engraving minus the title across the top. In so doing he ignored the fact that Rowlandson never claimed to have wielded a gun or physically resisted her captors.

Figure 9.
This crude woodcut, depicting Rowlandson fleeing the burning garrison house, appeared in the 1771 edition of *The Sovereignty and Goodness of God.*

A

NARRATIVE

OF THE

CAPTIVITY, SUFFERINGS AND REMOVES

OF

Mrs. *Mary Rowlandſon,*

Who was taken Priſoner by the INDIANS with ſeveral others, and treated in the moſt barbarous and cruel Manner by thoſe vile Savages : With many other remarkable Events during her TRAVELS.

Written by her own Hand, for her private Uſe, and now made public at the earneſt Deſire of ſome Friends, and for the Benefit of the afflicted.

BOSTON :

Printed and Sold at JOHN BOYLE's Printing-Office, next Door to the *Three Doves* in Marlborough Street 1773

Figure 10.
The title page of the 1773 edition once again represented Rowlandson wielding a rifle in defense of her home.

duced elements of fiction in order to heighten the text's allure for readers seeking a taste of terror or exoticism. Over time, the captivity motif spread beyond the narrative genre to imaginative literature, the stage, and, in the twentieth century, film.[112] The powerful cultural influence of this literature is evident to this day in our responses to contemporary captivities such as those of prisoners of war and hostages held by kidnappers or terrorists.

The genre of the captivity narrative as conventionally defined refers exclusively to accounts of non-Indians held by Indians. As such it juxtaposes Euro-American suffering to Native American aggression, subtly inverting the process of dispossession of natives by colonizers that was in fact the context for most narratives. Yet there are many accounts by and about Native Americans that testify to their own experiences as captives — which, after all, far outnumber those of whites among Indians — as well as captors. Our understanding of the cross-cultural dimensions of captivity will remain incomplete until the stories of the James Quanapohits, James Printers, and Weetamoos throughout American history are fully fleshed out and placed alongside the more familiar narratives of Euro-Americans.

Nevertheless, the vast outpouring of narratives testifies to the enduring appeal of the captivity experience as a means by which audiences can journey vicariously beyond the boundaries of their given cultural identities, reinforcing or loosening those boundaries, but, either way, returning to where they started. Directly and through her influence on the authors who came after her, Mary Rowlandson has taught generations of Americans how to imagine such an experience.

NOTES

[1]Sherburne F. Cook, "Interracial Warfare and Population Decline among the New England Indians," *Ethnohistory* 20 (1973), 1–24; U.S. Department of Commerce, Bureau of the Census, *Historical Statistics of the United States, Colonial Times to 1970,* 2 vols. (Washington, D.C.: U.S. Government Printing Office, 1975), 2:1168 (Series Z 1–19); Michael J. Puglisi, *Puritans Besieged: The Legacies of King Philip's War in the Massachusetts Bay Colony* (Lanham, Md.: University Press of America, 1991); Almon Wheeler Lauber, *Indian Slavery in the Colonial Times within the Present Limits of the United States* (New York: Columbia University, 1913); Evan Haefli and Kevin Sweeney, "Revisiting *The Redeemed Captive:* New Perspectives on the 1704 Attack on Deerfield," *William and Mary Quarterly,* 3d ser., 52 (1995), 3–46; T. H. Breen, "Wars, Taxes, and Political Brokers: The Ordeal of Massachusetts Bay, 1675–1692," in Breen, *Puritans and Adventurers: Change and Persistence in Early America* (New York: Oxford University Press, 1980), 68–80.

[2]Almira Larkin White, *Genealogy of the Descendants of John White of Wenham and Lancaster, Massachusetts, 1638–1900,* 4 vols. (Haverhill, Mass.: Chase Brothers, 1900–1909), 1:11, 13; 4:11; David L. Greene, "New Light on Mary Rowlandson," *Early American Literature* 20 (1985), 24.

[3]Robert G. Pope (ed.), *The Notebook of the Reverend John Fiske, 1644–1675,* Publications of the Colonial Society of Massachusetts, 47 (1974), 30.

[4]Pope, *Notebook,* 30.

[5]White, *Genealogy,* 1:9–10; 4:11.

[6]Pope, *Notebook,* 30–31; Mary Maples Dunn, "Saints and Sisters: Congregational and Quaker Women in the Early Colonial Period," *American Quarterly* 30 (1978), 589. I am grateful to Professor Laurel Thatcher Ulrich for pointing out to me that Joan White of Wenham was Mary Rowlandson's mother.

[7]David D. Hall (ed.), *The Antinomian Controversy, 1636–1638: A Documentary History* (Middletown, Conn.: Wesleyan University Press, 1968), 4–20; Dunn, "Saints and Sisters," 585–87.

[8]Pope, *Notebook,* 13–20 passim.

[9]White, *Genealogy,* 4:11–13, 15–21.

[10]Neal Salisbury, *Manitou and Providence: Indians, Europeans, and the Making of New England, 1500–1643* (New York: Oxford University Press, 1982), 22–30, 101–06, 183–84.

[11]Thomas Morton, *New English Canaan,* ed. Charles Francis Adams (Boston: Prince Society, 1883), 132–33. Golgotha, or Calvary, was the place where Jesus, and many others convicted by Roman authorities, were crucified.

[12]Salisbury, *Manitou and Providence,* 48–49, 147–50. On the early awareness by English traders of the Nipmucs, see Everett Emerson (ed.), *Letters from New England: The Massachusetts Bay Colony, 1629–1638* (Amherst: University of Massachusetts Press, 1976), 68; Morton, *New English Canaan,* 270–73.

[13]Salisbury, *Manitou and Providence,* 203–25.

[14]Nathaniel E. Shurtleff (ed.), *Records of the Governor and Company of the Massachusetts Bay in New England* (hereafter, *Mass. Recs.*) (Boston: W. White, 1853–54), 2:55–56; John Winthrop, *Winthrop's Journal: "History of New England," 1630–1649,* 2 vols. (New York: Charles Scribner's Sons, 1908), 2:160.

[15]*Mass. Recs.,* 1:327, 2:11; Winthrop, *Journal,* 2:154–55.

[16]Henry S. Nourse (ed.), *Early Records of Lancaster, Massachusetts, 1643–1725* (Lancaster, 1884), 13–15; Winthrop, *Journal,* 2:165.

[17]*Mass. Recs.,* 2:16; Nourse, *Early Records of Lancaster,* 308–309; Samuel Eliot Morison, "The Plantation of Nashaway—An Industrial Experiment," *Publications of the Colonial Society of Massachusetts* 27 (1932), 209–10, 213; David D. Hall, *The Faithful Shepard: A History of the New England Ministry in the Seventeenth Century* (Chapel Hill: University of North Carolina Press, 1972), 127–29.

[18]*Mass. Recs.,* 2:212.

[19]Nourse, *Early Records of Lancaster,* 17–19.

[20]*Mass. Recs.,* 2:55.

[21]*Mass. Recs.,* 3:365–66.

[22]*Mass. Recs.,* 3:302–04; Nourse, *Early Records of Lancaster,* 22–23; Winthrop, *Journal,* 2:343.

[23]Thomas Franklin Waters, *Ipswich in the Massachusetts Bay Colony,* 2 vols. (Ipswich, Mass.: Ipswich Historical Society, 1899), 1:493; George A. Schofield (ed.), *Ancient Records of Ipswich* (Ipswich, Mass.: G.A. Schofield, 1899), vol. 1 entries for 1646–50 passim; George Francis Dow (ed.), *Records and Files of the Quarterly Courts of Essex County, Massachusetts,* 4 vols. (Salem, Mass.: Essex Institute 1911–75), 1:37, 109, 112, 142, 143, 147, 168, 221, 233, 261 and n., 275–76, 277, 385, 387. Rowlandson also had defenders against his wife's claim. See Mary Beth Norton, *Founding Mothers and Fathers: Gendered Power and the Forming of American Society* (New York: Knopf, 1996), 91–95 passim.

[24]John L. Sibley, *Biographical Sketches of Graduates of Harvard University,* vol. 1, *1642–1658* (Cambridge, Mass.: Charles William Sever, 1873), 311–16.

[25] Nourse, *Early Records of Lancaster,* 62.

[26] Abijah P. Marvin, *History of the Town of Lancaster, Massachusetts, from the First Settlement to the Present Time, 1643–1879* (Lancaster, Mass.: Town of Lancaster, 1879), 95; Nourse, *Early Records of Lancaster,* 41; Joseph B. Felt, *History of Ipswich, Essex, and Hamilton,* (Cambridge, Mass.: C. Folsom, 1834), 23; Norton, *Founding Mothers and Fathers,* 18–19.

[27] Nourse, *Early Records of Lancaster,* 46–48.

[28] *Mass. Recs.,* 3:428; Nourse, *Early Records of Lancaster,* 50, 51, 55–56, 64, 76–77.

[29] Nourse, *Early Records of Lancaster,* 309; Samuel Sewall, *The Diary of Samuel Sewall, 1674–1729,* ed. M. Halsey Thomas 2 vols., (New York: Farrar, Straus, and Giroux, 1973), 1:372–73.

[30] William Cronon, *Changes in the Land: Indians, Colonists, and the Ecology of New England* (New York: Hill and Wang, 1983), 96–103; Neal Salisbury, "Indians and Colonists after the Pequot War: An Uneasy Balance," in Laurence M. Hauptman and James D. Wherry (eds.), *The Pequots in Southern New England: The Fall and Rise of an American Indian Nation* (Norman: University of Oklahoma Press 1990), 90.

[31] *Mass. Recs.,* 4(2):340; Henry S. Nourse (ed.), *Lancastriana,* 2 vols. (Clinton, Mass.: W. J. Coulter, 1900–1901), 1:7.

[32] Bernard Bailyn, *The New England Merchants in the Seventeenth Century* (Cambridge, Mass.: Harvard University Press, 1955), 55–56.

[33] Robert K. Diebold, "Joseph Rowlandson," in James A. Lavernier and Douglas R. Wilms (eds.), *American Writers before 1800,* 3 vols. (Westport, Conn.: Greenwood Press, 1983), 3:1245.

[34] *Mass. Recs.,* 4(2):556–57.

[35] Cronon, *Changes in the Land,* 88–89; Nourse, *Early Records of Lancaster,* 40–41; Daniel Gookin, *Historical Collections of the Indians in New England,* ed. Jeffrey Fiske (n.p.: Towtaid, 1970), 85; Salisbury, "Indians and Colonists after the Pequot War," 91–92.

[36] Cronon, *Changes in the Land,* 128–37; Virginia DeJohn Anderson, "King Philip's Herds: Indians, Colonists, and the Problem of Livestock in Early New England," *William and Mary Quarterly,* 3d ser., 51 (1994), 601–24.

[37] Douglas Edward Leach, *Flintlock and Tomahawk: New England in King Philip's War* (New York: Macmillan, 1958), 30–44.

[38] Gookin, *Historical Collections,* 85–87.

[39] Jill Lepore, "Dead Men Tell No Tales: John Sassamon and the Fatal Consequences of Literacy," *American Quarterly,* 46 (1994) 479–512; Lepore, "The Name of War: Waging, Writing, and Remembering Metacom's War" (Ph.D. diss., Yale University, 1995), 84–131; Leach, *Flintlock and Tomahawk,* 14–29.

[40] Leach, *Flintlock and Tomahawk,* 44–72 passim.

[41] Leach, *Flintlock and Tomahawk,* 72–84.

[42] Nourse, *Early Records of Lancaster,* 352.

[43] Leach, *Flintlock and Tomahawk,* 85–102, 112–44, 155–57.

[44] Patrick M. Malone, *The Skulking Way of War: Technology and Tactics among the New England Indians* (Lanham, Md.: Madison Books, 1991), 29–36, 42–66, 70–75.

[45] John Underhill, "Newes from America" (1638), *Massachusetts Historical Society Collections,* 3d ser., 6 (1837), 26.

[46] Adam J. Hirsch, "The Collision of Military Cultures in Seventeenth-Century New England," *Journal of American History* 74 (1988), 1187–1212; Allyn B. Forbes (ed.), *Winthrop Papers,* 5 vols. (Boston: Massachusetts Historical Society, 1929–47), 3:414; Malone, *Skulking Way of War,* 75–80.

[47] Daniel Gookin, "An Historical Account of the Doings and Sufferings of the Christian Indians in New England," *Archaeologia Americana, Transactions and Collections of the American Antiquarian Society* 2 (1836), 423–523; Leach, *Flintlock and Tomahawk,* 145–54; Malone, *Skulking Way of War,* 84–88; Jenny Hale Pulsipher, "Massacre at Hurtleberry Hill: Christian Indians and English Authority in Metacom's War," *William and Mary Quarterly,* 3d ser., 53 (1996), 459–86. On Bacon's Rebellion in Virginia, see Wilcomb E. Washburn, *The Governor and the Rebel: A History of Bacon's Rebellion in*

Virginia (Chapel Hill: University of North Carolina Press, 1957); Edmund S. Morgan, *American Slavery, American Freedom: The Ordeal of Colonial Virginia* (New York: Norton, 1975), 250–70.

[48] Leach, *Flintlock and Tomahawk*, 155–57; Francis Jennings, *The Invasion of America: Indians, Colonialism, and the Cant of Conquest* (Chapel Hill: University of North Carolina Press, 1975), 313–15.

[49] Gookin, "Historical Account," 487–90; Nourse, *Early Records of Lancaster*, 104–06; George M. Bodge, *Soldiers in King Philip's War*, 2d ed. (Leominster, Mass.: by the author, 1896), 353; Leach, *Flintlock and Tomahawk*, 157.

[50] Nourse, *Early Records of Lancaster*, 107.

[51] Henry S. Nourse (ed.), *The Narrative of the Captivity and Restoration of Mrs. Mary Rowlandson* (Lancaster, Mass.: J. Wilson and Son, 1903), 80.

[52] Nourse, *Early Records of Lancaster*, 109.

[53] Quoted in Edmund S. Morgan, "Light on the Puritans from John Hull's Notebooks," *New England Quarterly* 15 (1942), 97. I am grateful to Professor Morgan for calling my attention to this research note.

[54] *Mass. Recs.*, 5:75.

[55] Robert Kent Diebold, "A Critical Edition of Mrs. Mary Rowlandson's Captivity Narrative" (Ph.D. diss., Yale University, 1972), lxviii.

[56] Diebold, "Critical Edition," lxx.

[57] Salisbury, *Manitou and Providence*, 122, 199, 212–15, 229–35.

[58] Samuel G. Drake, *Biography and History of the Indians of North America*, 11th ed. (Boston: B. B. Mussey, 1851), 239–40, 241. Aside from her name, Onux, nothing is known of Quinnapin's third wife.

[59] Eric Spencer Johnson, " 'Some by Flatteries and Others by Threatenings': Political Strategies among Native Americans of Seventeenth-Century Southern New England" (Ph.D. diss., University of Massachusetts, Amherst, 1993), chap. 6.

[60] Drake, *Biography and History*, 187–89.

[61] Samuel G. Drake (ed.), *The Old Indian Chronicle* (Boston: S. A. Drake, 1867), 123.

[62] Laurel Thatcher Ulrich, *Good Wives: Image and Reality in the Lives of Women in Northern New England, 1650–1750* (New York: Knopf, 1982).

[63] Kathleen J. Bragdon, *The Native People of Southern New England, 1500–1650* (Norman: University of Oklahoma Press, 1996), 175–83.

[64] Ulrich, *Good Wives*, 34.

[65] Sewall, *Diary*, 1:372–73. On the more general use of Indian children as servants before Metacom's War, see Lawrence William Towner, "A Good Master Well Served: A Social History of Servitude in Massachusetts, 1620–1750" (Ph.D. diss., Northwestern University, 1955), 135–39 passim.

[66] Daniel K. Richter, "War and Culture: The Iroquois Experience," *William and Mary Quarterly* 40 (1983), 528–59; Haefli and Sweeney, "Revisiting *The Redeemed Captive.*"

[67] See, for example, James Axtell, "The White Indians of Colonial America," *William and Mary Quarterly* 32 (1975), 335–36; John Demos, *The Unredeemed Captive: A Family Story from Early America* (New York: Knopf, 1994); June Namias (ed.), *A Narrative of the Life of Mrs. Mary Jemison,* by James E. Seaver (Norman: Univeristy of Oklahoma Press, 1992). For a brief summary, see Kathryn Zabelle Derounian-Stodola and James Arthur Levernier, *The Indian Captivity Narrative, 1550–1900* (New York: Twayne, 1993), 5–8.

[68] Leach, *Flintlock and Tomahawk*, 161–63, 171–75, 179–80; Douglas Edward Leach, "The 'Whens' of Mary Rowlandson's Captivity," *New England Quarterly* 34 (1961), 356–63; Diebold, "Critical Edition," lxxi–lxxix; lxxxii–lxxxiii.

[69] Gookin, "Historical Account," 507–08; Drake, *Biography and History*, 240–41, 274–75, 330–31; Leach, *Flintlock and Tomahawk*, 150, 179.

[70] Gookin, "Historical Account," 475–76; Drake, *Biography and History*, 114–15, 265.

[71] Lepore, "The Name of War," 236–41.

[72]Cf. Leach, *Flintlock and Tomahawk,* 181, 199–241; Diebold, "Critical Edition," lxxxii, lxxxiv–lxxxvi.

[73]Diebold, "Critical Edition," xcv–xcvii.

[74]Leach, *Flintlock and Tomahawk,* 235–36; Lepore, "The Name of War," 289–90.

[75]Drake, *Biography and History,* 189.

[76]Samuel A. Green (ed.), *Diary by Increase Mather, March, 1675–December, 1676* (Cambridge, Mass.: J. Wilson and Son, 1900), 47; Sewall, *Diary,* 1:23; Drake, *Biography and History,* 241, 267.

[77]Drake, *Biography and History,* 115; Diebold, "Critical Edition," clxxii.

[78]Lauber, *Indian Slavery in Colonial Times,* 109–11, 125–31, 137–53.

[79]Drake, *Biography and History,* 273; Lauber, *Indian Slavery,* 144; Leach, *Flintlock and Tomahawk,* 245.

[80]Thomas L. Doughton, "Native American Presence and the Politics of Representation: Indians in Nineteenth-Century Massachusetts" (unpublished paper, 1996); Donna Keith Baron, et al., "They Were Here All Along: The Native American Presence in Lower Central New England in the Eighteenth and Nineteenth Centuries," *William and Mary Quarterly,* 3d ser., 53 (1996), 561–86.

[81]Neal Salisbury, "Toward the Covenant Chain: Iroquois and Southern New England Algonquians, 1637–1684," in Daniel Richter and James Merrell (eds.), *Beyond the Covenant Chain: The Iroquois and Their Neighbors in Indian North America, 1600–1800* (Syracuse: Syracuse University Press, 1987), 71; Haefli and Sweeney, "Revisiting *The Redeemed Captive,*" 14, 20–26.

[82]Haefli and Sweeney, "Revisiting *The Redeemed Captive,*" 9–26, 45.

[83]Nourse, *Early Records of Lancaster,* 119–20, 126; Sewall, *Diary,* 1:272; Puglisi, *Puritans Besieged,* 114–15.

[84]Leach, *Flintlock and Tomahawk,* 245.

[85]Nourse, *Early Records of Lancaster,* 125, 133–34, 147–48; Sewall, *Diary,* 1:376, 512, 530.

[86]See the list in Lepore, "The Name of War," 383–87.

[87]The principal texts are Increase Mather, *A Brief History of the War with the Indians in New-England* (London, 1676); Mather, *Newes from New-England* (London, 1676); Mather, *A Relation of the Troubles which have hapned in New-England, By Reason of the Indians there* (Boston, 1677); Hubbard, *A Narrative of the Troubles with the Indians in New-England* (Boston, 1677). On the rivalry between the two authors, see Anne Kusener Nelsen, "King Philip's War and the Hubbard-Mather Rivalry," *William and Mary Quarterly,* 3d ser., 27 (1970), 615–29; Michael G. Hall, *The Last American Puritan: The Life of Increase Mather, 1639–1723* (Middletown, Conn.: Wesleyan University Press, 1988), 112–26; Dennis R. Perry, " 'Novelties and Stile which All Out-do': William Hubbard's Historiography Reconsidered," *Early American Literature* 20 (1994), 166–82.

[88]Gookin, "Historical Account."

[89]Diebold, "Critical Edition," c; Kathryn Zabelle Derounian, "Puritan Orthodoxy and the 'Survivor Syndrome' in Mary Rowlandson's Indian Captivity Narrative," *Early American Literature* 22 (1987), 82–93; Mitchell Robert Breitwieser, *American Puritanism and the Defense of Mourning: Religion, Grief, and Ethnology in Mary White Rowlandson's Captivity Narrative* (Madison: University of Wisconsin Press, 1990).

[90]Sibley, *Biographical Sketches,* 1:313n.

[91]Gookin, "Historical Account."

[92]Gookin, "Historical Account," 456–61.

[93]Nourse (ed.), *Lancastriana,* 1:20; Greene, "New Light on Mary Rowlandson," 25, 27.

[94]Greene, "New Light on Mary Rowlandson," 28–30.

[95]Kathryn Zabelle Derounian, "The Publication, Promotion, and Distribution of Mary Rowlandson's Indian Captivity Narrative in the Seventeenth Century," *Early American Literature* 23 (1988), 240–43.

[96]Hall, *Last American Puritan,* 75; Green (ed.), *Diary by Increase Mather,* 25.

[97] Derounian, "Publication, Promotion, and Distribution," 240–41.

[98] Hall, *Last American Puritan,* 131–40; Derounian, "Publication, Promotion, and Distribution," 242.

[99] Derounian, "Publication, Promotion, and Distribution," 242.

[100] A type of sermon named for the Old Testament prophet Jeremiah, a jeremiad warned God's people of impending doom if they did not soon mend their ways. As such, it was widely used by New England ministers advocating spiritual reform during the late seventeenth century.

[101] In Nourse, *Narrative of the Captivity,* 121–45. Quote at 145.

[102] John Harvard Ellis, *The Works of Anne Bradstreet in Prose and Verse* (Charlestown, Mass.: A. E. Cutter, 1867), lxvi–lxvii. On the Hutchinson-Rowlandson comparison, cf. John D. Seelye, *Prophetic Waters: The River in Early American Life and Literature* (New York: Oxford University Press, 1977), 289–91.

[103] Diebold, "Critical Edition," clxiii–clxxviii.

[104] Derounian, "Publication, Promotion, and Distribution" 255–57; Frank Luther Mott, *Golden Multitudes: The Story of Best Sellers in the United States* (New York: Macmillan, 1947), 303; Derounian-Stodola and Levernier, *Indian Captivity Narrative,* 99.

[105] Some scholars have maintained that the second edition's unusually large number of spelling errors is evidence that its compositor was one for whom English was not a first language. See Diebold, "Critical Edition," clxx–clxxiv; Derounian, "Publication, Promotion, and Distribution," 245–46. But there are good reasons to doubt that Printer was any less competent a speller than most literate colonists. For example, the supplementary documents in this volume by John Easton, deputy governor of Rhode Island, and by the inhabitants of Lancaster are far less decipherable in their original form than is Rowlandson's narrative. Moreover, the preface is noticeably free of such errors. Although Printer worked from the Boston text of the narrative, there is no evidence that that edition had a preface, so the one part that he *may* have composed from scratch was that with the fewest errors.

[106] Diebold, "Critical Edition," clxxix–clxxxix.

[107] Sewall, *Diary,* 1:372–73

[108] Neal Salisbury, "Red Puritans: The 'Praying Indians' of Massachusetts Bay and John Eliot," *William and Mary Quarterly,* 3d ser., 31 (1974), 46.

[109] Greene, "New Light on Mary Rowlandson," 31–35.

[110] R.W.G. Vail, *The Voice of the Old Frontier* (Philadelphia: University of Pennsylvania Press, 1949), traces editions to the 1930s. See pp. 209, 290–91, 295, 366, 397–98, 407, 418–19, 456–59.

[111] Alvar Núñez Cabeza de Vaca, *Castaways,* ed. Enrique Pupo-Walker, trans. Frances M. López-Morillas (Berkeley: University of California Press, 1993), xi, xviii.

[112] See Derounian-Stodola and Levernier, *Indian Captivity Narrative,* for a useful introduction and overview.

PART TWO

The Document

THE
Soveraignty & Goodness
OF
GOD,
Together,
With the Faithfulness of His Promises
Displayed;
Being a
NARRATIVE
Of the *Captivity* and *Restauration* of
Mrs. *Mary Rowlandson.*

Commended by her, to all that desires to
know the Lords doings to, and
dealings with Her.

Especially to her dear Children and Relations,

The second Addition Corrected and amended.

Written by Her own Hand for Her private Use, and now
made Publick at the earnest Desire of some Friends,
and for the benefit of the Afflicted.

Deut. 32. 29, *See now that I, even I am he, and there is no*
God with me: I kill and I make alive, I wound and I heal,
neither is there any can deliver out of my hand.

CAMBRIDGE,
Printed by *Samuel Green,* 1 6 8 2.

The Sovereignty and Goodness of God
By Mary Rowlandson

The Preface to the Reader

It was on Tuesday, Feb. 1, 1675,[1] in the afternoon, when the *Narrhagansets* quarters (in or toward the *Nipmug* Country, whither they are now retyred for fear of the *English* Army lying in their own Country) were the second time beaten up by the Forces of the united Colonies,[2] who thereupon soon betook themselves to flight, and were all the next day pursued by the *English,* some overtaken and destroyed. But on *Thursday,* Feb. 3d, the *English* having now been six dayes on their march, from their head quarters, at *Wickford,* in the *Narrhaganset* Country, toward, and after the Enemy, and provision grown exceeding short, insomuch that they were fain to kill some Horses for the supply, especially of their *Indian* friends, they were necessitated to consider what was best to be done: And about noon (having hitherto followed the chase as hard as they might) a Councill was called, and though some few were of another mind, yet it was concluded by far the greater part of the Council of War, that the Army should desist the pursuit, and retire: the Forces of *Plimoth* and the *Bay*[3] to the next Town of the *Bay,* and *Connecticut* Forces to their own next Towns; which determination was immediately put in execution. The

[1] By the modern Gregorian calendar (already used everywhere in Europe outside of the British Isles), the date was February 11, 1676. Until the mid-eighteenth century, England observed the Julian calendar, in which the year began on March 25 instead of January 1 and which reckoned dates ten days earlier than the Gregorian calendar.
[2] The United Colonies of New England was a loose confederation consisting of the Puritan-dominated colonies of Massachusetts Bay, Connecticut, and Plymouth. It pointedly excluded religiously tolerant Rhode Island.
[3] The colony of Massachusetts Bay.

consequent whereof, as it was not difficult to be foreseen by those that knew the causless enmity of these *Barbarians,* against the *English,* and the malicious and revengefull spirit of these Heathen: so it soon proved dismall.

The *Narrhagansets* were now driven quite from their own Country, and all their provisions there hoarded up, to which they durst not at present return, and being so numerous as they were, soon devoured those to whom they went,[4] whereby both the one and other were now reduced to extream straits, and so necessitated to take the first and best opportunity for supply, and very glad, no doubt of such an opportunity as this, to provide for themselves, and make spoil of the *English* at once; and seeing themselves thus discharged of their pursuers, and a little refreshed after their flight, the very next week upon *Thurseday,* Feb. 10, they fell with mighty force and fury upon *Lancaster:* which small Town, remote from aid of others, and not being Gerisoned as it might, the Army being now come in, and as the time indeed required (the design of the *Indians* against that place being known to the *English* some time before),[5] was not able to make effectual resistance: but notwithstanding utmost endeavor of the Inhabitants, most of the buildings were turned into ashes; many People (Men, Women and Children) slain, and others captivated. The most solemn and remarkable part of this Trajedy, may that justly be reputed, which fell upon the Family of that reverend Servant of God, Mr. *Joseph Rolandson,* the faithfull Pastor of Christ in that place, who being gone down to the Councill of the *Massachusets* to seek aid for the defence of the place, at his return found the Town in flames, or smoke, his own house being set on fire by the Enemy, through the disadvantage of a defective Fortification, and all in it consumed: his precious yokefellow, and dear Children, wounded and captivated (as the issue evidenced, and following Narrative declares) by these cruel and barbarous Salvages. A sad Catestrophe! Thus all things come alike to all: None knows either love or hatred by all that is before him. It is no new thing for Gods precious ones to drink as deep as others, of the Cup of common Calamity: Take just Lot (yet captivated) for instance beside others.[6] But it is not my business to dilate on these things, but only in few words introductively to preface to the following script, which is a Narrative of the wonderfully awfull,

---

[4]Meaning that the Narragansett refugees quickly depleted their Nipmuck hosts' food supply.

[5]This is a reference to the report by James Quanapohit, or Quannapaquait, which appears on p. 119.

[6]See Genesis 14, esp. 12–16.

wise, holy, powerfull, and gracious providence of God, towards that worthy and precious Gentlewoman, the dear Consort of the said Reverend Mr. *Rowlandson,* and her Children with her, as in casting of her into such a waterless pit, so in preserving, supporting, and carrying through so many such extream hazards, unspeakable difficulties and disconsolateness, and at last delivering her out of them all, and her Surviving Children also. It was a strange and amazing dispensation, that the Lord should so afflict his precious Servant, and Hand maid. It was a strange, if not more, that he should so bear up the spirits of his Servant under such bereavements and of his handmaid under such captivity, travels and hardships (much too hard for flesh and blood) as he did, and at length deliver and restore. But he was their Saviour, who hath said, *When thou passest through the Waters, I will be with thee, and through the Rivers, they shall not overflow thee: When thou walkest through the fire thou shalt not be burnt, nor shall the flame kindle upon thee,* Isa. 43, ver. 2, and again, *He woundeth and his hands make whole. He shall deliver thee in six troubles, yea in seven there shall no evil touch thee. In Famine he shall redeem thee from Death, and in War from the power of the sword.* Job 5.18, 19, 20. Methinks this dispensation doth bear some resemblance to those of *Joseph, David* and *Daniel;* yea, and of the three Children too,[7] the Stories whereof do represent us with the excellent textures of divine providence, curious pieces of divine work: and truly so doth this, and therefore not to be forgotten, but worthy to be exhibited to, and viewed, and pondered by all, that disdain not to consider the operation of his hands.

The works of the Lord (not only of Creation, but of Providence also, especially those that do more peculiarly concern his dear ones, that are as the Apple of his Eye, as the Signet upon His Hand, the Delight of his Eyes, and the Object of his tenderest Care) are great, sought out of all those that have pleasure therein. And of these verily this is none of the least.

This Narrative was penned by the Gentlewoman her self, to be to her a memorandum of Gods dealing with her, that she might never forget, but remember the same, and the severall circumstances thereof, all the dayes of her life. A pious scope which deserves both commendation and imitation: Some friends having obtained a sight of it, could not but be so much affected with the many passages of working providence discovered therein as to judge it worthy of publick view, and altogether unmeet that such works of God should be hid from present and future Generations: And therefore though this Gentlewomans modesty would not thrust it

---

[7]See Daniel 3.

into the Press, yet her gratitude unto God made her not hardly per-swadable to let it pass, that God might have his due glory and others benefit by it as well as herself. I hope by this time none will cast any reflection upon this Gentlewoman, on the score of this publication of her affliction and deliverance. If any should, doubtless they may be reckoned with the nine lepers, of whom it is said, *Were there not ten cleansed, where are the nine? but one returning to give God thanks.*[8] Let such further know that this was a dispensation of publick note, and of universall concernment, and so much the more, by how much the nearer this Gentlewoman stood related to that faithfull Servant of God, whose capacity and employment was publick in the house of God, and his name on that account of a very sweet savour in the Churches of Christ. Who is there of a true Christian spirit, that did not look upon himself much concerned in this bereavement, this Captivity in the time thereof, and in this deliverance when it came, yea more than in many others; and how many are there, to whom so concerned, it will doubtless be a very acceptable thing to see the way of God with this Gentlewoman in the aforesaid dispensation, thus laid out and portrayed before their eyes.

To conclude, whatever any coy phantasies may deem, yet it highly concerns those that have so deeply tasted, how good the Lord is, to enquire with *David, What shall I render to the Lord for all his benefits to me? Psal.* 116. 12. He thinks nothing too great; yea, being sensible of his own disproportion to the due praises of God he calls in help. *Oh, magnifie the Lord with me, let us exalt his Name together,* Psal. 34. 3. And it is but reason, that our praises should hold proportion with our prayers: and that as many hath helped together by prayer for the obtaining of this Mercy, so praises should be returned by many on this behalf; And forasmuch as not the generall but particular knowledge of things make deepest impression upon the affections, this Narrative particularizing the several passages of this providence will not a little conduce thereunto. And therefore holy *David* in order to the attainment of that end, accounts himself concerned to declare what God has done for his soul, *Psal. 66.16. Come and hear, all ye that fear God, and I will declare what God hath done for my soul,* i.e. *for his life,* see v. 9, 10. *He holdeth our soul in life, and suffers not our feet to be moved, for thou our God hast proved us, thou hast tried us, as silver is tried.* Life-mercies, are heart-affecting mercies, of great impression and force, to enlarge pious hearts in the praises of God, so that such know not how but to talk of Gods acts, and to speak of and publish his wonderfull works. Deep troubles, when the waters come in unto thy soul, are

---

[8]See Luke 17:18–19.

wont to produce vowes: vowes must be paid. *It is better not vow, than vow and not to pay.*[9] I may say, that as none knows what it is to fight and pursue such an enemy as this, but they that have fought and pursued them: so none can imagine what it is to be captivated, and enslaved to such atheistical, proud, wild, cruel, barbarous, brutish (in one word) diabolicall creatures as these, the worst of the heathen; nor what difficulties, hardships, hazards, sorrows, anxieties and perplexities do unavoidably wait upon such a condition, but those that have tryed it. No serious spirit then (especially knowing anything of this Gentlewomans piety) can imagine but that the vows of God are upon her. Excuse her then if she come thus into publick, to pay those vows. Come and hear what she hath to say.

I am confident that no Friend of divine Providence will ever repent his time and pains spent in reading over these sheets, but will judg them worth perusing again and again.

Here *Reader,* you may see an instance of the Soveraignty of God, who doth what he will with his own as well as others; and who may say to him, *What dost Thou?*[10] Here you may see an instance of the faith and patience of the Saints, under the most heart-sinking tryals; here you may see, the promises are breasts full of consolation, when all the world besides is empty, and gives nothing but sorrow. That God is indeed the supream Lord of the world, ruling the most unruly, weakening the most cruel and salvage, granting his People mercy in the sight of the unmercifull, curbing the lusts of the most filthy, holding the hands of the violent, delivering the prey from the mighty, *and gathering together the out casts of* Israel. Once and again you have heard, but here you may see, *that power belongeth unto God;* that our God is the God of Salvation, and to him belong the issues from Death. That our God is in the Heavens, and doth whatever pleases him. Here you have *Sampsons* Riddle exemplified, and that great promise, *Rom.* 8. 28. verified, *Out of the Eater comes forth meat, and sweetness out of the strong;*[11] The worst of evils working together for the best good. How evident is it that the Lord hath made this Gentlewoman a gainer by all this affliction, that she can say, *'tis good for her, yea better that she hath been, than that she should not have been thus afflicted.*

Oh how doth God shine forth in such things as these!

Reader, if thou gettest no good by such a Declaration as this, the fault must needs be thine own. Read therefore, Peruse, Ponder, and from hence lay up something from the experience of another, against thine

---

[9] See Ecclesiastes 5:5.

[10] Job 9:12.

[11] Although Romans 8:28 refers to a promise by God, Samson's riddle and the passage quoted are found in Judges 14:14.

own turn comes, that so thou also through patience and consolation of the Scripture mayest have hope.

TER AMICAM[12]

A Narrative of the Captivity and Restauration of Mrs. Mary Rowlandson

On the tenth of February 1675,[13] Came the *Indians* with great numbers upon *Lancaster:* Their first coming was about Sun-rising; hearing the noise of some Guns, we looked out; several Houses were burning, and the Smoke ascending to Heaven. There were five persons taken in one house, the Father, and the Mother and a sucking Child, they knockt on the head; the other two they took and carried away alive. There were two others, who being out of their Garison upon some occasion were set upon; one was knockt on the head, the other escaped: Another there was who running along was shot and wounded, and fell down; he begged of them his life, promising them Money (as they told me) but they would not hearken to him but knockt him in head, and script him naked, and split open his Bowels. Another seeing many of the *Indians* about his Barn, ventured and went out, but was quickly shot down. There were three others belonging to the same Garison who were killed; the *Indians* getting up upon the roof of the Barn, had advantage to shoot down upon them over their Fortification. Thus these murtherous wretches went on, burning, and destroying before them.

At length they came and beset our own house, and quickly it was the dolefullest day that ever mine eyes saw. The House stood upon the edge of a hill; some of the *Indians* got behind the hill, others into the Barn, and others behind any thing that could shelter them; from all which places they shot against the House, so that the Bullets seemed to fly like hail; and quickly they wounded one man among us, then another, and then a third. About two hours (according to my observation, in that amazing time) they had been about the house before they prevailed to fire it (which they did with Flax and Hemp, which they brought out of the

---

[12]The approximate translation of this phrase is "thy three-fold friend," but subsequent editions corrected it to read *per amicum,* "by a friend," probably the rendering intended here.

[13]By our calendar, February 20, 1676. See note 1.

Barn, and there being no defence about the House, only two Flankers[14] at two opposite corners, and one of them not finished) they fired it once and one ventured out and quenched it, but they quickly fired again, and that took. Now is that dreadfull hour come, that I have often heard of (in time of War, as it was the case of others) but now mine eyes see it. Some in our house were fighting for their lives, others wallowing in their blood, the House on fire over our heads, and the bloody Heathen ready to knock us on the head, if we stirred out. Now might we hear Mothers & Children crying out for themselves, and one another, *Lord, What shall we do?* Then I took my Children[15] (and one of my sisters,[16] hers) to go forth and leave the house: but as soon as we came to the door and appeared, the *Indians* shot so thick that the bullets rattled against the House, as if one had taken an handfull of stones and threw them, so that we were fain to give back. We had six stout Dogs belonging to our Garrison, but none of them wou'd stir, though another time, if any *Indian* had come to the door, they were ready to fly upon him and tear him down. The Lord hereby would make us the more to acknowledge his hand, and to see that our help is alwayes in him. But out we must go, the fire increasing, and coming along behind us, roaring, and the Indians gaping before us with their Guns, Spears and Hatchets to devour us. No sooner were we out of the House, but my Brother in Law (being before wounded, in defending the house, in or near the throat) fell down dead, whereat the *Indians* scornfully shouted, and hallowed, and were presently upon him, stripping off his cloaths, the bulletts flying thick, one went through my side, and the same (as would seem) through the bowels and hand of my dear Child in my arms.[17] One of my elder Sisters Children, named *William,* had then his Leg broken, which the *Indians* perceiving, they knockt him on head. Thus were we butchered by those merciless Heathen, standing amazed, with the blood running down to our heels. My eldest Sister being yet in the House, and seeing those wofull sights, the Infidels haling Mothers one way, and Children another, and some wallowing in their blood: and her elder Son telling her that her Son *William* was dead, and my self was wounded, she said, And, *Lord, let me dy with them;* which was no sooner said, but she was struck with a Bullet, and fell down dead over the threshold. I hope she is reaping the fruit of her good labours, being faithfull to

[14]Projecting fortifications.

[15]Rowlandson had three children, Joseph, Jr. (b. 1661), Mary (b. 1665), and Sarah (b. 1669).

[16]Two of Rowlandson's sisters and their families were among the thirty-seven persons housed in the Rowlandson garrison.

[17]Her youngest child, Sarah.

the service of God in her place. In her younger years she lay under much trouble upon spiritual accounts, till it pleased God to make that precious scripture take hold of her heart, 2 *Cor.* 12. 9. *And he said unto me, my grace is sufficient for thee.* More than twenty years after I have heard her tell how sweet and comfortable that place was to her. But to return: the *Indians* laid hold of us, pulling me one way, and the Children another, and said, *Come go along with us;* I told them they would kill me: they answered, *If I were willing to go along with them, they would not hurt me.*

Oh the dolefull sight that now was to behold at this House! *Come, behold the works of the Lord, what desolations he has made in the Earth.*[18] Of thirty seven persons who were in this one House, none escaped either present death, or a bitter captivity, save only one, who might say as he, *Job* 1. 15. *And I only am escaped alone to tell the News.* There were twelve killed, some shot, some stab'd with their Spears, some knock'd down with their Hatchets. When we are in prosperity, Oh the little that we think of such dreadfull sights, and to see our dear Friends, and Relations ly bleeding out their heart-blood upon the ground. There was one who was chopt into the head with a Hatchet, and stripped naked, and yet was crawling up and down. It is a solemn sight to see so many Christians lying in their blood, some here, and some there, like a company of Sheep torn by Wolves. All of them stript naked by a company of hell-hounds, roaring, singing, ranting and insulting, as if they would have torn our very hearts out; yet the Lord by his Almighty power preserved a number of us from death, for there were twenty-four of us taken alive and carried captive.

I had often before this said, that if the *Indians* should come, I should chuse rather to be killed by them than be taken alive, but when it came to the tryal my mind changed; their glittering weapons so daunted my spirit, that I chose rather to go along with those (as I may say) ravenous Beasts, than that moment to end my dayes; and that I may the better declare what happened to me during that grievous Captivity, I shall particularly speak of the severall Removes we had up and down the Wilderness.

THE FIRST REMOVE[19]

Now away we must go with those Barbarous Creatures, with our bodies wounded and bleeding, and our hearts no less than our bodies. About a mile we went that night, up upon a hill within sight of the Town, where they intended to lodge. There was hard by a vacant house (deserted by the English before, for fear of the *Indians*). I asked them whither I might

---

[18]Psalm 46:8.
[19]For Rowlandson's "removes" during her captivity, see Figure 12 (p. 72).

not lodge in the house that night to which they answered, what will you love *English men* still? This was the dolefullest night that ever my eyes saw. Oh the roaring, and singing and danceing, and yelling of those black creatures in the night, which made the place a lively resemblance of hell. And as miserable was the waste that was there made, of Horses, Cattle, Sheep, Swine, Calves, Lambs, Roasting Pigs, and Fowls (which they had plundered in the Town) some roasting, some lying and burning, and some boyling to feed our merciless Enemies; who were joyfull enough though we were disconsolate. To add to the dolefulness of the former day, and the dismalness of the present night: my thoughts ran upon my losses and sad bereaved condition. All was gone, my Husband gone (at least separated from me, he being in the Bay;[20] and to add to my grief, the *Indians* told me they would kill him as he came homeward) my Children gone, my Relations and Friends gone, our House and home and all our comforts within door, and without, all was gone, (except my life) and I knew not but the next moment that might go too. There remained nothing to me but one poor wounded Babe, and it seemed at present worse than death that it was in such a pitiful condition, bespeaking Compassion, and I had no refreshing for it, nor suitable things to revive it.[21] Little do many think what is the savageness and brutishness of this barbarous Enemy, aye even those that seem to profess more than others among them,[22] when the *English* have fallen into their hands.

Those seven that were killed at *Lancaster* the summer before upon a Sabbath day, and the one that was afterward killed upon a week day, were slain and mangled in a barbarous manner, by One-ey'd *John,* and *Marlborough's* Praying *Indians,* which Capt. *Mosely* brought to *Boston,* as the *Indians* told me.[23]

THE SECOND REMOVE

But now, the next morning, I must turn my back upon the Town, and travel with them into the vast and desolate Wilderness, I knew not whither. It is not my tongue, or pen can express the sorrows of my heart, and bitterness of my spirit, that I had at this departure: but God was with me, in a

---

[20]In the eastern part of the colony, near the bay known as Massachusetts Bay.

[21]Seventeenth-century English people referred to small children by the gender-neutral pronoun "it," rather than "he" or "she."

[22]Meaning those Indians who profess Christianity.

[23]Rowlandson refers here to the attack on Lancaster of August 7, 1675, led by Nipmuc sachem Monoco ("One-eyed John"). As discussed in the Introduction, Captain Samuel Moseley's attempt to implicate the Christian Indians of Marlborough in the attack proved unsuccessful in court.

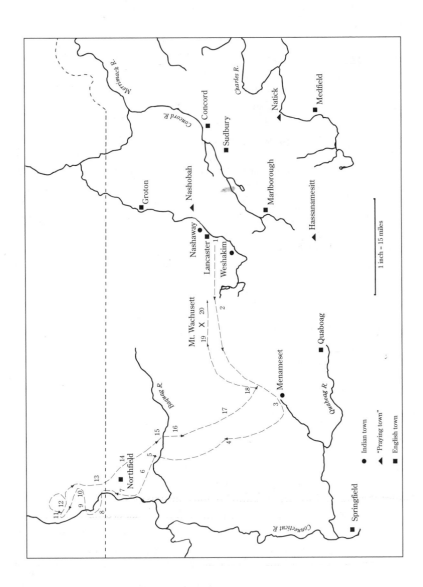

Merrimack R.

Concord R.

Charles R.

Groton ■

Nashobah ▲

Concord ■

Sudbury ■

Natick ▲

Medfield ■

Nashaway ●

Lancaster ■

Weshakim ●

Marlborough ■

Hassanamesitt ▲

Mt. Wachusett
X 20
19

1

2

Menameset ●

Quaboag ■

3

Quaboag R.

Bottag R.

18

17

16

15

14
Northfield ■

13

12

11

9 10

8

7

6

5

4

Connecticut R.

Springfield ■

1 inch = 15 miles

● Indian town
▲ "Praying town"
■ English town

wonderfull manner, carrying me along, and bearing up my spirit, that it did not quite fail. One of the *Indians* carried my poor wounded Babe upon a horse, it went moaning all along, I shall dy, I shall dy. I went on foot after it, with sorrow that cannot be exprest. At length I took it off the horse, and carried it in my arms till my strength failed, and I fell down with it: Then they set me upon a horse with my wounded Child in my lap, and there being no furniture[24] upon the horse back, as we were going down a steep hill, we both fell over the horses head, at which they like inhumane creatures laught, and rejoyced to see it, though I thought we should there have ended our dayes, as overcome with so many difficulties. But the Lord renewed my strength still, and carried me along, that I might see more of his Power; yea, so much that I could never have thought of, had I not experienced it.

After this it quickly began to snow, and when night came on, they stopt: and now down I must sit in the snow, by a little fire, and a few boughs behind me, with my sick Child in my lap; and calling much for water, being now (through the wound) fallen into a violent Fever. My own wound also growing so stiff, that I could scarce sit down or rise up; yet so it must be, that I must sit all this cold winter night upon the cold snowy ground, with my sick Child in my armes, looking that every hour would be the last of its life; and having no Christian friend near me, either to comfort or help me. Oh, I may see the wonderfull power of God, that my Spirit did not utterly sink under my affliction: still the Lord upheld me with his gracious and mercifull Spirit, and we were both alive to see the light of the next morning.

THE THIRD REMOVE

The morning being come, they prepared to go on their way: One of the Indians *got up upon a horse, and they set me up behind him, with my poor sick Babe in my lap.* A very wearisome and tedious day I had of it; what with my own wound, and my Childs being so exceeding sick, and in a lamentable condition with her wound. It may be easily judged what a poor feeble condition we were in, there being not the least crumb of refreshing that came within either of our mouths, from *Wednesday* night to *Satur-*

[24]Saddle, stirrups, bridle, reins, and so forth.

Figure 12 *(left).* **Mary Rowlandson's "Removes"**

day night, except only a little cold water.[25] This day in the afternoon, about an hour by Sun, we came to the place where they intended, *viz.* an Indian town called *Wenimesset,* northward of *Quabaug.*[26] When we were come, Oh the number of Pagans (now merciless enemies) that there came about me, that I may say as *David,* Psal 27. 13, *I had fainted, unless I had believed, &c.* The next day was the Sabbath: I then remembered how careless I had been of Gods holy time: how many Sabbaths I had lost and misspent, and how evilly I had walked in Gods sight; which lay so close unto my spirit, that it was easie for me to see how righteous it was with God to cut off the thread of my life, and cast me out of his presence forever. Yet the Lord still shewed mercy to me, and upheld me; and as he wounded me with one hand, so he healed me with the other. This day there came to me one *Robert Pepper* (a man belonging to *Roxbury*) who was taken in Captain *Beers* his fight,[27] and had been now a considerable time with the *Indians;* and up with them almost as far as *Albany* to see king *Philip,* as he told me, and was now very lately come into these parts. Hearing, I say, that I was in this *Indian* Town, he obtained leave to come and see me. He told me, he himself was wounded in the leg at Captain *Beers* his Fight; and was not able some time to go, but as they carried him, and as he took Oaken leaves and laid to his wound, and through the blessing of God he was able to travel again. Then I took Oaken leaves and laid to my side, and with the blessing of God it cured me also; yet before the cure was wrought, I may say, as it is in *Psal.* 38. 5, 6. *My wounds stink and are corrupt, I am troubled, I am bowed down greatly, I go mourning all the day long.* I sat much alone with a poor wounded Child in my lap, which moaned night and day, having nothing to revive the body, or cheer the spirits of her, but in stead of that, sometimes one *Indian* would come and tell me in one hour, that your *Master* will knock your Child in the head, and then a second, and then a third, your *Master* will quickly knock your Child in the head.

This was the comfort I had from them, miserable comforters are ye all,[28] *as he said.* Thus nine days I sat upon my knees, with my Babe in my lap, till my flesh was raw again; my Child being even ready to depart this sor-

---

[25]But they were given at least one small piece of food, which neither of them ate during this period, as Rowlandson later reveals (p. 92).

[26]Wenimesset was a Nipmuc town more commonly called Menameset. Like Nashaway, Quabaug was the name both of a Nipmuc town and of a nearby English settlement. Rowlandson is most likely referring to the latter, which was subsequently renamed Brookfield.

[27]Captain Richard Beers and his troops were attacked near Northfield, Massachusetts, in September 1675.

[28]Job 16:2.

rowful world, they bade me carry it out to another Wigwam (I suppose because they would not be troubled with such spectacles) Whither I went with a very heavy heart, and down I sat with the picture of death in my lap. About two houres in the night, my sweet Babe, like a lamb departed this life, on *Feb. 18. 1675,* It being about six *yeares,* and *five months* old. It was *nine dayes* from the first wounding, in this miserable condition, without any refreshing of one nature or other, except a little cold water. I cannot but take notice, how at another time I could not bear to be in the room where any dead person was, but now the case is changed; I must and could ly down by my dead Babe, side by side all the night after. I have thought since of the wonderfull goodness of God to me, in preserving me in the use of my reason and senses, in that distressed time, that I did not use wicked and violent means to end my own miserable life. In the morning, when they understood that my child was dead they sent for me home to my Masters Wigwam: (by my Master in this writing, must be understood *Quanopin,* who was a *Saggamore,*[29] and married King *Philips* wives Sister; not that he first took me, but I was sold to him by another *Narhaganset Indian,* who took me when first I came out of the Garison). I went to take up my dead child in my arms to carry it with me, but they bid me let it alone: there was no resisting, but goe I must and leave it. When I had been at my masters *wigwam,* I took the first opportunity I could get, to go look after my dead child: when I came I askt them what they had done with it? then they told me it was upon the hill: then they went and shewed me where it was, where I saw the ground was newly digged, and there they told me they had buried it: *There I left that Child in the Wilderness, and must commit it, and my self also in this Wilderness-condition, to him who is above all.* God having taken away this dear Child, I went to see my daughter *Mary,* who was at this same *Indian Town,* at a *Wigwam* not very far off, though we had little liberty or opportunity to see one another: she was about ten years old, & taken from the door at first by a *Praying Indian* & afterward sold for a gun. When I came in sight, she would fall a weeping; at which they were provoked, and would not let me come near her, but bade me be gone; which was a heart-cutting word to me. I had one Child dead, another in the Wilderness, I knew not where, the third they would not let me come near to: *Me* (as he said) *have ye bereaved of my children,* Joseph *is not, and* Simeon *is not, and ye will take* Benjamin *also, all these things are against me.*[30] I

---

[29] On Quinnapin, see the Introduction, esp. pp. 25–26. A sagamore was a sachem, or political leader.

[30] Genesis 42:36.

could not sit still in this condition, but kept, walking from *one* place to another. And as I was going along, my heart was even overwhelm'd with the thoughts of my condition, and that I should have Children, *and a Nation which I knew not ruled over them.* Whereupon I earnestly entreated the Lord, that he would consider my low estate, and shew me a token for good, and if it were his blessed will, some sign and hope of some relief. And indeed quickly the Lord answered, in some measure, my poor prayers: for as I was going up and down mourning and lamenting my condition, my Son came to me, and asked me how I did; I had not seen him before, since the destruction of the Town, and I knew not where he was, till I was informed by himself, that he was amongst a smaller parcel of *Indians,* whose place was about six miles off; with tears in his eyes, he asked me whether his sister *Sarah* was dead; and told me he had seen his sister *Mary;* and prayed me, that I would not be troubled in reference to himself. The occasion of his coming to see me at this time, was this: There was, as I said, about six miles from us, a smal Plantation of *Indians,* where it seems he had been during his Captivity: and at this time, there were some Forces of the *Indians* gathered out of our company, and some also from them (among whom was my Sons master) to go to assault and burn *Medfield:* In this time of the absence of his master, his dame brought him to see me. I took this to be some gracious answer to my earnest and unfeigned desire. The next day, *viz.* to this, the *Indians* returned from *Medfield,* all the company, for those that belonged to the other smal company, came through the Town that now we were at. But before they came to us, Oh! the outragious roaring and hooping that there was: They began their din about a mile before they came to us. By their noise and hooping they signified how many they had destroyed (which was at that time twenty three). Those that were with us at home, were gathered together as soon as they heard the hooping, and every time that the other went over their number, these at home gave a shout, that the very Earth rung again: And thus they continued till those that had been upon the expedition were come up to the *Sagamores Wigwam;* and then, Oh, the hideous insulting and triumphing that there was over some *Englishmens* scalps that they had taken (as their manner) and brought with them. I cannot but take notice of the wonderfull mercy of God to me in those afflictions, in sending me a Bible. One of the *Indians* that came from *Medfield* fight, had brought some plunder, came to me, and asked me, if I wou'd have a Bible, he had got one in his basket. I was glad of it, and asked him, whether he thought the *Indians* would let me read? He answered, yes: So I took the Bible, and in that melancholy time, it came into my mind to read first the 28. *Chap.* of *Deut.* which I did, and when I had read it, my dark heart wrought on this manner, *That there was no mercy for me, that the blessings were gone, and the curses come in their room, and that I had lost my opportunity.* But the Lord helped me still to go on reading till I came to *Chap.* 30 the seven first verses, where I found, *There was mercy promised again, if we would return to him by repentance; and though we were scattered from one end of the Earth to the other, yet the Lord would gather us together, and turn all those curses upon our Enemies.* I do not desire to live to forget this Scripture, and what comfort it was to me.

Now the *Indians* began to talk of removing from this place, some one way, and some another. There were now besides my self nine *English* Captives in this place (all of them Children, except one Woman). I got an opportunity to go and take my leave of them; they being to go one way, and I another, *I asked them whether they were earnest with God for deliverance;* they told me, they did as they were able, and it was some comfort to me, that the Lord stirred up *Children to look to him.* The Woman *viz.* Goodwife *Joslin*[31] told me, she should never see me again, and that she could find in her heart to run away; I wisht her not to run away by any means, for we were near *thirty miles* from any *English Town,* and she very big with Child, and had but one week to reckon; and another Child in her Arms, two years old, and bad Rivers there were to go over, and we were feeble, with our poor and coarse entertainment. I had my Bible with me, I pulled it out, and asked her whether she would read; we opened the Bible and lighted on *Psal.* 27. in which Psalm we especially took notice of that, *ver. ult.,*[32] *Wait on the Lord, Be of good courage, and he shall strengthen thine heart, wait I say on the Lord.*

THE FOURTH REMOVE

And now I must part with that little company I had. Here I parted from my daughter *Mary,* (whom I never saw again till I saw her in *Dorchester,* returned from Captivity), and from four little Cousins and Neighbours, some of which I never saw afterward: the Lord only knows the end of them. Amongst them also was that poor Woman before mentioned, who came to a sad end, as some of the company told me in my travel: She having much grief upon her Spirit, about her miserable condition, being so near her time, she would be often asking the Indians to let her go home; they not being willing to that, and yet vexed with her importunity, gath-

---

[31]Ann Joslin, also captured in the Rowlandson garrison.
[32]Last verse.

ered a great company together about her, and stript her naked, and set her in the midst of them; and when they had sung and danced about her (in their hellish manner) as long as they pleased, they knockt her on head, and the child in her arms with her: when they had done that, they made a fire and put them both into it, and told the other Children that were with them, that if they attempted to go home, they would serve them in like manner: The Children said, she did not shed one tear, but prayed all the while. But to return to my own Journey; we travelled about half a day or little more, and came to a desolate place in the Wilderness, where there were no *Wigwams* or *Inhabitants* before; we came about the middle of the afternoon to this place; cold and wet, and snowy, and hungry, and weary, and no refreshing, for man, but the cold ground to sit on, and our poor *Indian cheer.*

Heart-aking thoughts here I had about my poor Children, who were scattered up and down among the wild beasts of the forrest: My head was light and dizzy (either through hunger or hard lodging, or trouble or all together) my knees feeble, my body raw by sitting double night and day, that I cannot express to man the affliction that lay upon my Spirit, but the Lord helped me at that time to express it to himself. I opened my Bible to read, and the Lord brought that precious scripture to me, *Jer.* 31. 16. *Thus saith the Lord, refrain thy voice from weeping, and thine eyes from tears, for thy work shall be rewarded, and they shall come again from the land of the Enemy.* This was a sweet Cordial to me, when I was ready to faint, many and many a time have I sat down, and wept sweetly over this Scripture. At this place we continued about four dayes.

THE FIFTH REMOVE

The occasion (as I thought) of their moving at this time, was, the English *Army, it being near and following them:* For they went, as if they had gone for their lives, for some considerable way, and then they made a stop, and chose some of their stoutest men, and sent them back to hold the *English* army in play whilst the rest escaped: And then, *like Jehu, they marched on furiously,*[33] with their old, and with their young: some carried their old decrepit mothers, some carried one, and some another. Four of them carried a great *Indian* upon a Bier;[34] but going through a thick Wood with

---

[33]See II Kings 9:20.

[34]A bier is a framework for carrying either a corpse or an exalted person. This is a rare reference to a New England sachem being carried this way. The practice was far more common among Indians in the Southeast.

him, they were hindered, and could make no haste; whereupon they took him upon their backs, and carried him, one at a time, till they came to *Bacquaug* River.[35] Upon a *Friday,* a little after noon we came to this River. When all the company was come up, and were gathered together, I thought to count the number of them, but they were so many, and being somewhat in motion, it was beyond my skil. In this travel, because of my wound, I was somewhat favored in my load; I carried only my knitting work and two quarts of parched meal: Being very faint I asked my mistriss[36] to give me one spoonfull of the meal, but she would not give me a taste. They quickly fell to cutting dry trees, to make Rafts to carry them over the river: and soon my turn came to go over: By the advantage of some brush which they had laid upon the Raft to sit upon, I did not wet my foot (which many of themselves at the other end were mid-leg deep) which cannot but be acknowledged as a favour of God to my weakened body, it being a very cold time. I was not before acquainted with such kind of doings or dangers. *When thou passeth through the waters I will be with thee, and through the rivers they shall not overflow thee,* Isai. 43. 2. A certain number of us got over the River that night, but it was the night after the Sabbath before all the company was got over. On the *Saturday* they boyled an old Horses leg which they had got, and so we drank of the broth, as soon as they thought it was ready, and when it was almost all gone, they filled it up again.

The first week of my being among them, I hardly ate any thing; the second week, I found my stomach grow very faint for want of something; and yet it was very hard to get down their filthy trash: but the third week, though I could think how formerly my stomach would turn against this or that, and I could starve and die before I could eat such things, yet they were sweet and savory to my taste. I was at this time knitting a pair of white cotton stockins for my mistriss: and had not yet wrought upon a Sabbath day; when the Sabbath came they bade me go to work; I told them it was the Sabbath-day, and desired them to let me rest, and told them I would do as much more tomorrow; to which they answered me, they would break my face. And here I cannot but take notice of the strange providence of God in preserving the heathen: They were many hundreds, old and young, some sick, and some lame, many had *Papooses* at their backs, the greatest number at this time with us, were *Squaws,* and they travelled with all they had, bag and baggage, and yet they got over this River aforesaid; and on *Munday* they set their *Wigwams* on fire, and

---

[35]Now known as Miller's River.
[36]Weetamoo, whom Rowlandson will later refer to as Wettimore.

away they went: On that very day came the *English* Army after them to this River, and saw the smoak of their *Wigwams,* and yet this River put a stop to them. God did not give them courage or activity to go over after us; we were not ready for so great a mercy as victory and deliverance; if we had been, God would have found out a way for the *English* to have passed this River, as well as for the *Indians* with their *Squaws* and *Children,* and all their Luggage: *Oh, that my People had hearkened to me, and* Israel *had walked in my ways, I should soon have subdued their Enemies, and turned my hand against their Adversaries,* Psal. 81. 13, 14.

THE SIXTH REMOVE

On Munday *(as I said) they set their* Wigwams *on fire, and went away.* It was a cold morning, and before us there was a great Brook with ice on it; some waded through it, up to the knees & higher, but others went till they came to a Beaver dam, and I amongst them, where through the good providence of God, I did not wet my foot. I went along that day mourning and lamenting, leaving farther my own Country, and travelling into the vast and howling *Wilderness,* and I understood something of *Lot*'s Wife's Temptation, *when she looked back:*[37] we came that day to a great Swamp, by the side of which we took up our lodging that night. When I came to the brow of the hill, that looked toward the Swamp, I thought we had been come to a great *Indian* Town (though there were none but our own Company). The *Indians* were as thick as the trees: it seemed as if there had been a thousand Hatchets going at once: if one looked before one, there was nothing but *Indians,* and behind one, nothing but *Indians,* and so on either hand, I my self in the midst, and no Christian soul near me, *and yet how hath the Lord preserved me in safety! Oh the experience that I have had of the goodness of God, to me and mine!*

THE SEVENTH REMOVE

After a restless and hungry night there, we had a wearisome time of it the next day. The Swamp by which we lay, was, as it were, a deep Dungeon, and an exceeding high and steep hill before it. Before I got to the top of the hill, I thought my heart and legs, and all would have broken, and failed me. What through faintness, and soreness of body, it was a grievous day

[37]See Genesis 19:26.

of travel to me. As we went along, I saw a place where *English* cattle had been: that was comfort to me, such as it was: quickly after that we came to an *English* Path, which so took with me, that I thought I could have freely lyin down and dyed. That day, a little after noon, we came to *Squakheag*, where the *Indians* quickly spread themselves over the deserted *English* fields, gleaning what they could find; some pickt up ears of Wheat that were crickled down, some found ears of *Indian* Corn, some found Ground-nuts, and others sheaves of Wheat that were frozen together in the shock, and went to threshing of them out. My self got two ears of *Indian* Corn, and whilst I did but turn my back, one of them was stolen from me, which much troubled me. There came an *Indian* to them at that time, with a basket of Horse-liver. I asked him to give me a piece: *What,* sayes he *can you eat Horse-liver?* I told him, I would try, if he would give a piece, which he did, and I laid it on the coals to roast; but before it was half ready they got half of it away from me, so that I was fain to take the rest and eat it as it was, with the blood about my mouth, and yet a savory bit it was to me: *For to the hungry Soul, every bitter thing is sweet.*[38] A solemn sight me thought it was, to see Fields of wheat and *Indian* Corn forsaken and spoiled: and the remainders of them to be food for our merciless Enemies. That night we had a mess of wheat for our Supper.

THE EIGHTH REMOVE

On the morrow morning we must go over the River, *i.e.* Connecticot, to meet with King *Philip,* two *Cannoos* full, they had carried over, the next Turn I myself was to go; but as my foot was upon the *Cannoo* to step in, there was a sudden out-cry among them, and I must step back; and instead of going over the River, I must go four or five miles up the River farther Northward. Some of the *Indians* ran one way, and some another. The cause of this rout was, as I thought, their espying some *English Scouts,* who were thereabout. In this travel up the river, about noon the Company made a stop, and sat down; some to eat, and others to rest them. As I sate amongst them, musing of things past, my Son *Joseph* unexpectedly came to me: we asked of each others welfare, bemoaning our dolefull condition, and the change that had come upon us. We had Husband and Father, and Children, and Sisters, and Friends, and Relations, and House, and Home, and many Comforts of this Life: but now we may

[38]Proverbs 27:7.

say, as Job, *Naked came I out of my Mothers Womb, and naked shall I return: The Lord gave, and the Lord hath taken away, Blessed be the Name of the Lord.*[39] I asked him whither he would read; he told me, he earnestly desired it. I gave him my Bible, and he lighted upon that comfortable scripture, Psal. 118. 17, 18. *I shall not dy but live, and declare the works of the Lord: the Lord hath chastened me sore, yet he hath not given me over to death.* Look here, *Mother* (sayes he), did you read this? And here I may take occasion to mention one principall ground of my setting forth these Lines: even as the Psalmist sayes, *To declare the Works of the Lord,* and His wonderfull Power in carrying us along, preserving us in the *Wilderness,* while under the Enemies hand, and returning of us in safety again. And His goodness in bringing to my hand so many comfortable and suitable Scriptures in my distress. But to Return, We travelled on till night; and in the morning, we must go over the River to *Philip's* crew. When I was in the Cannoo, I could not but be amazed at the numerous crew of Pagans that were on the Bank on the other side. When I came ashore, they gathered all about me, I sitting alone in the midst: I observed they asked one another questions, and laughed, and rejoyced over their Gains and Victories. Then my heart began to fail: and I fell a weeping which was the first time to my remembrance, that I wept before them. Although I had met with so much Affliction, and my heart was many times ready to break, yet could I not shed one tear in their sight: but rather had been all this while in a maze, and like one astonished: but now I may say as, Psal. 137. 1. *By the rivers of* Babylon, *there we sat down: yea, we wept when we remembered Zion.* There one of them asked me, why I wept, I could hardly tell what to say: yet I answered, they would kill me: No, said he, none will hurt you. Then came one of them and gave me two spoon-fulls of Meal to comfort me, and another gave me half a pint of Pease; which was more worth than many Bushels at another time. Then I went to see King *Philip,* he bade me come in and sit down, and asked me whether I would smoke (a usual Complement now adayes amongst Saints and Sinners) but this no way suited me. For though I had formerly used Tobacco, yet I had left it ever since I was first taken. *It seems to be a bait, the devil lays to make men loose their precious time:* I remember with shame, how formerly, when I had taken two or three pipes, I was presently ready for another, such a bewitching thing it is: But I thank God, he has now given me power over it; surely there are many who may be better imployed than to ly sucking a stinking Tobacco-pipe.

[39]Job 1:21.

Now the *Indians* gather their Forces to go against *North-Hampton:* over-night one went about yelling and hooting to give notice of the design. Whereupon they fell to boyling of Ground-nuts, and parching of Corn (as many as had it) for their Provision: and in the morning away they went. *During my abode in this place,* Philip *spake to me to make a shirt for his boy, which* I *did, for which he gave me a shilling:* I *offered the money to my master, but he bade me keep it: and with it* I *bought a piece of Horse flesh.* Afterwards he asked me to make a Cap for his boy, for which he invited me to Dinner. I went, and he gave me a Pancake, about as big as two fingers; it was made of parched wheat, beaten, and fryed in Bears grease, but I thought I never tasted pleasanter meat in my life. There was a *Squaw* who spake to me to make a shirt for her *Sannup,*[40] for which she gave me a piece of Bear. Another asked me to knit a pair of Stockins, for which she gave me a quart of Pease: I boyled my Pease and Bear together, and invited my master and mistriss to dinner, but the proud Gossip, because I served them both in one Dish, would eat nothing, except one bit that he gave her upon the point of his knife. Hearing that my son was come to this place, I went to see him, and found him lying flat upon the ground: I asked him how he could sleep so? He answered me, *That he was not asleep, but at Prayer;* and lay so, that they might not observe what he was doing. I pray God he may remember these things now he is returned in safety. At this Place (the Sun now getting higher) what with the beams and heat of the Sun, and the smoak of the *Wigwams,* I thought I should have been blind, I could scarce discern one *Wigwam* from another. There was here one *Mary Thurston* of *Medfield,* who seeing how it was with me, lent me a Hat to wear: but as soon as I was gone, the *Squaw* (who owned that *Mary Thurston*) came running after me, and got it away again. *Here was the* Squaw *that gave me one Spoonfull of Meal.* I put it in my Pocket to keep it safe: yet notwithstanding somebody stole it, but put five *Indian* Corns in the room of it: which Corns were the greatest Provisions I had in my travel for one day.

The *Indians* returning from *North-Hampton,* brought with them some Horses, and Sheep, and other things which they had taken: I desired them, that they would carry me to *Albany,* upon one of those horses, and sell me for powder: for so they had sometimes discoursed. I was utterly hopless of getting home on foot, the way that I came. I could hardly bear to think of the many weary steps I had taken, to come to this place.

---

[40]Married man, in this case her husband.

THE NINTH REMOVE

But instead of going either to *Albany* or homeward, we must go five miles up the River, and then go over it. Here we abode a while. Here lived a sorry *Indian,* who spoke to me to make him a shirt, when I had done it, he would pay me nothing. But he living by the River side, where I often went to fetch water, I would often be putting of him in mind, and calling for my pay: at last he told me if I would make another shirt, for a *Papoos* not yet born, he would give me a knife, which he did when I had done it. I carried the knife in, and my master asked me to give it him, and I was not a little glad that I had any thing that they would accept of, and be pleased with. When we were at this place, my Masters maid came home, she had been gone *three weeks* into the *Narrhaganset Country,* to fetch Corn, where they had stored up some in the ground: she brought home about a peck and half of corn. This was about the time that their great captain, *Naananto,* was killed in the *Narrhaganset Country.*[41] *My Son being now about a mile from me, I asked liberty to go and see him, they bade me go, and away I went: but quickly lost my self, travelling over Hills and through Swamps, and could not find the way to him.* And I cannot but admire at the wonderfull power and goodness of God to me, in that, though I was gone from home, and met with all sorts of *Indians,* and those I had no knowledge of, and there being no Christian soul near me; yet not one of them offered the least imaginable miscarriage to me. I turned homeward again, and met with my master, he shewed me the way to my Son: When I came to him I found him not well: and withall he had a boyl on his side, which much troubled him: We bemoaned one another a while, as the Lord helped us, and then I returned again. When I was returned, I found myself as unsatisfied as I was before. I went up and down mourning and lamenting: and my spirit was ready to sink, with the thoughts of my poor Children: my Son was ill, and I could not but think of his mournfull looks, and no Christian Friend was near him, to do any office of love for him, either for Soul or Body. And my poor Girl, I knew not where she was, nor whither she was sick, or well, or alive, or dead. I repaired under these thoughts to my Bible (my great comfort in that time) and that Scripture came to my hand, *Cast thy burden upon the Lord, and He shall sustain thee,* Psal. 55. 22.

But I was fain to go and look after something to satisfie my hunger, and going among the *Wigwams,* I went into one, and there found a *Squaw*

---

[41]The death of the leading Narragansett sachem, better known as Canonchet, was a severe blow to the morale of the anti-English Indians.

who shewed herself very kind to me, and gave me a piece of Bear. I put it into my pocket, and came home, but could not find an opportunity to broil it, for fear they would get it from me, and there it lay all that day and night in my stinking pocket. In the morning I went to the same *Squaw*, who had a Kettle of Ground-nuts boyling: I asked her to let me boyle my piece of Bear in her Kettle, which she did, and gave me some Ground-nuts to eat with it: and I cannot but think how pleasant it was to me. I have sometimes seen Bear baked very handsomely among the *English*, and some like it, but the thought that it was Bear, made me tremble: but now that was savoury to me that one would think was enough to turn the stomach of a bruit Creature.

One bitter cold day, I could find no room to sit down before the fire: I went out, and could not tell what to do, but I went into another Wigwam, *where they were also sitting round the fire, but the* Squaw *laid a skin for me, and bid me sit down, and gave me some Ground-nuts, and bade me come again: and told me they would buy me, if they were able, and yet these were strangers to me that I never saw before.*

THE TENTH REMOVE

That day a small part of the Company removed about three quarters of a mile, intending further the next day. When they came to the place where they intended to lodge, and had pitched their *Wigwams,* being hungry I went again back to the place we were before at, to get something to eat: being encouraged by the *Squaws* kindness, who bade me come again; when I was there, there came an *Indian* to look after me, who when he had found me, kicked me all along: I went home and found Venison roasting that night, but they would not give me one bit of it. Sometimes I met with favour, and sometimes with nothing but frowns. 2

THE ELEVENTH REMOVE

The next day in the morning they took their Travel, intending a dayes journey up the River. I took my load at my back, and quickly we came to wade over the River: and passed over tiresome and wearisome hills. One hill was so steep that I was fain to creep up upon my knees, and to hold by the twiggs and bushes to keep myself from falling backward. My head also was so light, that I usually reeled as I went; but I hope all these wearisome steps that I have taken, are but a forewarning to me of the heavenly rest. *I know, O Lord, that thy Judgements are right, and that thou in faithfulness hast afflicted me,* Psal. 119. 71.[42]

THE TWELFTH REMOVE

It was upon a Sabbath-day morning, that they prepared for their Travel. This morning I asked my master whither he would sell me to my husband; he answered me *Nux,*[43] which did much rejoyce my spirit. My mistriss, before we went, was gone to the burial of a *Papoos,* and returning, she found me sitting and reading in my Bible; she snatched it hastily out of my hand, and threw it out of doors; I ran out and catch it up, and put it into my pocket, and never let her see it afterward. Then they packed up their things to be gone, and gave me my load: I complained it was too heavy, whereupon she gave me a slap in the face, and bade me go; I lifted up my heart to God, hoping the Redemption was not far off: and the rather because their insolency grew worse and worse.

But the thoughts of my going homeward (for so we bent our course) much cheared my Spirit, and made my burden seem light, and almost nothing at all. But (to my amazement and great perplexity) the scale was soon turned: for when we had gone a little way, on a sudden my mistress gives out, she would go no further, but turn back again, and said, I must go back again with her, and she called her *Sannup,* and would have had him gone back also, but he would not, but said, *He would go on, and come to us again in three dayes.* My Spirit was upon this, I confess, very impatient, and almost outragious.[44] I thought I could as well have dyed as went back: I cannot declare the trouble that I was in about it; but yet back again I must go. As soon as I had an opportunity, I took my Bible to read, and that quieting Scripture came to my hand, *Psal. 46. 10. Be still, and know that I am God.* Which stilled my spirit for the present: But a sore time of tryal, I concluded, I had to go through. My master being gone, who seemed to me the best friend that I had of an *Indian,* both in cold and hunger, and quickly so it proved. Down I sat, with my heart as full as it could hold, and yet so hungry that I could not sit neither: but going out to see what I could find, and walking among the Trees, I found six *Acorns,* and two *Ches-nuts,* which were some refreshment to me. Towards Night I gathered me some sticks for my own comfort, that I might not lie a-cold:

---

[42]Actually, Psalm 119:75.

[43]Yes.

[44]Meaning that she almost burst out in a rage. Weetamoo was undoubtedly turning back because her own child, who would die shortly (see p. 91), was too sick to travel.

but when we came to ly down they bade me go out, and ly somewhere else, for they had company (they said) come in more than their own: I told them, I could not tell where to go, they bade me go look; I told them, if I went to another *Wigwam* they would be angry, and send me home again. Then one of the Company drew his sword, and told me he would run me through if I did not go presently. Then was I fain to stoop to this rude fellow, and to go out in the night, I knew not whither. *Mine eyes have seen that fellow afterwards walking up and down* Boston, *under the appearance of a* Friend-Indian, *and severall others of the like Cut.* I went to one *Wigwam,* and they told me they had no room. Then I went to another, and they said the same; at last an old *Indian* bade me come to him, and his *Squaw* gave me some Ground-nuts; she gave me also something to lay under my head, and a good fire we had: and through the good providence of God, I had a comfortable lodging that night. In the morning, another *Indian* bade me come at night, and he would give me six Ground-nuts, which I did. We were at this place and time about two miles from *Connecticut River.* We went in the morning to gather Ground-nuts, to the River, and went back again that night. I went with a good load at my back (for they when they went, though but a little way, would carry all their trumpery with them) I told them the skin was off my back, but I had no other comforting answer from them than this, *That it would be no matter if my head were off too.*

THE THIRTEENTH REMOVE

Instead of going toward the Bay, *which was that I desired, I must go with them five or six miles down the River into a mighty Thicket of Brush: where we abode almost a fortnight.* Here one asked me to make a shirt for her Papoos for which she gave me a mess of Broth, which was thickened with meal made of the Bark of a Tree, and to make it the better, she had put into it about a handfull of Pease, and a few roasted Ground-nuts. I had not seen my son a pritty while, and here was an *Indian* of whom I made inquiry after him, and asked him when he saw him: he answered me, that such a time his master roasted him, and that himself did eat a piece of him, as big as his two fingers, and that he was very good meat: *But the Lord upheld my Spirit, under this discouragement; and I considered their* 3 *horrible addictedness to lying, and that there is not one of them that makes the least conscience of speaking of truth.* In this place, on a cold night, as I lay by the fire, I removed a stick that kept the heat from me, a *Squaw* moved it down again, at which I lookt up, and she threw a handfull of ashes in mine eyes: I thought I should have been quite blinded, and have never seen more: but lying down, the water run out of my eyes, and carried the dirt with it, that by the morning, I recovered my sight again. Yet upon this, and the like occasions, I hope it is not too much to say with Job, *Have pitty upon me, have pitty upon me, O ye my friends, for the Hand of the Lord has touched me.*[45] And here I cannot but remember how many times sitting in their *Wigwams,* and musing on things past, I should suddenly leap up and run out, as if I had been at home, forgetting where I was, and what my condition was: But when I was without, and saw nothing but *Wilderness,* and *Woods,* and a company of barbarous heathens: my mind quickly returned to me, which made me think of that, spoken concerning *Sampson,* who said, *I will go out and shake myself as at other times, but he wist not that the Lord was departed from him.*[46] About this time I began to think that all my hopes of Restoration would come to nothing. I thought of the *English* Army, and hoped for their coming, and being taken by them, but that failed also. I hoped to be carried to *Albany,* as the *Indians* had discoursed before, but that failed also. I thought of being sold to my Husband, as my master spake, but in stead of that, my master himself was gone, and I left behind, so that my Spirit was now quite ready to sink. I asked them to let me go out and pick up some sticks, that I might get alone, *And poure out my heart unto the Lord.* Then also I took my Bible to read, but I found no comfort here neither, which many times I was wont to find: *So easie a thing it is with God to dry up the Streames of Scripture-comfort from us.* Yet I can say, that in all my sorrows and afflictions, God did not leave me to have my impatience work towards himself, as if his wayes were unrighteous. *But I knew that he laid upon me less than I deserved.* Afterward, before this dolefull time ended with me, I was turning the leaves of my Bible, and the Lord brought to me some Scriptures, which did a little revive me, as that Isai. 55. 8. *For my thoughts are not your thoughts, neither are your wayes my ways, saith the Lord.* And also that, *Psal.* 37. 5. *Commit thy way unto the Lord, trust also in him, and he shall bring it to pass.* About this time they came yelping from *Hadly,* where they had killed three *English men,* and brought one Captive with them, *viz. Thomas Read.* They all gathered about the poor Man, asking him many Questions. I desired also to go and see him; and when I came, he was crying bitterly, supposing they would quickly kill him. Whereupon I asked one of them, whether they intended to kill him; he answered me, they would not: He being a little cheared with that, I asked him about the wel-fare of my *Hus-*

---

[45]Job 19:21.
[46]Judges 16:20.

band, he told me he saw him such a time in the *Bay,* and he was well, but very melancholly. By which I certainly understood (though I suspected it before) that whatsoever the *Indians* told me respecting him was vanity and lies. Some of them told me, he was dead, and they had killed him: some said he was Married again, and that the Governour wished him to marry; and told him he should have his choice, and that all perswaded I was dead. So like were these barbarous creatures to him who was a lyar from the beginning.

As I was sitting once in the *Wigwam* here, *Philips* Maid came in with the Child in her arms, and asked me to give her a piece of my Apron, to make a flap for it, I told her I would not: then my Mistress bade me give it, but still I said no: the maid told me if I would not give her a piece, she would tear a piece off it: I told her I would tear her Coat then, with that my Mistriss rises up, and takes up a stick big enough to have killed me, and struck at me with it, but I stepped out, and she struck the stick into the Mat of the Wigwam. But while she was pulling of it out, I ran to the Maid and gave her all my Apron, and so that storm went over.

Hearing that my Son was come to this place, I went to see him, and told him his Father was well, but very melancholly: he told me he was as much grieved for his Father as for himself; I wondred at his speech, for I thought I had enough upon my spirit in reference to my self, to make me mindless of my Husband and every one else: they being safe among their Friends. He told me also, that a while before, his Master (together with other *Indians*) were going to the *French* for *Powder;* but by the way the *Mohawks* met with them, and killed four of their Company which made the rest turn back again,[47] for which I desired that my self and he may bless the Lord; for it might have been worse with him, had he been sold to the *French,* than it proved to be in his remaining with the *Indians.*[48]

I went to see an *English* Youth in this place, one *John Gilberd* of *Springfield.* I found him lying without dores, upon the ground; I asked him how he did? He told me he was very sick of a flux,[49] with eating so much blood: They had turned him out of the *Wigwam,* and with him an *Indian Papoos,* almost dead, (whose Parents had been killed) in a bitter cold day, with-

---

[47]Having been at war with most New England Indians for the preceding decade, the Mohawks found common cause with the colonists upon the outbreak of King Philip's War.

[48]Rowlandson fears the French in Canada because they are Catholic. Puritans regarded the Pope as the Anti-Christ and Catholicism as a form of spiritual slavery.

[49]Dysentery.

out fire or clothes: the young man himself had nothing on, but his shirt and wast-coat. This sight was enough to melt a heart of flint. There they lay quivering in the Cold, the youth round like a dog, the *Papoos* stretcht out, with his eyes and nose and mouth full of dirt, and yet alive, and groaning. I advised John to go and get to some fire: he told me he cou'd not stand, but I perswaded him still, lest he should ly there and die: and with much adoe I got him to a fire, and went my self home. As soon as I was got home, his Masters Daughter came after me, to know what I had done with the *English man,* I told her I had got him to a fire in such a place. Now had I need to pray *Pauls* prayer, 2 Thess. 3. 2. *That we may be delivered from unreasonable and wicked men.* For her satisfaction I went along with her, and brought her to him; but before I got home again, it was noised about, that I was running away and getting the *English* youth, along with me; that as soon as I came in, they began to rant and domineer: asking me where I had been, and what I had been doing? and saying they would knock him on the head: I told them, I had been seeing the *English Youth,* and that I would not run away, they told me I lyed, and taking up a Hatchet, they came to me, and said they would knock me down if I stirred out again; and so confined me to the *Wigwam.* Now may I say with *David,* 2 Sam. 24. 14. *I am in a great strait.* If I keep in, I must dy with hunger, and if I go out, I must be knockt in head. This distressed condition held that day, and half the next; *And then the Lord remembered me, whose mercyes are great.* Then came an *Indian* to me with a pair of stockings that were too big for him, and he would have me ravel them out, and knit them fit for him. I shewed my self willing, and bade him ask my mistriss if I might go along with him a little way; she said yes, I might, but I was not a little refresht with that news, that I had my liberty again. Then I went along with him, and he gave me some roasted Ground-nuts, which did again revive my feeble stomach.

    Being got out of her sight, I had time and liberty again to look into my Bible: *Which was my Guid by day, and my Pillow by night.* Now that comfortable Scripture presented itself to me, *Isa.* 54. 7. *For a small moment have I forsaken thee, but with great mercies will I gather thee.* Thus the Lord carried me along from one time to another, and made good to me this precious promise, and many others. Then my Son came to see me, and I asked his master to let him stay a while with me, that I might comb his head, and look over him, for he was almost overcome with lice. He told me, when I had done, that he was very hungry, but I had nothing to relieve him; but bid him go into the Wigwams as he went along, and see if he could get any thing among them. Which he did, and it seems tarried a little too long; for his Master was angry with him, and beat him, and then sold him. Then he came running to tell me he had a new Master, and that he had given him some Ground-nuts already. Then I went along with him to his new Master who told me he loved him: and he should not want. So his master carried him away, & I never saw him afterward, till I saw him at *Pascataqua* in *Portsmouth.*

That night they bade me go out of the *Wigwam* again: my Mistrisses Papoos was sick, and it died that night, and there was one benefit in it, that there was more room. I went to a *Wigwam,* and they bade me come in, and gave me a skin to ly upon, and a mess of Venison and Ground-nuts, which was a choice Dish among them. On the morrow they buried the *Papoos,* and afterward, both morning and evening, there came a company to mourn and howle with her: though I confess, I could not much condole with them. Many sorrowfull dayes I had in this place: often getting alone; *like a Crane, or a Swallow, so did I chatter: I did mourn as a Dove, mine eyes fail with looking upward. Oh, Lord, I am oppressed; undertake for me,* Isa. 38. 14. I could tell the Lord as *Hezekiah,* ver. 3. *Remember now O Lord, I beseech thee, how I have walked before thee in truth.*[50] Now had I time to examine all my wayes: my Conscience did not accuse me, of un-righteousness toward one or other: yet I saw how in my walk with God, I had been a careless creature. As *David* said, *Against thee, thee only have I sinned:* & I might say with the poor Publican, *God be merciful unto me a sinner.*[51] On the Sabbath-dayes, I could look upon the Sun and think how People were going to the house of God, to have their Souls refresht; & then home, and their bodies also; but I was destitute of both; & might say as the poor Prodigal, *he would fain have filled his belly with the husks that the Swine did eat, and no man gave unto him,* Luke 15. 16. For I must say with him, *Father I have sinned against heaven, and in thy sight,* ver. 21.[52] I remembered how on the night before & after the Sabbath, when my Family was about me, and Relations and Neighbours with us, we could pray and sing, and then refresh our bodies with the good creatures of God; and then have a comfortable Bed to ly down on: but in stead of all this, I had only a little Swill for the body, and then like a Swine, must ly down on the ground. I cannot express to man the sorrow that lay upon my Spirit, the Lord knows it. Yet that comfortable Scripture would often come to my mind, *For a small moment have I forsaken thee, but with great mercies will I gather thee.*[53]

---

[50]Hezekiah speaks these words in Isaiah 38:3.
[51]Psalm 51:4 and Luke 18:13, respectively.
[52]Like the quotation immediately preceding, in Luke 15.
[53]Isaiah 54:7.

THE FOURTEENTH REMOVE

Now must we pack up and be gone from this Thicket, bending our course toward the Bay-towns, I haveing nothing to eat by the way this day, but a few crumbs of Cake, that an *Indian* gave my girle the same day we were taken.[54] She gave it me, and I put it in my pocket; there it lay, till it was so mouldy (for want of good baking) that one could not

[54]Rowlandson here contradicts her statement on pp. 73–74 that no one gave her or her daughter any food.

Figure 13.
This modern replica represents the kind of wigwam used by many southern New England Indians before and during the seventeenth century.

tell what it was made of; it fell all to crumbs, & grew so dry and hard, that it was like little flints; & this refreshed me many times, when I was ready to faint. It was in my thoughts when I put it into my mouth; that if ever I returned, I would tell the World what a blessing the Lord gave to such mean food. As we went along, they killed a *Deer,* with a young one in her, they gave me a piece of the *Fawn,* and it was so young and tender, that one might eat the bones as well as the flesh, and yet I thought it very good. When night came on we sate down; it rained, but they quickly got up a Bark Wigwam, where I lay dry that night. I looked out in the morning, and many of them had lain in the rain all night, I saw by their Reaking. Thus the Lord dealt mercifully with me many times, and I fared better than many of them. In the morning they took the blood of the *Deer,* and put it into the Paunch, and so boyled it; I could eat nothing of that, though they ate it sweetly. And yet they were so nice[55] in other things, that when I had fetcht Water, and had put the Dish I dipt the water with, into the Kettle of water which I brought, they would say, they would knock me down; for they said, it was a sluttish trick.

THE FIFTEENTH REMOVE

We went on our Travel. I having got one handfull of Ground-nuts, for my support that day, they gave me my load, and I went on cheerfully (with the thoughts of going homeward) haveing my burden more on my back than my spirit: we came to *Baquaug River* again that day, near which we abode a few dayes. Sometimes one of them would give me a Pipe, another a little Tobacco, another a little Salt: which I would change for a little Victuals. I cannot but think what a Wolvish appetite persons have in a starving condition: for many times when they gave me that which was hot, I was so greedy, that I shou'd burn my mouth, that it would trouble me hours after, and yet I should quickly do the same again. And after I was thoroughly hungry, I was never again satisfied. For though sometimes it fell out, that I got enough, and did eat till I could eat no more, yet I was as unsatisfied as I was when I began. And now could I see that Scripture verified (there being many Scriptures which we do not take notice of, or understand till we are afflicted) *Mic.* 6. 14. *Thou shalt eat and not be satisfied.* Now I might see more than ever before, the miseries that sin hath brought upon us: Many times I should be ready to run out against the Hea-

---

[55]Nice, in the archaic sense of fastidious, difficult to please.

then, but the Scripture would quiet me again, *Amos,* 3. 6, *Shal there be evil in the City, and the Lord hath not done it?* The Lord help me to make a right improvement of His Word, and that I might learn that great lesson, *Mic.* 6. 8, 9. *He hath showed thee (Oh Man) what is good, and what doth the Lord require of thee, but to do justly, and love mercy, and walk humbly with thy God? Hear ye the rod, and who hath appointed it.*

THE SIXTEENTH REMOVE

We began this Remove with wading over Baquag *River: the water was up to the knees, and the stream very swift, and so cold that I thought it would have cut me in sunder.* I was so weak and feeble, that I reeled as I went along, and thought there I must end my dayes at last, after my bearing and getting through so many difficulties; the *Indians* stood laughing to see me staggering along: but in my distress the Lord gave me experience of the truth, and goodness of that promise, *Isai.* 43. 2. *When thou passest through the Waters, I will be with thee, and through the Rivers, they shall not overflow thee.* Then I sat down to put on my stockins and shoes, with the teares running down mine eyes, and many sorrowfull thoughts in my heart, but I gat up to go along with them. Quickly there came up to us an *Indian,* who informed them, that I must go to *Wachusett* to my master, for there was a Letter come from the Council to the *Sagamores,* about redeeming the Captives, and that there would be another in fourteen dayes, and that I must be there ready.[56] My heart was so heavy before that I could scarce speak or go in the path; and yet now so light, that I could run. My strength seemed to come again, and recruit my feeble knees, and aking heart: yet it pleased them to go but one mile that night, and there we stayed two dayes. In that time came a company of *Indians* to us, near thirty, all on horse-back. My heart skipt within me, thinking they had been *English men* at the first sight of them, for they were dressed in *English* Apparel, with Hats, white Neckcloths, and Sashes about their waists, and Ribbonds upon their shoulders: but when they came near, there was a vast difference between the lovely faces of Christians, and the foul looks of these Heathens, which much damped my spirit again.

---

[56]This is the letter from Governor John Leverett to the "Indian Sagamores" (Document 6).

THE SEVENTEENTH REMOVE

A comfortable Remove it was to me, because of my hopes. They gave me a pack, and along we went chearfully; but quickly my will proved more than my strength; having little or no refreshing my strength failed me, and my spirit were almost quite gone. Now may I say with *David,* Psalm 119.[57] 22, 23, 24. *I am poor and needy, and my heart is wounded within me. I am gone like the shadow when it declineth: I am tossed up and down like the locusts; my knees are weak through fasting, and my flesh faileth of fatness.* At night we came to an *Indian Town,* and the *Indians* sate down by a *Wigwam* discoursing, but I was almost spent, and could scarce speak. I laid down my load, and went into the *Wigwam,* and there sat an *Indian* boyling of *Horses feet* (they being wont to eat the flesh first, and when the feet were old and dried, and they had nothing else, they would cut off the feet and use them). I asked him to give me a little of his Broth, or Water they were boiling in; he took a dish, and gave me one spoonful of Samp,[58] and bid me take as much of the Broth as I would. Then I put some of the hot water to the Samp, and drank it up, and my spirit came again. He gave me also a piece of the Ruff or Ridding of the small Guts,[59] and I broiled it on the coals; and now may I say with *Jonathan, See, I pray you, how mine eyes have been enlightened, because I tasted a little of this honey,* 1 *Sam.* 14. 29. Now is my Spirit revived again, though means be never so inconsiderable, yet if the Lord bestow his blessing upon them, they shall refresh both Soul and Body.

THE EIGHTEENTH REMOVE

We took up our packs and along we went, but a wearisome day I had of it. As we went along I saw an *English-man* stript naked, and lying dead upon the ground, but knew not who it was. Then we came to another *Indian Town,* where we stayed all night. In this Town there were four *English Children,* Captives; and one of them my own Sisters.[60] I went to see how she did, and she was well, considering her Captive-condition. I would have tarried that night with her, but they that owned her would not suffer it. Then I went into another *Wigwam,* where they were boyling Corn and

---

[57] Actually, Psalm 109.

[58] A corn porridge.

[59] That is, parts that were rough (difficult or distasteful to eat) or had been gotten rid of because they were considered inedible.

[60] That is, her sister's child.

Beans, which was a lovely sight to see, but I could not get a taste thereof. Then I went to another *Wigwam,* where there were two of the *English Children;* the *Squaw* was boyling *Horses feet,* then she cut me off a little piece, and gave one of the *English Children* a piece also. Being very hungry I had quickly eat up mine, but the Child could not bite it, it was so tough and sinewy, but lay sucking, gnawing, chewing and slobbering of it in the mouth and hand, then I took it of the Child, and ate it myself, and savoury it was to my taste. Then I may say as *Job Chap.* 6. 7. *The things that my soul refused to touch, are as my sorrowful meat.* Thus the Lord made that pleasant refreshing, which another time would have been an abomination. Then I went home to my mistresses *Wigwam;* and they told me I disgraced my master with begging, and if I did so any more, they would knock me in the head: I told them, they had as good knock me in the head as starve me to death.

THE NINETEENTH REMOVE

They said, when we went out, that we must travel to Wachuset *this day.* But a bitter weary day I had of it, travelling now three dayes together, without resting any day between. At last, after many weary steps, I saw *Wachuset* hills, but many miles off. Then we came to a great *Swamp,* through which we travelled, up to the knees, in mud and water, which was heavy going to one tyred before. Being almost spent, I thought I should have sunk down at last, and never gat out; but I may say, as in Psal. 94. 18. *When my foot slipped, thy mercy, O Lord, held me up.* Going along, having indeed my life, but little spirit, *Philip,* who was in the Company, came up and took me by the hand, and said, *Two weeks more and you shal be Mistress again.* I asked him, if he spake true? He answered, Yes, *and quickly you shall come to your master again;* who had been gone from us three weeks. After many weary steps we came to *Wachuset,* where he was: and glad I was to see him. He asked me, *When I washt me?* I told him not this month, then he fetcht me some water himself, and bid me wash, and gave me the Glass to see how I lookt; and bid his *Squaw* give me something to eat: so she gave me a mess of Beans and meat, and a little Groundnut Cake. I was wonderfully revived with this favour shewed me, *Psal.* 106. 46, *He made them also to be pittied, of all those that carried them Captives.*

My master had three *Squaws,* living sometimes with one, and sometimes with another one, this old Squaw, at whose *Wigwam* I was, and with whom my master had been those three weeks. Another was *Wettimore,* with whom I had lived and served all this while: A severe and proud Dame she was, bestowing every day in dressing herself neat as much time as any of the Gentry of the land: powdering her hair, and painting her face, going with Neck-laces, with Jewels in her ears, and Bracelets upon her hands: When she had dressed her self, her work was to make Girdles of *Wampom* and *Beads.* The third *Squaw* was a younger one, by whom he had two *Papooses.* By that time I was refresht by the old *Squaw,* with whom my master was, *Wettimores* Maid came to call me home, at which I fell a weeping. Then the old *Squaw* told me, to encourage me, that if I wanted victuals, I should come to her, and that I should ly there in her *Wigwam.* Then I went with the maid, and quickly came again and lodged there. The *Squaw* laid a Mat under me, and a good Rugg over me; the first time I had any such kindness shewed me. I understood that *Wettimore* thought, that if she should let me go and serve with the old *Squaw,* she would be in danger to loose, not only my service, but the redemption-pay also. And I was not a little glad to hear this; being by it raised in my hopes, that in Gods due time there would be an end of this sorrowfull hour. Then in came an *Indian,* and asked me to knit him three pair of Stockins, for which I had a Hat, and a silk Handkerchief. Then another asked me to make her a shift, for which she gave me an Apron.

Then came *Tom* and *Peter,* with the second Letter from the Council, about the Captives.[61] Though they were *Indians,* I gat them by the hand, and burst out into tears; my heart was so full that I could not speak to them; but recovering my self, I asked them how my husband did, and all my friends and acquaintance? they said, *They are all very well, but melancholy.* They brought me two Biskets, and a pound of Tobacco. The Tobacco I quickly gave away; when it was all gone, one asked me to give him a pipe of Tobacco, I told him it was all gone; then began he to rant and threaten. I told him when my Husband came I would give him some: *Hang him Rogue (sayes he) I will knock out his brains, if he comes here.* And then again, in the same breath they would say, *That if there should come an hundred without Guns, they would do them no hurt.* So unstable and like mad men they were. So that fearing the worst, I durst not send to my Husband, though there were some thoughts of his coming to Redeem and fetch me, not knowing what might follow; *For there was little more trust to them than to the master they served.* When the Letter was come, the *Saggamores* met to consult about the Captives, and called me to them to enquire how much my husband would give to redeem me, when I came I sate down among them, as I was wont to do, as their man-

---

[61]No copies of this letter are known to exist.

ner is: Then they bade me stand up, and said, *they were the General Court.*[62] They bid me speak what I thought he would give. Now knowing that all we had was destroyed by the *Indians,* I was in a great strait: I thought if I should speak of but a little, it would be slighted, and hinder the matter; if of a great sum, I knew not where it would be procured: yet at a venture, I said *Twenty pounds,*[63] yet desired them to take less; but they would not hear of that, but sent that message to *Boston,* that for *Twenty pounds* I should be redeemed.[64] It was a Praying-*Indian* [65]that wrote their Letter for them. There was another Praying *Indian,* who told me, that he had a brother, that would not eat Horse; his conscience was so tender and scrupulous (though as large as hell, for the destruction of poor *Christians*). Then he said, he read that Scripture to him, 2 Kings, 6. 25. *There was a famine in* Samaria, *and behold they besieged it, until an Asses head was sold for fourscore pieces of silver, and the fourth part of a Kab*[66] *of Doves dung, for five pieces of silver.* He expounded this place to his brother, and shewed him that it was lawfull to eat that in a Famine which is not at another time. And now, says he, he will eat horse with any *Indian* of them all. There was another Praying-*Indian,* who when he had done all the mischief that he could, betrayed his own Father into the *English* hands, thereby to purchase his own life. Another Praying-*Indian* was at *Sudbury-fight,* though, as he deserved, he was afterward hanged for it.[67] There was another Praying *Indian,* so wicked and cruel, as to wear a string about his neck, strung with *Christians* fingers. Another Praying-*Indian,* when

[62]The General Court was the name of Massachusetts Bay's legislature.

[63]The equivalent in 1991 U.S. currency would be about $437, based on calculations derived from John J. McCusker, *Money and Exchange in Europe and America, 1600–1775: A Handbook* (Chapel Hill: University of North Carolina Press, 1978), 139 (for converting Massachusetts pounds to pounds sterling), and McCusker, *How Much Is That in Real Money? A Historical Price Index for Use as a Deflator of Money Values in the Economy of the United States* (Worcester, Mass.: American Antiquarian Society, 1992), 313 (for converting pounds sterling to dollars).

[64]See Document 7. Rowlandson's elaborate explanation of the ransom price she set suggests that she may have been criticized for it by some colonists.

[65]James Printer.

[66]An ancient Hebrew unit of measurement, equivalent to about two liters or 3.5 pints.

[67]The battle of Sudbury, apparently fought while the two Nipmuc messengers were in the Indian camp, was the last major clash engaged in by Rowlandson's captors. As she indicates, it marked a further step in the demoralization of the anti-English forces.

Figure 14 *(right).* **Paul Revere, Portrait of King Philip (Metacom), 1772**

Created soon after Metacom's death, this engraving owes more to European conventions regarding the depiction of Native Americans than it does to evidence or understanding of its subject. Note the similarity of Metacom's pose to that of Ninigret on p. 39.

PHILIP. *KING* of Mount Hope.

they went to *Sudbury-fight,* went with them, and his *Squaw* also with him, with her *Papoos* at her back. Before they went to that fight, they got a company together to *Powaw;* the manner was as followeth. There was one that kneeled upon a *Deer-skin,* with the company round him in a ring who kneeled, and striking upon the ground with their hands, and with sticks, and muttering or humming with their mouths, besides him who kneeled in the ring, there also stood one with a Gun in his hand: Then he on the *Deer-skin* made a speech, and all manifested assent to it: and so they did many times together. Then they bade him with the Gun go out of the ring, which he did, but when he was out, they called him in again; but he seemed to make a stand, then they called the more earnestly, till he returned again: Then they all sang. Then they gave him two Guns, in either hand one: And so he on the *Deer-skin* began again; and at the end of every sentence in his speaking, they all assented, humming or muttering with their mouthes, and striking upon the ground with their hands. Then they bade him with the two Guns go out of the ring again; which he did, a little way. Then they called him in again, but he made a stand; so they called him with greater earnestness; but he stood reeling and wavering as if he knew not whither he should stand or fall, or which way to go. Then they called him with exceeding great vehemency, all of them, one and another: after a little while he turned in, staggering as he went, with his Armes stretched out, in either hand a Gun. As soon as he came in, they all sang and rejoyced exceedingly a while. And then he upon the *Deer-skin,* made another speech unto which they all assented in a rejoicing manner: and so they ended their business, and forthwith went to *Sudbury-fight.*[68] To my thinking they went without any scruple, but that they should prosper, and gain the victory: And they went out not so rejoycing, but they came home with as great a Victory. For they said they had killed two Captains, and almost an hundred men. One *English-man* they brought along with them: and he said, it was too true, for they had made sad work at *Sudbury,* as indeed it proved. Yet they came home without that rejoicing and triumphing over their victory, which they were wont to shew at other times, but rather like Dogs (as they say) which have lost their ears. Yet I could not perceive that it was for their own loss of men: They said, they had not lost above five or six: and I missed none, except in one *Wigwam.* When they went, they acted as if the Devil had

[68]The powwow Rowlandson has described was a prebattle ceremony of some kind. Although she was ostensibly appalled at the fact that it was organized by a Christian Indian, her detailed description betrays a deeper fascination. Note that the ceremony also modified precolonial tradition in its use of guns.

told them that they should gain the victory: and now they acted, as if the Devil had told them they should have a fall. Whither it were so or no, I cannot tell, but so it proved, for quickly they began to fall, and so held on that Summer, till they came to utter ruine. They came home on a Sabbath day, and the *Powaw* that kneeled upon the *Deer-skin* came home (I may say, without abuse) as black as the Devil.[69] When my master came home, he came to me and bid me make a shirt for his *Papoos,* of a holland-laced Pillowbeer.[70] About that time there came an *Indian* to me and bid me come to his *Wigwam,* at night, and he would give me some Pork & Ground-nuts. Which I did, and as I was eating, another *Indian* said to me, he seems to be your good Friend, but he killed two *Englishmen* at *Sudbury,* and there lie their Cloaths behind you: I looked behind me, and there I saw bloody Cloaths, with Bullet holes in them; yet the Lord suffered not this wretch to do me any hurt; Yea, instead of that, he many times refresht me: five or six times did he and his *Squaw* refresh my feeble carcass. If I went to their *Wigwam* at any time, they would alwayes give me something, and yet they were strangers that I never saw before. Another *Squaw* gave me a piece of fresh Pork, and a little Salt with it, and lent me her Pan to Fry it in; and I cannot but remember what a sweet, pleasant and delightfull relish that bit had to me, to this day. So little do we prize common mercies when we have them to the full.

THE TWENTIETH REMOVE

It was their usual manner to remove, when they had done any mischief, lest they should be found out: and so they did at this time. We went about three or four miles, and there they built a great *Wigwam,* big enough to hold an hundred *Indians,* which they did in preparation to a great day of Dancing. They would say now amongst themselves, that the *Governour* would be so angry for his loss at Sudbury, that he would send no more about the Captives, which made me grieve and tremble. My Sister being not far from the place where we now were, and hearing that I was here, desired her master to let her come and see me, and he was willing to it, and would go with her: but she being ready before him, told him she would go before, and was come within a Mile or two of the place; Then he overtook her, and began to rant as if he had been mad; and made her go back again in the Rain; so that I never saw her till I saw her in

---

[69] Among New England natives, a powwow referred both to certain kinds of ceremonies and to the spiritual healers, or shamans, who conducted them.
[70] That is, from a pillowcase of a type of linen cloth that originated in the Netherlands.

Charlestown. But the Lord requited many of their ill doings, for this *Indian* her master, was hanged afterward at *Boston.* The *Indians* now began to come from all quarters, against their merry dancing day. Among some of them came one *Goodwife Kettle:*[71] I told her my heart was so heavy that it was ready to break: so is mine too, said she, but yet said, I hope we shall hear some good news shortly. I could hear how earnestly my Sister desired to see me, and I as earnestly desired to see her: and yet neither of us could get an opportunity. My Daughter was also now about a mile off, and I had not seen her in nine or ten weeks, as I had not seen my Sister since our first taking. I earnestly desired them to let me go and see them: yea, I intreated, begged, and perswaded them, but to let me see my Daughter; and yet so hard hearted were they, that they would not suffer it. They made use of their tyrannical power whilst they had it: but through the Lord's wonderful mercy, their time was now but short.

On a Sabbath day, the Sun being about an hour high in the afternoon, came Mr. John Hoar[72] *(the Council permitting him, and his own foreward spirit inclining him) together with the two forementioned Indians,* Tom *and* Peter, *with their third Letter from the Council.* When they came near, I was abroad: though I saw them not, they presently called me in, and bade me sit down and not stir. Then they catched up their Guns, and away they ran, as if an Enemy had been at hand; and the Guns went off apace. I manifested some great trouble, and they asked me what was the matter? I told them, I *thought they had killed the* English-man (for they had in the mean time informed me that an *English-man* was come), they said, *No;* They shot over his Horse, and under, and before his Horse; and they pusht him this way and that way, at their pleasure, shewing what they could do: Then they let them come to their *Wigwams.* I begged of them to let me see the *English man,* but they would not. But there was I fain to sit their pleasure. When they had talked their fill with him, they suffered me to go to him. We asked each other of our welfare, and how my Husband did, and all my Friends? He told me they were all well, and would be glad to see me. Amongst other things which my Husband sent me, there came a pound of *Tobacco:* which I sold for nine shillings in Money: for many of the *Indians* for want of *Tobacco,* smoaked *Hemlock,* and *Ground-Ivy.* It was a great mistake in any, who thought I sent for *Tobacco:* for through the favour of God, that desire was overcome. I now asked them, whither I should go home with Mr. *Hoar?* They answered

---

[71]Elizabeth Kettle, also captured at Lancaster.
[72]See Document 9. John Hoar was a Concord lawyer enlisted by Joseph Rowlandson to redeem Mary.

No, one and another of them: and it being night, we lay down with that answer; in the morning, Mr. *Hoar* invited the *Saggamores* to Dinner; but when we went to get it ready, we found that they had stollen the greatest part of the Provision Mr. *Hoar* had brought, out of his Bags, in the night: *And we may see the wonderfull power of God, in that one passage, in that when there was such a great number of the* Indians *together, and so greedy of a little good food; and no* English *there, but Mr. Hoar and my self: that there they did not knock us in the head, and take what we had: there being not only some Provision, but also Trading-cloth, a part of the twenty pounds agreed upon: But instead of doing us any mischief, they seemed to be ashamed of the fact, and said, it were some* Matchit[73] Indian *that did it.* Oh, that we could believe that there is nothing too hard for God! God shewed his Power over the Heathen in this, *as he did over the hungry Lyons when* Daniel *was cast into the Den.* Mr. *Hoar* called them betime to Dinner, but they ate very little, they being so busie in dressing themselves, and getting ready for their Dance: which was carried on by eight of them, four *Men* and four *Squaws;* My master and mistriss being two. He was dressed in his Holland shirt, with great Laces sewed at the tail of it, he had his silver Buttons, his white Stockins, his Garters were hung round with Shillings, and he had Girdles of *Wampom upon his head and shoulders.* She had a Kersey[74] Coat, and covered with Girdles of *Wampom* from the Loins upward: her armes from her elbows to her hands were covered with Bracelets; there were handfulls of Neck-laces about her neck, and severall sorts of Jewels in her ears. She had fine red Stockins, and white Shoos, her hair powdered and face painted Red, that was alwayes before Black. And all the Dancers were after the same manner. There were two other singing and knocking on a Kettle for their musick. They keept hopping up and down one after another, with a Kettle of water in the midst, standing warm upon some Embers, to drink of when they were dry. They held on till it was almost night, throwing out *Wampom* to the standers by. At night I asked them again, if I should go home? They all as one said No, except my Husband would come for me. When we were lain down, my Master went out of the *Wigwam,* and by and by sent in an *Indian* called *James the Printer,* who told Mr. *Hoar,* that my Master would let me go home tomorrow, if he would let him have one pint of Liquors. Then Mr. *Hoar* called his own *Indians, Tom* and *Peter,* and bid them go and see whither he would promise before them three: and if he would, he should have it; which he did, and he had it. Then *Philip*

---

[73]Bad.
[74]A kind of coarse cloth woven from wool.

smelling the business cal'd me to him, and asked me what I would give him, to tell me some good news, and speak a good word for me. *I told him, I could not tell what to give him, I would anything I had, and asked him what he would have?* He said, two Coats and twenty shillings in Mony, and half a bushel of seed Corn, and some Tobacco. I thanked him for his love: but I knew the good news as well as the crafty *Fox.* My Master after he had had his drink, quickly came ranting into the *Wigwam* again, and called for Mr. *Hoar,* drinking to him, and saying, *He was a good man:* and then again he would say, *Hang him, Rogue:* Being almost drunk, he would drink to him, and yet presently say he should be hanged. Then he called for me, I trembled to hear him, yet I was fain to go to him, and he drank to me, shewing no incivility. He was the first *Indian* I saw drunk all the while that I was amongst them. At last his *Squaw* ran out, and he after her, round the *Wigwam,* with his money jingling at his knees: But she escaped him: But having an old *Squaw* he ran to her: and so through the Lords mercy, we were no more troubled that night. *Yet I had not a comfortable nights rest: for I think I can say, I did not sleep for three nights together.* The night before the Letter came from the Council, I could not rest, I was so full of feares and troubles, God many times leaving us most in the dark, when deliverance is nearest: yea, at this time I could not rest, night nor day. The next night I was overjoyed, Mr. *Hoar* being come, and that with such good tidings. The third night I was even swallowed up with all thoughts of things, *viz.* that ever I should go home again; and that I must go, leaving my Children behind me in the *Wilderness;* so that sleep was now almost departed from mine eyes.

On *Tuesday morning* they called their *General Court* (as they call it) to consult and determine, whether I should go home or no: And they all as one man did seemingly consent to it, that I should go home; except *Philip,* who would not come among them.[75]

But before I go any further, I would take leave to mention a few remarkable passages of providence, which I took special notice of in my afflicted time.

1. *Of the fair opportunity lost in the long March, a little after the* Fort-fight,[76] *when our* English Army *was so numerous, and in pursuit of the* Enemy, *and so near as to take several and destroy them: and the* Enemy *in such distress for food, that our men might track them by their rooting in*

---

[75]Metacom opposed the Nipmuc strategy of using the captives' release as a means of opening more general peace negotiations with the English.

[76]Rowlandson refers here to the English attack of the Narragansett Great Swamp Fort in December 1675, and the subsequent Narragansett exodus to Nipmuc country.

the earth for Ground-nuts whilest they were flying for their lives. I say, that then our Army should want Provision, and be forced to leave their pursuit and return homeward: and the very next week the *Enemy* came upon our *Town,* like Bears bereft of their whelps, or so many ravenous Wolves, rending us and our Lambs to death. But what shall I say? God seemed to leave His People to themselves, and order all things for His own holy ends. *Shall there be evil in the City and the Lord hath not done it? They are not grieved for the affliction of* Joseph, *therefore shal they go Captive, with the first that go Captive. It is the Lords doing, and it should be marvelous in our eyes.*[77]

2. I cannot but remember how the Indians *derided the slowness, and dulness of the* English *Army, in its setting out.* For after the desolations at *Lancaster* and *Medfield,* as I went along with them, they asked me when I thought the *English* Army would come after them? I told them I could not tell: It may be they will come in *May,* said they. Thus did they scoffe at us, as if the *English* would be a quarter of a year getting ready.

3. Which also I have hinted before, when the English *Army with new supplies were sent forth to pursue after the enemy, and they understanding it, fled before them till they came to* Baquaug *River, where they forthwith went over safely: that that River should be impassable to the* English. I can but admire to see the wonderfull providence of God in preserving the heathen for farther affliction to our poor Countrey. They could go in great numbers over, but the *English* must stop: God had an over-ruling hand in all those things.

_4. It was thought, if their corn were cut down, they would starve and dy with hunger: and all their Corn that could be found, was destroyed, and they driven from that little they had in store, into the Woods in the midst of Winter;* and yet how to admiration did the Lord preserve them for his Holy ends, and the destruction of many still amongst the *English!* Strangely did the Lord provide for them; that I did not see (all the time I was among them) one Man, Woman, or Child, die with hunger.[78]

Though many times they would eat that, that a Hog or a Dog would hardly touch; yet by that God strengthened them to be a scourge to His People.

The chief and commonest food was Ground-nuts: They eat also Nuts and Acorns, Harty-choaks,[79] Lilly roots, Ground-beans, and several other weeds and roots, that I know not.

---

[77]Amos 3:6; 6:6–7; Psalm 118:23.

[78]Rowlandson has described earlier an Indian child on the verge of death from hunger (pp. 89–90) and mentioned the death of Weetamoo's child (p. 91).

[79]Artichokes, undoubtedly Jerusalem artichokes, a plant harvested by Indians throughout eastern North America and the Mississippi Valley.

They would pick up old bones, and cut them to pieces at the joynts, and if they were full of wormes and magots, they would scald them over the fire to make the vermine come out, and then boile them, and drink up the Liquor, and then beat the great ends of them in a Morter, and so eat them. They would eat Horses guts, and ears, and all sorts of wild Birds which they could catch: also Bear, Venison, Beaver, Tortois, Frogs, Squirrels, Dogs, Skunks, Rattle-snakes; yea, the very Bark of Trees; besides all sorts of creatures, and provision which they plundered from the *English*. I can but stand in admiration to see the wonderful power of God, in providing for such a vast number of our Enemies in the *Wilderness,* where there was nothing to be seen, but from hand to mouth. Many times in a morning, the generality of them would eat up all they had, and yet have some further supply against what they wanted. It is said, *Psal.* 81. 13, 14. *Oh, that my People had hearkened to me, and* Israel *had walked in my wayes, I should soon have subdued their Enemies, and turned my hand against their Adversaries.* But now our perverse and evil carriages in the sight of the Lord, have so offended Him, that instead of turning His hand against them, the Lord feeds and nourishes them up to be a scourge to the whole Land.

    5. *Another thing that I would observe is, the strange providence of God, in turning things about when the* Indians *were at the highest, and the* English *at the lowest.* I was with the Enemy eleven weeks and five dayes, and not one Week passed without the fury of the Enemy, and some desolation by fire and sword upon one place or other. They mourned (with their black faces) for their own losses, yet triumphed and rejoyced in their inhumane, and many times devilish cruelty to the *English.* They would boast much of their Victories; saying, that in two hours time they had destroyed such a *Captain,* and his *Company* at such a place; and such a *Captain* and his *Company* in such a place; and such a *Captain* and his *Company* in such a place; and boast how many *Towns* they had destroyed, and then scoffe, and say, *They had done them a good turn, to send them to Heaven so soon.* Again, they would say, *This summer that they would knock all the Rogues in the head, or drive them into the Sea, or make them flie the Countrey:* thinking surely, *Agag*-like, *The bitterness of Death is past.*[80] Now the Heathen begins to think all is their own, and the poor Christians hopes to fail (as to man) and now their eyes are more to God, and their hearts sigh heaven-ward: and to say in good earnest, *Help Lord, or we perish:*[81] When the Lord had brought his people to this, that they saw no help in any thing

---

[80]I Samuel 15:32.
[81]Matthew 8:25.

but himself: then he takes the quarrel into his own hand: and though they had made a pit, in their own imaginations, as deep as hell for the Christians that Summer, yet the Lord hurll'd themselves into it. And the Lord had not so many wayes before to preserve them, but now he hath as many to destroy them.

But to return again to my going home, where we may see a remarkable change of Providence: At first they were all against it, except my Husband would come for me; but afterwards they assented to it, and seemed much to rejoyce in it; some askt me to send them some Bread, others some Tobacco, others shaking me by the hand, offering me a Hood and Scarfe to ride in; not one moving hand or tongue against it. Thus hath the Lord answered my poor desire, and the many earnest requests of others put up unto God for me. In my travels an *Indian* came to me, and told me, if I were willing, he and his *Squaw* would run away, and go home along with me: I told him *No:* I was not willing to run away, but desired to wait Gods time, that I might go home quietly, and without fear. And now God hath granted me my desire. O the wonderfull power of God that I have seen, and the experience that I have had: *I have been in the midst of those roaring Lyons, and Salvage Bears, that feared neither God, nor Man, nor the Devil, by night and day, alone and in company: sleeping all sorts together, and yet not one of them ever offered me the least abuse of unchastity to me, in word or action.*[82] Though some are ready to say, I speak it for my own credit; *But I speak it in the presence of God, and to His glory.*[83] Gods power is as great now, and as sufficient to save, as when he preserved *Daniel* in the Lions den; or the three *Children* in the fiery Furnace. I may well say as his *Psal.* 107. 1, 2, *Oh give thanks unto the Lord for He is good, for his mercy endureth for ever.* Let the Redeemed of the Lord say so, whom He hath redeemed from the hand of the Enemy, especially that I should come away in the midst of so many hundreds of Enemies quietly and peacably, and not a Dog moving his tongue. So I took my leave of them, and in coming along my heart melted into tears, more then all the while I was with them, and I was almost swallowed up with the thoughts that ever I should go home again. About the Sun going down, Mr. *Hoar,* and my self, and the two *Indians* came to *Lancaster,* and a solemn sight it was to me. There had I lived many comfortable years amongst my Relations and Neighbours, and now not one *Christian* to be

---

[82]While most colonists feared otherwise, there is no record of any sexual violation of captive women by Native Americans anywhere in eastern North America.

[83]This sentence is another indication that Rowlandson was writing in part to counter her detractors.

seen, nor one house left standing. We went on to a Farm house that was yet standing, where we lay all night: and a comfortable lodging we had, though nothing but straw to ly on. The Lord preserved us in safety that night, and raised us up again in the morning, and carried us along, that before noon, we came to *Concord*. Now was I full of joy, and yet not without sorrow: joy to see such a lovely sight, so many *Christians* together, and some of them my Neighbours: There I met with my Brother, and my Brother in Law, who asked me, if I knew where his Wife was? Poor heart! he had helped to bury her, and knew it not; she being shot down by the house was partly burnt: so that those who were at *Boston* at the desolation of the *Town,* and came back afterward, and buried the dead, did not know her. Yet I was not without sorrow, to think how many were looking and longing, and my own Children amongst the rest, to enjoy that deliverance that I had now received, and I did not know whither ever I should see them again. Being recruited with food and raiment we went to *Boston* that day, where I met with my dear Husband, but the thoughts of our dear Children, one being dead, and the other we could not tell where, abated our comfort each to other. I was not before so much hem'd in with the merciless and cruel Heathen, but now as much with pittiful, tender-hearted and compassionate Christians. In that poor, and destressed, and beggerly condition I was received in, I was kindly entertained in severall Houses: so much love I received from several (some of whom I knew, and others I knew not) that I am not capable to declare it. But the Lord knows them all by name: *The Lord reward them seven fold into their bosoms of his spirituals, for their temporals!* The *twenty pounds* the price of my redemption was raised by some *Boston* Gentlemen, and Ms.[84] *Usher,* whose bounty and religious charity, I would not forget to make mention of. Then Mr. *Thomas Shepard* of *Charlestown* received us into his House, where we continued eleven weeks; and a Father and Mother they were to us. And many more tender-hearted Friends we met with in that place. We were now in the midst of love, yet not without much and frequent heaviness of heart for our poor Children, and other Relations, who were still in affliction. The week following, after my coming in, the Governour[85] and Council sent forth to the *Indians* again; and that not without success; for they brought in my Sister, and Good-wife Kettle: Their not knowing where our Children were, was a sore tryal to us still, and yet we were not without secret hopes that we should see them

---

[84]This usage was almost certainly unintended, but is here left as printed because it is unclear whether Rowlandson was referring to a *Mr.* or a *Mrs.* Usher. Rowlandson's many editors over the past three centuries have been divided as to Usher's identity and gender.

[85]The governor of Massachusetts Bay, John Leverett.

again. That which was dead lay heavier upon my spirit, than those which were alive and amongst the Heathen; thinking how it suffered with its wounds, and I was in no way able to relieve it; and how it was buried by the Heathen in the *Wilderness* from among all Christians. We were hurried up and down in our thoughts, sometimes we should hear a report that they were gone this way, and sometimes that; and that they were come in, in this place or that: We kept enquiring and listening to hear concerning them, but no certain news as yet. About this time the Council had ordered a day of publick *Thanks-giving:* though I thought I had still cause of mourning, and being unsettled in our minds, we thought we would ride toward the *Eastward,* to see if we could hear anything concerning our Children. And as we were riding along (God is the wise disposer of all things) between *Ipswich* and *Rowley* we met with Mr. *William Hubbard,*[86] who told us that our Son *Joseph* was come in to Major *Waldrens,*[87] and another with him, which was my Sisters Son. I asked him how he knew it? He said, the Major himself told him so. So along we went till we came to *Newbury;* and their Minister being absent, they desired my Husband to preach the *Thanks-giving* for them; but he was not willing to stay there that night, but would go over to *Salisbury,* to hear further, and come again in the morning; which he did, and Preached there that day. At night, when he had done, one came and told him that his Daughter was come in at *Providence*: Here was mercy on both hands: Now hath God fulfilled that precious Scripture which was such a comfort to me in my distressed condition. When my heart was ready to sink into the Earth (my Children being gone I could not tell whither) and my knees trembled under me, *And I was walking through the valley of the shadow of Death:* Then the Lord brought, and now has fulfilled that reviving word unto me: Thus saith the Lord, *Refrain thy voice from weeping, and thine eyes from tears, for thy work shall be rewarded,* saith the Lord, *and they shall come again from the Land of the Enemy.*[88] Now we were between them, the one on the *East,* and the other on the *West*: Our Son being nearest, we went to him first, to *Portsmouth,* where we met with him, and with the Major also: who told us he had done what he could, but could not redeem him under *seven*

---

[86]Hubbard was a minister at Ipswich, Massachusetts, who became one of the more prominent historians of the war. He had also helped prosecute Joseph Rowlandson for libel a quarter century earlier. See the Introduction.

[87]Major Richard Waldron of Dover, New Hampshire, who became infamous a few months later for luring a large number of Nipmucs and other Indians into disarming under the pretext of peace, then capturing them and selling many into slavery. See Evan Haefli and Kevin Sweeney, "Revisiting *The Redeemed Captive:* New Perspectives on the 1704 Attack on Deerfield," *William and Mary Quarterly* 52 (1995): 22–23.

[88]Jeremiah 31:16.

pounds; which the good People thereabouts were pleased to pay. The Lord reward the Major, and all the rest, though unknown to me, for their labour of Love. My Sisters Son was redeemed for *four pounds,* which the Council gave order for the payment of. Having now received one of our Children, we hastened toward the other: going back through *Newbury,* my Husband Preached there on the *Sabbath-day:* for which they rewarded him many fold.

On *Munday* we came to Charlestown, where we heard that the Governour of *Road-Island*[89] had sent over for our Daughter, to take care of her, being now within his Jurisdiction: which should not pass without our acknowledgments. But she being nearer *Rehoboth* than *Road-Island,* Mr. *Newman*[90] went over, and took care of her, and brought her to his own House. And the goodness of God was admirable to us in our low estate, in that he raised up passionate Friends on every side to us, when we had nothing to recompance any for their love. The *Indians* were now gone that way, that it was apprehended dangerous to go to her: But the Carts which carried Provision to the *English* Army, being guarded, brought her with them to *Dorchester,* where we received her safe: blessed be the Lord for it, *For great is his Power, and he can do whatsoever seemeth him good.* Her coming in was after this manner: She was travelling one day with the *Indians,* with her basket at her back; the company of *Indians* were got before her, and gone out of sight, all except one *Squaw;* she followed the *Squaw* till night, and then both of them lay down, having nothing over them but the heavens, and under them but the earth. Thus she travelled three dayes together, not knowing whither she was going: having nothing to eat or drink but water, and green *Hirtle-berries.* At last they came into *Providence,* where she was kindly entertained by several of that *Town.* The *Indians* often said, that I should never have her under *twenty pounds:* But now the Lord hath brought her in upon free-cost, and given her to me the second time. The Lord make us a blessing indeed, each to others. Now have I seen that Scripture also fulfilled, *Deut.* 30. 4, 7. *If any of thine be driven out to the outmost parts of heaven, from thence will the Lord thy God gather thee, and from thence will he fetch thee. And the Lord thy God will put all these curses upon thine enemies, and on them which hate thee, which persecuted thee.* Thus hath the Lord brought me and mine out of that horrible pit, and hath set us in the midst of tender-hearted and compassionate Christians. It is the desire of my soul, that we may walk worthy of the mercies received, and which we are receiving.

---

[89]William Coddington.
[90]Noah Newman, a minister of Rehoboth.

Our family being now gathered together (those of us that were living) the South Church *in* Boston *hired an House for us: Then we removed from Mr.* Shepards, *those cordial Friends, and went to* Boston, *where we continued about three quarters of a year: Still the Lord went along with us, and provided graciously for us.* I thought it somewhat strange to set up House-keeping with bare walls; but as *Solomon* says, *Mony answers all things;*[91] and that we had through the benevolence of Christian-friends, some in this *Town,* and some in that, and others: And some from *England,* that in a little time we might look, and see the House furnished with love. The Lord hath been exceeding good to us in our low estate, in that when we had neither house nor home, nor other necessaries, the Lord so moved the hearts of these and those towards us, that we wanted neither food, nor raiment for our selves or ours, *Prov.* 18. 24. *There is a Friend which sticketh closer than a Brother.* And how many such Friends have we found, and now living amongst? And truly such a Friend have we found him to be unto us, in whose house we lived, *viz.* Mr. *James Whitcomb,*[92] a Friend unto us near hand, and afar off.

I can remember the time, when I used to sleep quietly without workings in my thoughts, whole nights together, but now it is other wayes with me. When all are fast about me, and no eye open, but his who ever waketh, my thoughts are upon things past, upon the awfull dispensation of the Lord towards us; upon his wonderfull power and might, in carrying of us through so many difficulties, in returning us in safety, and suffering none to hurt us. I remember in the night season, how the other day I was in the midst of thousands of enemies, & nothing but death before me: It is then hard work to perswade myself, that ever I should be satisfied with bread again. But now we are fed *with the finest of the Wheat,* and, as I may say, *with honey out of the rock:*[93] In stead of the Husk, we have the fatted Calf:[94] The thoughts of these things in the particulars of them, and of the love and goodness of God towards us, make it true of me, what David said of himself, *Psal.* 6. 6. *I watered my couch with my tears.* Oh! the wonderfull power of God that mine eyes have seen, affording matter enough for my thoughts to run in, that when others are sleeping mine are weeping.

I have seen the extrem vanity of this World: One hour I have been in health, and wealth, wanting nothing: But the next hour in sickness and wounds, and death, having nothing but sorrow and affliction.

---

[91]Ecclesiastes 10:19.

[92]A wealthy Boston resident whose business dealings included buying and selling Indian slaves. See Document 14.

[93]Psalm 81:16.

[94]See Luke 15:11–32.

Before I knew what affliction meant, I was ready sometimes to wish for it. When I lived in prosperity, having the comforts of the World about me, my relations by me, my Heart chearfull: and taking little care for any thing; and yet seeing many, whom I preferred before my self, under many tryals and afflictions, in sickness, weakness, poverty, losses, crosses, and cares of the World, I should be sometimes jealous least I should have my portion in this life, and that Scripture would come to my mind, *Heb.* 12. 6. *For whom the* **Lord** *loveth he chasteneth, and scourgeth every Son whom he receiveth.* But now I see the Lord had his time to scourge and chasten me. The portion of some is to have their afflictions by drops, now one drop and then another; but the dregs of the Cup, the Wine of astonishment: like a sweeping rain that leaveth no food, did the Lord prepare to be my portion. Affliction I wanted, and affliction I had, full measure (I thought) pressed down and running over; yet I see, when God calls a Person to any thing, and through never so many difficulties, yet he is fully able to carry them through and make them see, and say they have been gainers thereby. And I hope I can say in some measure, As *David* did, *It is good for me that I have been afflicted.*[95] The Lord hath shewed me the vanity of these outward things. That they are the *Vanity of vanities, and vexation of spirit;*[96] that they are but a shadow, a blast, a bubble, and things of no continuance. That we must rely on God himself, and our whole dependance must be upon him. If trouble from smaller matters begin to arise in me, I have something at hand to check my self with, and say, why am I troubled? It was but the other day that if I had had the world, I would have given it for my freedom, or to have been a Servant to a Christian. I have learned to look beyond present and smaller troubles, and to be quieted under them, as *Moses* said, *Exod.* 14. 13. *Stand still and see the Salvation of the Lord.*

FINIS.

[95]Psalm 119:71.
[96]Ecclesiates 1:2, 14.

PART THREE

Related Documents

METACOM ON THE CAUSES OF ANGLO-INDIAN WAR

1

JOHN EASTON

Excerpt from "A Relacion of the Indyan Warre"

1675

The selection that follows is the most comprehensive statement that we have of the case against the English in 1675. As the clouds of war gathered in mid-June, Deputy Governor John Easton and several other Rhode Islanders arranged to meet the Wampanoag sachem, Metacom ("King Philip"), and his councillors in hopes of resolving differences between the two sides. The natives had reason to expect that they might receive a fair hearing of their grievances. Because of its policies of religious toleration and fairness in its dealings with Native Americans, Rhode Island had been excluded from the United Colonies of New England, which consisted of the more militantly Puritan Massachusetts Bay, Connecticut, and Plymouth. Easton's own family had been expelled from Massachusetts as followers of Antinomian radical Anne Hutchinson when he was a youth, and later the family converted to Quakerism with its beliefs of nonviolence. Nevertheless, as Easton makes clear, his loyalties were fundamentally English. In his account of the meeting, he recorded the Wampanoags' many grievances—grievances that had accumulated, especially within the preceding five years, to the point where war appeared the only possible solution. Although the natives were clearly intrigued by Easton's proposals for having the conflict mediated by outsiders, he could do nothing to address their complaints against the United Colonies. About one week later, Wampanoag warriors began attacking English homes in Swansea, Plymouth colony, and the war was on. As Easton made clear to Metacom during their meeting, Rhode Island would side with the other English if and when war broke out.

For forty years' time reports and jealousies of war had been very frequent that we did not think that a war was breaking forth, but about a week

---

John Easton, "A Relacion of the Indyan Warre" (1675; pub. 1858; reprinted in Charles H. Lincoln, ed., *Narratives of the Indian Wars, 1675–1699*, New York, 1913), 8–12.

before it did we had cause to think it would. Then to endeavor to prevent it, we sent a man to Philip that if he would come to the ferry we would come over to speak with him. About four mile we had to come thither. Our messenger come to them, they not aware of it behaved themselves as furious but suddenly appeased when they understood who he was and what he came for. He called his council and agreed to come to us came himself unarmed and about forty of his men armed. Then five of us went over. Three were magistrates. We sat very friendly together. We told him our business was to endeavor that they might not receive or do wrong. They said that was well they had done no wrong, the English wronged them, we said we knew the English said they[1] wronged them and the Indians said the English wronged them but our desire was the quarrel might rightly be decided in the best way, and not as dogs decided their quarrels. The Indians owned that fighting was the worst way then they propounded how right might take place, we said by arbitration. They said all English agreed against them and so by arbitration they had had much wrong, many square miles of land so taken from them for English would have English Arbitrators, and once they were persuaded to give in their arms, that thereby jealousy might be removed and the English having their arms would not deliver them as they had promised, until they consented to pay 100 pounds, and now they had not so much land or money, that they were as good be killed as leave all their livelihood.[2] We said they might choose a Indian king,[3] and the English might choose the governor of New York that neither had cause to say either were parties in the difference.[4] They said they had not heard of that way and said we honestly spoke so we were persuaded if that way had been tendered they would have accepted. We did endeavor not to hear their complaints, said it was not convenient for us now to consider of, but to endeavor to prevent war, said to them when in war against English blood was spilled that engaged all Englishmen for we were to be all under one king.[5] We knew what their complaints would

---

[1]The Indians.

[2]In 1671 Plymouth, fearing increased Wampanoag militance, extracted an agreement from a reluctant Metacom to disarm his followers. But many Wampanoags maintained that the agreement did not apply to them, and there is some reason to suppose that it initially covered only those present at the conference and not, as the colony subsequently claimed, all Wampanoags.

[3]The English often referred to Indian sachems with whom they dealt diplomatically as "kings" and "queens," implicitly acknowledging the sovereignty of the nations that these sachems led.

[4]It is unlikely that the United Colonies would have agreed to have New York Governor Edmund Andros negotiate for them because of his colony's claim on Connecticut and Massachusetts territory west of the Connecticut River.

[5]The confusing last part of this sentence appears to mean that once English blood was spilled, all English would unite against the perpetrators.

be, and in our colony had removed some of them in sending for Indian rulers in what the crime concerned Indian lives which they very lovingly accepted and agreed with us to their execution and said they were able to satisfy their subjects when they knew an Indian suffered duly, but said in what was only between their Indians and not in townships that we had purchased, they would not have us prosecute and that they had a great fear to have any of their Indians should be called or forced to be Christian Indians. They said that such were in everything more mischievous, only dissemblers, and then the English made them not subject to their kings, and by their lying to wrong their kings. We knew it to be true, and we promising them that however in government to Indians all should be alike and that we knew it was our kings will it should be so, that although we were weaker than other colonies, they having submitted to our king to protect them others dared not otherwise to molest them. So they expressed they took that to be well, that we had little cause to doubt but that to us under the king they would have yielded to our determinations in what any should have complained to us against them, but Philip charged it to be dishonesty in us to put off the hearing the complaints; therefore we consented to hear them. They said they had been the first in doing good to the English, and the English the first in doing wrong, said when the English first came their king's father was as a great man and the English as a little child, he constrained other Indians from wronging the English and gave them corn and showed them how to plant and was free to do them any good and had let them have a 100 times more land, then now the king had for his own people,[6] but their king's brother when he was king came miserably to die by being forced to court as they judged poisoned,[7] and another greivance was if 20 of their honest Indians testified that a Englishman had done them wrong, it was as nothing, and if but one of their worst Indians testified against any Indian or their king when it pleased the English that was sufficient. Another grievance was when their kings sold land the English would say it was more than they agreed to and a writing must be proof against all them, and sum of their kings had done wrong to sell so much. He left his people none and some being given to drunkeness the English made them drunk and then cheated them in bargains, but now their kings were forewarned not for to part with land for nothing in comparison to the value thereof. Now whom the English had owned for king or queen

---

[6]The Wampanoags here refer their sachem ("king") Ousamequin, also known as Massasoit, who maintained friendly relations with Plymouth colony from 1621, soon after its founding, until his death in 1662.

[7]Ousamequin was succeeded by his eldest son, Wamsutta (also known as Alexander), who suddenly and mysteriously died soon thereafter while returning from a conference with Plymouth officials. Upon his death, Metacom succeeded to the sachemship.

they[8] would disinherit, and make another king that would give or sell them their land, that now they had no hopes left to keep any land. Another grievance the English cattle and horses still increased that when they removed 30 miles from where English had anything to do, they could not keep their corn from being spoiled, they never being used to fence, and thought when the English bought land of them that they would have kept their cattle upon their own land. Another grievance the English were so eager to sell the Indians liquors that most of the Indians spent all in drunkeness and then ravened upon[9] the sober Indians and they did believe often did hurt the English cattle, and their kings could not prevent it. We knew before these were their grand complaints, but then we only endeavored to persuade that all complaints might be righted without war, but could have no other answer but that they had not heard of that way for the Governor of York and an Indian king to have the hearing of it. We had cause to think if that had been tendered it would have been accepted. We endeavored that however they should lay down their arms for the English were too strong for them. They said then the English should do to them as they did when they were too strong for the English. So we departed without any discourteousness, and suddenly had letter from Plimouth Governor they intended in arms to conform[10] Philip, but no information what that was they required or what terms he refused to have their quarrel decided, and in a weeks time after we had been with the Indians the war thus begun.

[8]The English.
[9]Seized, plundered.
[10]Force into subjection.

THE PERILS OF WAR

2

*The Examination and Relation
of James Quannapaquait*

January 24, 1675

*Despite facing the antagonism of most colonists and terrible imprisonment
on barren Deer Island, many Christian and other Indians tried to remain
neutral or openly supported the English. Two examples of the latter were
James Quanapohit (referred to in this document as Quannapaquait) and*

J. H. Temple, *History of North Brookfield* (North Brookfield, 1887), 112–18.

Job Kattananit, who were released from the island in order to spy for the colonists among their fellow Nipmucs. With both English and Indians suspicious of their motives and actions, they undertook their missions at great personal risk. The following report from Quanapohit, whose last name was sometimes rendered by English writers as Quannepaquait or Quanapaug, was given at Daniel Gookin's home after Quanapohit arrived there with news of the anti-English Indians, including their planned attack on Lancaster. The report shows how the war sometimes divided people from the same community, such as Quanapohit and Monoco, and indicates that the principal motive for attacking towns like Lancaster was for their stores of corn. Dated January 24, 1675 (Old Style calendar), it makes clear that the English knew of the Indians' plans to attack Lancaster three weeks in advance but ignored the intelligence because they did not trust its source. Finally, it shows that the Indians who worked on behalf of the colonists were not simply acquiescing to English rule but were acting out of concern for the welfare of their families and communities, whose situations, whether in enemy hands or on Deer Island, were desperate.

An examination of the original manuscript at the Connecticut Archives makes clear that the square brackets were inserted by the original recorder, apparently to distinguish his clarifying additions from Quanapohit's actual words. Ellipses indicate a space where the manuscript is illegible.

The examination & relation of James Quannapaquait, allias James Rumny-Marsh beeing one of the christian Indians belonging to Natick; taken the 24th day of Janry 1675–6, on wch day hee returned from his jorney, [for this man and another called Job of Magungoog, a christian man also] were sent forth by order of the councill of Massachusetts upon the last of December, [as spyes], to discover the enemyes quarters & motions & his state & condition, & to gaine what intelegence they could; for wch end they had particuler instruction. Though when first they were moved to goe this jorny, they saw it would bee a hazardous undertaking, & that they should runne the hazard of their lives in it, yet they were willing to venture upon these & like considerations, (1, that they might declare their readines to serve the English. 2^{ly} one of them namly Job had 3 children [even all he had] that were carried away with the Hassanameshe[11] indians &, as he conceived were with the enemy, & he was willing to know

---

[11]Hassanamesit.

their state as wel as the condition of the praying indians of Hassameske & Magunkoog that were hee thought in the power of the enimy. 3^d They hoped to sugest somthing in order to the enemies submission to the English & making peace if they found the enimy in a temper fit for it & if that could bee effected then they hoped the poor christian Indians at the Deer Island & in other places posibly might bee restored to their places againe, & bee freed from much suffering they are now in by this warre, & therby the jelosyes that the English have now of them might bee removed, these & other reasons induced them to runne this adventure for wch also if they returned in safty they had a promise of a reward.

They doubted the indian enimy would mistrust them for spyes, & that they would move them [to] fight for them against the English, unto which doubts they were advised to tell the Indian enemy a lamentable story [& that agreable to truth] of their deepe sufferings by the English; that Job was imprisoned severall daies [as hee was] where hee suffered much, though hee had served the English faithfully as an interprter & in actull armes being with the Mohegins at the fight neare Secunke with Philip,[12] the begining of August last, but imprisonment & suspitions the English had of him was part of his reward for that service to the English. And as for the other, James, he & his brother went out with Captian Prentis with their horses & armes at the first going out against Philipp in June & had done faithfull service for the English as his captains had testified by their certificate & continued in their service many weekes & was in severall fights, & that his bro: Thomas had kild one of Philip's cheefe men & brought in his head to the Governor of Boston, & had also in the service by accident lost the use of his left hand, & that both James and his brother Thomas had since in November last [beeing called to it] was out with Captain Syll in the Nipmuck contry & [as his captaine had certified] had performed faithfull service; & was instrumentall to recover an English captive Peter Bentt's servant from the enimey, & his brother savd the lives of two English men at a wigwam at Pakachooge, vizt[13] Mr Mackarty, servant, a surgeon to Captian Henchman, & one Goodwin, a soldier of Charlestowne, as they both could & would testify. Yet after all these services both they & their wives & children & all their country men that lived at Naticke were mistrusted by the English & thereupon [at a few houres warning] brought away from their place & fort & houses at Naticke & carried down in boats to Deare Island, leaving & loosing much of their substance, catle, swine, horse & corn, & at the Iland were exposed to

---

[12]That is, Kattananit had fought on the side of the Mohegans and English against Metacom in a battle near the latter's stronghold at Seekonk.
[13]Namely.

great sufferings haveing litle wood for fuell, a bleak place & poore wigwams such as they could make a shift to make themselves with a few matts, & here at the iland had very little provision, many of them, & divers other sorrowes & troubles they were exposed to, & were about 350 soules, men women & children; & that now haveing an opperutny to get off the iland they came to see how things were with the indians in the woods; & if they preferred them to fight with & for them they were advised to manifest all readines & forwardnes & not shew any aversenes.[14] Things being thus prepared these 2 spyes were sent away without armes excepting hatchetts & with a little parcht meal for provision, & they tooke their jorny from Cambridge the 30th of December, & from Natick they set forth the 31th of December being Friday early in the morning. That day they past through the woods directly to Hassomesed where they lodged that night; on Saterday morn, being the first of Janury they past over Nipmuck River & lodged at Manchage that night. On the 2 Janury they went forward to Maanexit wch is about 10 miles & there they met with seaven Indians of the enimy: some of them had armes; having confered with these indians they were conducted by those indians next day to Quabaage old fort where they met severall other Indians of their company's; & by them the next day were conducted to the enemies quarters which is about twenty miles northward of Quabauge old fort at a place called Menemesseg, which is about 8 miles north of where Captain Hutchison & Captain Wheeler was woonded & several men with them slayn (in the begining of August last) as these indians informed them. At this place among these Indians they found all the christian Indians belonging to Hassannmiske & Magunhooge wich are[15] about forty men & about 80 women & children. These praying indians were carried away by the enemy somewhat willingly, others of them unwillingly, as they told him. For before they went away they were in a great strait, for if they came to the English they knew they shold be sent to Deere Iland, as others were, & their corne beeing at such a distance about 40 miles from Boston it could not bee caried to susteyne their lives & so they should bee in danger to famish, & others feard they should bee sent away to Barbados, or other places. And to stay at Hassanamesho these indians our enemies[16] would not permit them, but said they must have the corne, but promised them if they would goe with them they should not die but bee preserved; these being in this condition most of

---

[14]That is, if the anti-English Indians wanted Quanapohit and Kattananit to fight the English, the two spies should pretend to go along.

[15]That is, which number.

[16]That is, the Indian enemies of the English.

them thought it best to go with them though they feared death every way: only Tukuppawillin [the minister] he lamented much & his aged father the deacon & son and som others & would faine have come back to the English after they were gone as far as Manchange but the enimy mockt him, for crying & drew him . . . the rest that were unwilling along with them: These things our spies understood from the p[raying] indians here. The enimys that hee was among & live at the afforesaid places are in . . . small townes about 20 wigwams at a place & they are all within 3 miles com[pass], and to consist of about 300 fighting men besides duble as many women & children . . . they have no fort, but wigwams only, some covred with barks & som with matts. The Indians that are heare are the Nipmuck indians, the Quabaag indians, the Paca-[choog] indians, the Weshakum & Nashaway indians. The cheef sagomeres & captains are Mawtaamp, John with one eye[17] & Sam [of Weshukum or Nashaway] Sagamore John [having one leg bigger than the other] of Pakachooge. Here also is Matoonus & his sons. Of the Hassanamesho & christian Indians, he saw here Captain Tom allias Wattasakomponin & his son Nehimiah. They say that the enimy have solic[it]ed them to take armes & fight against the English but they told James they would not fight against the English, they will rather die. Here he also saw Tukuppawillin their pastor & his aged father their deacon, whome he saith mourn greatly & daily read the bible which is their greatest comfort. Also he there saw James Printer brother to the minister, & Joseph & Sa . . . two brethern [sons to Robin of Hassameshe deceased]. Hee also saw Pumhamun & Jacob of Magunkoog with divers others that he could have mentioned but those are the principal.

Some of the Indians [our enimies] mistrusted that these two men were spies, especially Matoonus & his sonnes & some others: these solicited James to borrow his hatchet & his knife [when he saw they needed none] which made him cautious of himselfe & suspitious of their evill intention to him, but James [at the second towne] he came to meet with John with one eye, of Weshakum [a stout captaine among them] this man knew James & said thou hast been with me in the warr with the Mauhaks & I know thou art a valiant man & therefore none shall wrong thee nor kill thee here, but they shall first kill me. Therefore abide at my wigwam & I will protect thee. So this man entertained him kindly, & protected him. Job his companion stayd at Pumhams wigwame wher his 3 children were kept: hee and Job aboad with these indians severall daies

17Monoco.

& sometimes went forth to hunt deere not farr off & returnd againe. Hee laboured to gaine what information hee could of their affayres, & was informed by Capt John [with one eye] his host & others said things, viz. That Philip was quartered this winter within halfe a dayes jorny . . . fort Albany [The same thing is certified by a letter from Major Andros Governor of New York sent Mr Leet deputy Governor of Connecticut dated 5th January (75) which letter being sent to Governor Winthrop by Mr Leet was read in our Councill on Thursday last 23 instant. This also may tend to confirme the truth of James his intelegence, as wel as divers other passages both before & aftermentioned]. Moreover they informed our spy that the Hadly Northampton & Spinkfield[18] Indians had their winter quarters between them & Philip & som quartered at Squakeake. They told him also that a cheefe captaine named —— of Hadley & Northampton indians, who was a valiant man, had been a chiefe captaine in the Mawhak warre had attempted to kill Philip & intended to do it; alleaging that Philip had begun a warr with the English that had brought great trouble upon them.[19] Hee saieth that these Indians told him that it was som of their number that were in the Nipmuck country to get the corn & that the English came upon them in the wigwam at Hassunnamesuke & there they killed two Englishmen, & that they had got & caried away all the corne at Pakuahooge & in the Nipmuck country unto their quarters, upon which they had lived this winter, & upon beef & pork they had killed about Quaboage, & venison [of which there is great store in those parts & by reason of the deep snow there beeing mid thigh deep] it is easy to kill deare without gunns. He saieth that ere long, when their beefe & porke & deare is spent & gon, that they wilbe in want of corne, but they intend then to com down upon the English townes, of Lancaster Marlborow Grotaon, & particulely they intend first to cut off Lancaster bridge, & then say they there can be no releef com to them from Boston, the people cannot escape & there they hope to have corne enough. Hee saieth they have store of armes, & have a gunsmith among them, a lame man that is a good workman & keeps their gunns well fixt. They have some armes among them that they tooke in the 2 fights when Captain Beeares & Captain Lothrop was slayne.[20] As for amunition they have some but not great store that he saw: Captian John with one eye shewed him a small

---

[18]Springfield.

[19]This is the earliest record of antagonism against Metacom from within the ranks of the anti-English Indians.

[20]A reference to two successful ambushes of English troops in the Connecticut River Valley in September 1675.

kettle full of powder about half a peck & 2 hornes full besides. Hee asked them where they got their ammuntion, hee answered some we had from the English were kild, & som from Fort Albany, but (said he) the Dutch wil not sell us powder; but wee give our bever & wompon to the Mawhakes & they buy it & let us have it of them. They told him that they had sent to the Wompeages & Mawquas to aid them in the spring, that the Wampeages promised them help, but the Maquaws said they were not willing to fight with English, but they would fight with the Mohegins & Pequots that were brethern to the English.[21] Further hee saieth that they told him that the Frenchman that was at Boston this sumer [viz. Monsieur Normanvile] was with Philip & his company as hee went back at their quarter about Pokomtuck, after he returnd from Boston. And that in their sight hee burned certene papers that hee said were letters from Boston to the French, saying what shall I doe with these papers any longer. Hee said to the Indians I would not have you burne the English mill, nor the meeting houses, nor the best houses for we [ie the French] intend to be with you in the spring before planting time & I will bring three hundred of your countrymen that are hunters & have been three years at the French. And we will bring armes & ammunition enough, for wee intend to helpe you against the English & posses our selves of Keneckticut river & other English plantations, and our King [ie the French King] will send shipps to stopp supplyes from coming by sea [from their King] to Boston.[22]

Hee saieth that they told him that the Pennakooge indians were quartered about the head of the Keneticut river, & had not at all ingaged in any fight with the English, & would not, their sagamors Wannalancet & others restrayned the young men (who had an opptunity to have destroyd many of Capt Moselys men when he was at Pennakooge last sumer but their sagamores would not suffer them to shoot a gunne).[23]

Further he saieth that he understood by the cheefe men & old men that they were inclinable to have peace againe with the English, but the young men [who are their principal soldiers] say we wil have no peace

---

[21]Wompeages probably refers to the Wappingers of the Hudson River Valley. Mawquaws, Maquaws, and Maquas were used frequently by the English to refer to the Mohawks. This sale of arms and the expression of Mohawk willingness to fight the pro-English Mohegans and Pequots were made prior to January 1676, when the Mohawks actively entered the war on the English side.

[22]Little is known of the visit to New England by the French official, Normanville, and this is the only account of his meeting with Metacom, held near Pocumtuck on the Connecticut River.

[23]The Pennacook Indians of the Merrimack River had withdrawn to northern New England precisely in order to avoid the war.

wee are all or most of us alive yet & the English have kild very few of us last summer; why shall wee have peace to bee made slaves, & either be kild or sent away to sea to Barbadoes &c. Let us live as long as wee can & die like men, & not live to bee enslaved. Hee saieth there is an English man a young man amongst them alive named Robert Pepper[24] who, being woonded in the legg in the fight when Captain Beares was kild, hid himselfe in the crotch of a great tree that lay on the ground, where an Indian called Sam Sagamore of Nashaway found him alive & tooke him prisoner & hee became his master. Hee lay lame severll weekes but beeing well used by his master & means used hee is now wel recovered. Hee saieth that once since hee was wel his master [carring him abroad with him] left him at Squakeake neare where hee was taken prisoner, his Master wishing him to goe to the English [whither there was a cart way led]. But Robert Pepper told James hee was afrayd his master did it but to try his fidelity to him to intrap him, & that if he should have gon away towards the English they would have intercepted him & so his life had beene in danger, so he went after his master & enquired after him & at last found him out, he saith Rob Peper would be glad to escape home and hopes hee shall meet with an oppertunity, when the Indians march nearer the English. James said his master told him hee would send him home when hee had convenient opptunety. Also hee was informed that there are two more English men prisoners with Philip & Hadly Indians, one is of Boston servant to a ship carpenter Grenhough, and the other he remembers not his name.

Hee saieth, that before hee & Job came among those indians they told them the Narragants had sent in one or 2 English scalps, but these indians would not receive them, but shot at their messenger & said they were English mens friends all last summer & would not creditt their first messangers.[25] After there came other messengers from Narragansetts & brought more heads [he saw twelve scalpes of English hangd upon trees], that then these Indians beeleved the Narragansset & receved the scalps & paid them [as their manner is], & now they beeleved that the Naragansitts & English are at warre, of which they are glad. The Narragansets told these indians that the English had had fight with them, & killed about forty fighting men & one Sachem, & about 300 old men women & children were kild & burnt in the wigwams, most of which were destroyd. They told him that the Narragansetts said the Mohegins & Pequitts Indi-

---

[24]Pepper appears briefly in Rowlandson's narrative, during the third remove. See p. 74.
[25]The Narragansetts had remained neutral until the English attacked their Great Swamp Fort in December 1675, hence the Nipmucs' initial distrust.

ans killed & woonded of them, as many as the English had kild. Being questioned by Mr. Danforth whether hee could learne whether the Narragansetts had ayded & assisted Philip & his companey in the summer against the English, hee answered that hee understood by those indians that they had not, but lookt on them as freinds to the English all along til now & their enemies. Hee saieth that hee was informed that the Nargansets said that an Inglish man one Joshua Tift[26] was among them when they had their fight at the English, & that he did them good service & kild & woonded 5 or 6 English in that fight, & that before they wold trust him he had kild a miller an English man at Narragansit, & brought his scalpe to them. Also hee said that the Naragansits told these indians that one William that lives in those parts brought them some powder & offered them all his catle for provisions desiring only that his life might bee spared & his children & grandchildren. These Narragansits solicited these indians[27] to send them som help [. . . they knew them to be stout soldiers], they promised to send with them 20 men to goe with them to see how things were, & they determined to begin their jorny last Saturday [ie 22th January] and they also resolved to take Job with them to Narraganset indians; and upon the same day Mawtaamp the sagamor said hee would goe with another company up to Phillip, to informe him & those Indians of the breach betwene the English & Narragansitts & he said that James [our spy] should goe along with him to Philipp to acquaint him of the state of affayres among the English & praying indians. James said to Mataamp I am willing to goe to Philip but not at this present because Philip knowes that I fought against him on the English side at Mount Hope & other places, & hee will not beeleve that I am realy turned to his party, unles I first do some exployt & kill some English men & carry their heads to him. Let me have opportunity to doe somthing of this nature before I goe to Philip. This answer of James seemed to satisfy the sagamore Mawtaump. But James doubting notwithstanding, that he might change his mind and take him with him when hee went, hee was resolved to endevor an escape before the time they intended the jorny, especially considering what Tachupawillin told him in secret that Philip had given order to his men that if they met with these John Hunter, James Speen, this James & Thomas Quannupaquit [brethren & Andrew Pitamee & Peter Ephraim they bring them to him or put them to death].

---

[26]Joshua Tift, or Tefft, was the only colonist known to have actively fought against the English. English troops captured him in January 1676, and he was convicted of treason, hanged, and his body drawn and quartered.
[27]That is, the Nipmucs with whom Quanapohit was staying.

Accordingly James moved Job [his companion] to contrive a way for an escape. Job concealed his purpose, and upon Wensday the 19th of this instant they 2 early in the morne went out as if they would goe a hunting for deare, as they had don at other times & returnd againe [James having goten about a pint of nokake[28] of Symon Squa one of the praying indians]. They beeing in the woods hunted for deere & killd 4 deare & as they traveld to & fro they percevd that by som footing of indians that some did watch their motions, so towards night they being neare a pond they drew the deer at the pond & tooke up their quarters in thicke swampe & there made a fire & dresd some of the venison, but no other indians came to them; so about 3 oclock before day, James said to Job now let us escape away if wee can. But Job said I am not willing to goe now, because my children are here and I will stay longer. If God please hee can preserve my life; if not I am willing to die. I will therfore goe backe againe to the indians & goe along with the company to the Naragansitt, & if I returne I will use what policy I can to get away my children. If I live, about . . . weeks hence I will com back & I will com to Naticke & therfore if you can, take 4 or 5 indians to meet me there. I shall if I live by that time get more intelligence of affayres. Then James said to him, I must now goe away for I am not like to have a better opptunity, & if they should carry mee to Philip I shall die. But I am sorry for you Job, lest when I am gon they will kill you for my sake; but you may tel them I runne away from you & was afrayd to goe to Philip before I had don some exployt. So they parted — & James our spy came homeward travilling through the woods night & day untill he came to Naticke to James Spene wigwam, who lives their to looke to som aged & sick folks that were not in capacity to be brought downe to Deare Iland, & on Lord's day came to Serjant Williams at the village & by him was conducted to & so to Boston before the Councel the same day which was the 24th day of this instnt Janury 1675 where his examination & relation was written by 2 scribes: & though this may a little differ from others in some particulars yet for substance it is the same.[29]

Moreover hee said that hee heard that the Narragansit were marched upp into the woods toward Quantesit & they were in company & the first company of above 200 among them were several woonded werre come

---

[28]A dried meal often carried by Indians when traveling because a portion of any size could be broken off and mixed with water.

[29]The other, briefer version was recorded by Daniel Gookin and published as "James Quanapaug's Information" in *Massachusetts Historical Society Collections,* 1st ser., 6 (1799), 205–08.

before the Narragansit come up to these Indians:—being omitted
beefore it is put in heare.

3

Town of Lancaster, Petition to the Governor and Council of Massachusetts
March 11, 1675

The consequences of Massachusetts's ignoring James Quanapohit's report were experienced first by the town of Lancaster. Although Job Kattananit's last-minute warning averted an even worse disaster, the town was virtually crippled by the attack. Moreover, the colony's leaders were unwilling to increase Lancaster's protection afterward, believing that it had to put its resources into pursuing the enemy. This petition, dated March 11—just one month after the attack in which Mary Rowlandson was captured—details the psychological as well as material condition of the town's remaining inhabitants. The governor and council approved the petition and, by the end of the month, Lancaster was completely abandoned.

To the Honerd Govrnor and Counseill

The humble petition of the poor destressed people of Lancaster, humbley sheweth, that since the enemy made such sad & dismall havocke amongst our deare friends & Brethren, & we that are left who have our lives for a[30] pray sadly sensible of Gods Judgment upon us, this with the destresse we are now in does embolden us to present our humble Requests to your Honors, hoping our Conditions may be considered by you and our Requests find acceptance with you, our state is very deplorable, in our Incapacity to subsist, as to Remove away we can not, the enemy has so Encompassed us, otherwise for want of help our cattle being the most of them carried away by the barberous heathen, & to stay disenabled for want of food, the Towns people are Generally gone who

---

[30]Clearly, there is a word missing here.

Henry S. Nourse, ed., *The Narrative of the Captivity and Restoration of Mrs. Mary Rowlandson* (Lancaster, Mass., 1903), 80–81.

felt the Judgment but light, & had theyr catle left them with theyr estats, but we many of us here in this prison, have not bread to last us one month & our other provision spent and gone, for the generality, our Town is drawn into two Garisons wherein are by the Good favours of your Honors eighteen soldiers, which we gladly mayntayn soe long as any thing lasts, & if your Honors should call them off, we are certaynly a bayt for the enemy if God do not wonderfully prevent, therefore we hope as God has made you fathers over us so you will have a fathers pitty to us & extend your care over us who are your poor destressed subjects. We are sorrowful to Leave the place, but hopelesse to keep it unless mayntayned by the Cuntrey,[31] it troubles our sperits to give any Incuridgment to the enemy, or leave any thing for them to promote their wicked designe, yet better save our Lives than lose Life and Estate both, we are in danger emenent, the enemy lying Above us, nay on both sides of us, as does plainly Apeare. Our womens cries does daily Increase beyond expression which does not only fill our ears but our hearts full of Greefe, which makes us humbly Request your Honors to send a Gard of men & that if you please so command we may have Carts. About fourteen will Remove the whole, eight of which has been present long at Sudbury but never came for want of a small guard of men, the whole that is, all that are in the one Garison, Kept in Major Willards house, which is all from your Honors most humble servents and suppliants.

Lancaster March 11th. 1675/76

> JACOB FARRAR
> JOHN HOUGHTON Sen[r]
> JOHN MOORE
> JOHN WHITTCOMB
> JOB WHITTCOMB
> JOHNATHAN WHITTCOMB
> JOHN HOUGHTON Jun[r]
> CYPRIAN STEEVENS

The other one Garison are in the like destresse & so humbly desire your like pitty & fatherly care, having widows and many fatherless children. The Number of Carts to Carey away this garrison is twenty Carts. Your Honors Humble Petitioners.

> JOHN PRESCOTT Sen[r]
> THO. SAWYER Sen[r]
> THO SAWYER Jun[r]

[31]The colony.

JONATHAN PRESCOTT
THO WILLDER
JOHN WILLDER
SARAH WHEELER wid
WIDOW FARBANKS
JOHN RIGBY
NATHANIELL WILDER
JOHN ROOPER
WIDOW ROOPER

4

JOB KATTANANIT

Petition to the Governor and Council of Massachusetts

February 14, 1675

*Job Kattananit, James Quanapohit's partner in espionage, delayed his return
to the English side until February 9, the night before the attack on Lancaster.
Having performed his duty for the English, Kattananit then asked permission
to return to their opponents' lands on a more personal mission — to rescue his
children and perhaps other Nipmuc Christians who had been seized by anti-
English Indians at their town of Hassanamesit. His petition, dated February
14 — just four days after the Lancaster attack — is the document that follows.
The petition was granted, but anti-Indian hysteria among the English
remained Kattananit's most serious obstacle. When Massachusetts Bay
decided, in March 1675, that its army could resume using friendly Indians,
Kattananit was enlisted to join a contingent of troops with the understanding
that he could leave them at an appropriate time to conduct his search. However, Samuel Moseley led a protest movement among the soldiers, who feared
that Kattananit would inform the enemy of their movements. The resulting
delays caused Kattananit to miss a scheduled rendezvous with a contact
behind the lines, so he was unable to locate his children. Fortunately, he and
they were safely united by the time the war was over.*

Josiah H. Temple, *History of Framingham, Massachusetts* (Framingham, Mass., 1887),
67–68.

The humble petition of Job Kattananit.

Whereas your poor suplyant hath been abroad in your Honours service among the Indian enemies, and have given a true and faithful account of what I could learn among them according to my Instructions; And in my Journey I found my three children with the enemy, together with some of my friends that continue their fidelity to God and to the English, and do greatly mourn for their condition, and long and desire to return to the English if you please, to let them live where or how you will please appoint: And to this end some few of them have agreed with me to meet them at Hassanamesit about the full of the moon, and to endeavor to bring my children with them—My humble request and supplication is that you will please to admit your poor servant: (And if you please to send an Englishman or two with me I shall be glad, but if that cannot be done, then to admit me and James Speen,[32] to go forth to see and meet and bring in my poor children and some few Godly Christians among them; and if they do escape we shall meet them and return within 3 or 4 days, if God please; but if we cannot meet them then I shall conclude they cannot escape, and so shall immediately return; and if your Honours please shall go forth with the army to the enemies' quarters, or to do any other service I can for your Honours and the country and go to the hazard of my life and shall be very thankful to your Honours for this favor.

[32] A Christian Massachusett Indian from the town of Natick.

5

Indians' Letter to English Troops at Medfield

1675

Shortly after Rowlandson was seized, members of her captors' party attacked and burned the town of Medfield, Massachusetts. When English troops arrived they found a grim message left on a bridge post by the fleeing natives, a message showing that the attackers knew just what the war's stakes were and where the English were most vulnerable. That the

Daniel Gookin, "An Historical Account of Doings and Sufferings of the Christian Indians in New England," *Transactions and Collections of the American Antiquarian Society* 2 (1836), 494.

note was written in English underscored the fact that learning and using the ways of "civilization" did not invariably lead Indians to repudiate their own cultural identities.

Know by this paper, that the Indians that thou hast provoked to wrath and anger, will war this twenty one years if you will; there are many Indians yet, we come three hundred at this time. You must consider the Indians lost nothing but their life; you must lose your fair houses and cattle.

THE REDEMPTION OF MARY ROWLANDSON

6

JOHN LEVERETT

Letter to "Indian Sagamores"
March 31, 1676

The process by which Rowlandson and other captives at Mt. Wachusett were ransomed was delicate and protracted. At the center were Nipmuc Indians on both sides of the conflict. Christian Nipmucs who had remained loyal to the English, even while confined to Deer Island, carried communications back and forth between the English and the Indian captors. Although the captives were held by Narragansetts, Wampanoags, and Nipmucs, it was the Nipmuc sachems who negotiated for all the captors. While the sachems could not write their own letters, they were able to call on Nipmucs in their own ranks for this task. These scribes were Nipmucs who had become literate in English while attending mission schools and who, while embracing much in the religion and culture of the English, chose to remain with their own people when war erupted in 1675. It is instructive that although Mary Rowlandson acknowledges the role played by certain Nipmucs in securing her release, she ignores their contributions when sounding her blanket indictments of all Christian Indians.

Henry S. Nourse, ed., *The Narrative of the Captivity and Restoration of Mrs. Mary Rowlandson* (Lancaster, Mass., 1903), 96.

*The process leading to Rowlandson's release began after Joseph Row-
landson persuaded Concord lawyer John Hoar to intervene on his behalf
among the Christians recently released from Deer Island. Hoar recruited Tom
Dublet (also known as Nepanet) to carry the following letter from Leverett.*

For the Indian Sagamores & people that are in warre against us. Intelligence is come to us that you have some English, especially women and
children in Captivity among you. We have therefore sent the messenger
offering to redeem them either for payment in goods or wampum or by
exchange of prisoners. We desire your answer by this our messenger
what price you demand for every man woman and child, or if you will
exchange for Indians. If you have any among you that can write your
answer to this our message, we desire it in writing; and to that end have
sent, paper pen and incke by the messenger. If you lett our messenger
have free access to you, freedome of a safe returne, we are willing to doe
the like by any messenger of yours, provided he come unarmed, and carry
a white flag upon a staffe, visible to be seen which we take as a flag of
truce, and is used by civilized nations in time of warre, when any messengers are sent in a way of treaty, which we have done by our messenger. In testimony whereof I have set my hand & seal.

JOHN LEVERETT *Gov*

Boston 31 March 1676.   Passed by the Council

EDWARD RAWSON *Secy*

7

SAM ET AL.

Letter to John Leverett

April 12, 1676

*In this letter, dated April 12, 1676, "Sam" (Shoshanim or Uskattuhgun)
and his colleagues were unwilling to make concessions to their opponents.
In the first part, their reply to Leverett, they insist that the English must send
two messengers, apparently recognizing the risks in placing responsibility*

Henry S. Nourse, ed., *The Narrative of the Captivity and Restoration of Mrs. Mary Rowlandson*
(Lancaster, Mass., 1903), 96–97.

for such weighty matters in the hands of a single person. They also call attention to the heavy losses suffered thus far by the English. They then add an extraordinary postscript in which they directly address Joseph Rowlandson and John Kettle, informing them of the conditions of their captive family members and including, as proof that they lived, the signs of Rowlandson's sister, Hannah Divoll, and Kettle's wife, Elizabeth. They add a request, ostensibly from Mary Rowlandson, that Joseph send her three pounds of tobacco. He replied by sending her a pound with each of the two subsequent letters. In connection with her receipt of the second shipment, Mary notes in her narrative that the request was fraudulent, for she had given up tobacco since being captured.

The letter also provides a window on the complexities of literacy in colonial New England. It reminds us that there were Indians such as Peter Jethro who could read and write in the colonists' language, however imperfectly. At the same time, the marks of Divoll and Kettle point to the fact that many colonists (about 10 percent of the men and 40 percent of the women) were unable to write even their own names. Like the Indian leaders, they had to entrust their written sentiments to scribes. Note that Rowlandson's request does not carry her signature; clearly, Shoshanim knew better than to show her what was being communicated.

We now give answer by this one man, but if you like my answer send one more man besides this one Tom Nepanet, and you send with all true heart and with all your mind by two men, because you know and we know your heart grew sorrowful with crying for your lost many many hundred men and all your house and all your land, and woman, child, and cattle, as all your thing that you have lost and on your backside stand.

SAM *Sachem*
KUTQUEN and   Peter Jethro
QUANOHIT *Sagamores*   *Scribe*

Mr Rowlandson, your wife and all your child is well but one dye. Your sister is well and her 3 child. John Kittel, your wife and all your child is all well, and all them prisoners taken at Nashua[33] is all well.

Mr Rowlandson, see your loving sister his[34] hand C Hanah

---

[33]The sachems here refer to Lancaster by its original name, Nashaway.
[34]Sister's.

And old Kettel wif his[35] hand T

Brother Rowlandson, pray send thre pound of Tobacco for me, if you can my loving husband pray send thre pound of tobacco for me.

This writing by your enemies

SAMUEL USKATTUHGUN and
GUNRASHIT, *two Indian Sagamores*

[35]Kettle's wife's.

8

JAMES PRINTER ET AL.

Letter to John Leverett et al.

ca. April 1676

The colony's response to the preceding letter has been lost, but the following reply to it from the Indians shows that the English did add a second messenger, a Nipmuc named Tatiquinea, or Peter Conway. The letter also indicates that the English, in the letter now lost, expressed particular interest in ransoming Mary Rowlandson among the many captives held at Mt. Wachusett. It sets her ransom at twenty pounds, as established by Rowlandson herself under pressure from her captors. Note that the Indians' attitude has softened somewhat since their last letter. While perhaps in part a response to the tone of the lost English letter, it also reflects the Indians' growing recognition after the battle of Sudbury that they would be unable to defeat the English. The letter, as the subsequent English response indicates, was written for the sachems by James Printer, who would later compose the type for Rowlandson's narrative.

For the Governor and the Council at Boston

The Indians, Tom Nepennomp and Peter Tatatiqunea hath brought us letter from you about the English Captives, especially for Mrs Rolanson;

Henry S. Nourse, ed., *The Narrative of the Captivity and Restoration of Mrs. Mary Rowlandson* (Lancaster, Mass., 1903), 97–98.

the answer is I am sorrow that I have don much to wrong you and yet I say the falte is lay upon you, for when we began quarrel at first with Plimouth men I did not think that you should have so much truble as now is: therefore I am willing to hear your desire about the Captives. Therefore we desire you to send Mr Rolanson and goodman Kettel: (for their wives) and these Indians Tom and Peter to redeem their wives, they shall come and goe very safely: Whereupon we ask Mrs Rolanson, how much your husband willing to give for you she gave an answer 20 pounds in goodes but John Kittels wife could not tell. and the rest captives may be spoken of hereafter.

9

Letter from Massachusetts Governor's Council to "Indian Sachems"

April 28, 1676

To judge from the tone of the following letter alone, the English were so dissatisfied with the Indians' previous reply that they were unwilling to concede anything further. But we know from Rowlandson's narrative and other sources that in fact they made a major concession when sending this letter. For while not sending Joseph Rowlandson or John Kettle, they did send an Englishman—John Hoar—with power to negotiate. On May 2, Hoar returned to Concord with a freed Mary Rowlandson. Elizabeth Kettle was released along with some other captives several weeks later.

To the Indian Sachems about Wachusets.
     We received your letter by Tom and Peter, which doth not answer ours to you: neither is subscribed by the sachems nor hath it any date, which we know your scribe James Printer doth well understand should be. wee have sent the said Tom & Peter againe to you expecting you will speedily give us a plaine & direct answer to our last letter, and if you have anything more to propound to us we desire to have it from you under your

Henry S. Nourse, ed., *The Narrative of the Captivity and Restoration of Mrs. Mary Rowlandson* (Lancaster, Mass., 1903), 98.

hands, by these our messengers, and you shall have a speedy answer. Dated the 28th, April, 1676.

POSTWAR JUSTICE

10

ANDREW PITTIMEE ET AL.

Petition to the Governor and Council of Massachusetts

June 1676

As the war wound down in the early summer of 1676, many anti-English Indians surrendered or were captured by colonial authorities, while others simply returned to their villages or fled the region altogether. The English then set out to determine which Indians within their grasp deserved punishment. The following two documents center on three Nipmuc families captured, like James Printer, by anti-English natives at Hassanamesit and pressured to join the war against the colonists. Focusing particularly on Hassanamesit's magistrate, Wuttasacomponom, or Captain Tom, they demonstrate just how difficult distinguishing friends from enemies could be. The petition is especially noteworthy because the accused Indians' loyalty is supported by James Quanapohit (here rendered as Quanahpohkit) and Job Kattananit as well as three other prominent pro-English natives.

To the Honourable the Govournour and Councill of the Massachusetts Colony, Assembled at Boston this[36] *of June 1676:*

The humble petition of Andrew Pittimee, Quanahpohkit, alias James Rumney Marsh,[37] John Magus, and James Speen, officers unto the Indian souldiers, now in your service, with the consent of the rest of the Indian souldiers being about eighty men;

[36]The date is missing from this document.
[37]James Quanapohit.

Daniel Gookin, "An Historical Account of the Doings and Sufferings of the Christian Indians in New England," *Transactions and Collections of the American Antiquarian Society* 2 (1836), 527–28.

Humbly imploreth your favour and mercies to be extended to some of the prisoners taken by us, (most of them) near Lancaster, Marlborough, &c: In whose behalf we are bold to supplicate your Honoures. And wee have three reasons for this our humble supplication; first, because the persons we beg pardon for, as we are informed, are innocent; and have not done any wrong or injury unto the English, all this war time, only were against their wills, taken and kept among the enemy. Secondly, because it pleased your Honours to say to some of us, to encourage us to fidelity and activity in your service, that you would be ready to do any thing for us, that was fitt for us to ask and you to grant. Thirdly, that others that are out, and love the English, may be encouraged to come in. More that we humbly intercede for, is the lives and libertyes of those few of our poor friends and kindred, that, in this time of temptation and affliction, have been in the enemy's quarters; we hope it will be no griefe of heart to you to shew mercy, and especially to such who have (as we conceive) done no wrong to the English. If wee did think, or had any ground to conceive that they were naught, and were enemies to the English, we would not intercede for them, but rather bear our testimony against them, as we have done. We have (especially some of us) been sundry times in your service to the hazzard of our lives, both as spyes, messengers, scouts, and souldiers, and have through God's favour acquitted ourselves faithfully, and shall do as long as we live endeavour with all fidelitie to fight in the English cause, which we judge is our cause, and also God's cause, to oppose the wicked Indians, enemies to God and all goodness. In granting this our humble request, you will much oblige us who desire to remain

Your Honoures Humble and Faithful Servants,

> ANDREW PITTIMEE,
> JAMES QUANAPOHKIT,
> JOB,[38]
> JOHN MAGUS,
> JAMES SPEEN.

The persons we supplicate for, are Capt. Tom, his son Nehemiah, his wife and two children, John Uktuck, his wife and children, Maanum and her child.

And if the Council please not to answer our desires in granting the lives and liberties of all these, yett if you shall please to grant the women and children, it will be a favour unto us.

---

[38]Job Kattananit, whose name was not included with those of the other petitioners at the head of the document.

11

Massachusetts Council to James Quanapohit et al.

1676

The Council replied to the Christian Indians' petition by granting mercy to the women and children cited but forcefully rejecting their plea on behalf of Wuttascomponom. (The disposition of Nehemiah and John Uktuck is not made clear.) In heralding the justice and benevolence of English rule over Indians, they refer to the experience of the Pequot Indians of Connecticut since their defeat by the English in 1637. Under the declaration made in the final paragraph, James Printer and a number of other Nipmucs surrendered and, after being cleared of charges of actively supporting the anti-English cause, regained their freedom.

In Answer to the Petition of James Quanhpohkit, James Speen, Job, Andrew Pittimee, and Jno. Magus.

Capt. Tom being a lawful prisoner at warr, there needs no further evidence for his conviction; yet hee having had liberty to present his plea before the Councill why he should not be proceeded against accordingly, instead of presenting any thing that might alleviate his withdrawing from the government of the English and joyning with the enemy, it doth appeare by sufficient evidence that hee was not only (as is credibly related by some Indians present with him) an instigator to others over whom he was by this government made a Captain, but was also actually present and an actor in the devastation of some of our plantations; and therefore it cannot consist with the honour and justice of authority to grant him a pardon.

Whereas the Council do, with reference to the Petitioners, grant them the lives of the women and children by them mentioned. And, further, the Councill do hereby declair, that, as they shall be ready to show favour in sparing the lives and liberty of those that have been our enemys, on their comeing in and submission of themselves to the English Government and your disposal, the reality and complacency of the government towards the Indians sufficiently appearing in the provisions they have made, and tranquility that the Pequots have injoyed under them for over forty years; so

---

Daniel Gookin, "An Historical Account of the Doings and Sufferings of the Christian Indians in New England," *Transactions and Collections of the American Antiquarian Society* 2 (1836), 528–29.

also it will not be availeable for any to plead in favour for them that they have been our friends while found and taken among our enemyes.

Further the Councill do hereby declare that none may expect priviledge bye his declaration, that come not in and submit themselves in 14 days next coming.

By the Council,

EDW. RAWSON, *Clerke.*

12

MATTAMUCK ET AL.

Letter to John Leverett et al.

July 6, 1676

The two months following Rowlandson's release were disastrous for the Nipmucs. In a desperate quest for food, they and their allies scattered to favored fishing grounds and to their cornfields. As a result, they became more vulnerable to attacks than when they were at mass encampments such as the one at Mt. Wachusett. English troops and allied natives set about attacking Indian camps and villages and either killing or enslaving whomever they could. On June 7, one such raid yielded the wives and children of Shoshanim and Mattaump, another Nipmuc sachem, who were later sold into slavery and sent to the West Indies. Before then Shoshanim and the other sachems wrote a letter whose tone reflects how desperate their situation had become.

To all Englishmen and Indians, all of you hear Mr Waban and Mr Eliott.[39]

July 6 1676. Mr John Leverett, my Lord, Mr Waban, and all the chief men our Brethren Praying to God: We beseech you all to help us: my wife she is but one, but there be more Prisoners, which we pray you keep well: Mattamuck his wife we entreat you for her, and not onely that man, but it is the Request of two Sachems, Sam Sachem of Weshakum, and the

[39]Waban was principal sachem/magistrate of the praying town of Natick. John Eliot was the leading missionary to Indians in Massachusetts Bay.

Henry S. Nourse, ed., *The Narrative of the Captivity and Restoration of Mrs. Mary Rowlandson* (Lancaster, Mass., 1903), 100–01.

Pakashoag Sachem.[40] And that further you will consider about the making Peace: We have spoken to the people of Nashobah (viz Tom Dublet and Peter) that we would agree with you and make covenant of Peace with you. We have been destroyed by your soldiers, but still we Remember it now to sit still: do you consider it again: we do earnestly entreat you, that it may be so by Jesus Christ. O let it be so: Amen Amen.

> MATTAMUCK his MARK N
> SAM SACHEM his MARK X
> SIMON POTTOQUAM *Scribe*
> UPPANIPPAQUUM his C
> PAKASHOKAG his MARK &

My Lord Mr Leverett at Boston, Mr Waban, Mr Eliott, Mr Gookin, and Council, hear ye. I went to Connecticot about the Captives, that I might bring them into your hands, and when we were almost there the English had destroyed those Indians. When I heard it I returned back again: then when I came home, we were also destroyed: After we were destroyed then Philip and Quanipun went away into their own Countrey againe: and I knew they were much afraid, because of our offer to joyn with the English, and therefore they went back into their own Countrey and I know they will make no warre: therefore because when some English men came to us Philip and Quanipun sent to kill them: but I said if any kill them, I'll kill them.

> Sam Sachem

Written by SIMON BOSHOKUM *Scribe*

[40]Shoshanim ("Sam Sachem") was sachem of the Nipmuc towns of Nashaway and Weshakim. Pakachoag was also a Nipmuc town.

13

A Memorandum of Indian Children Put Forth into Service to the English

August 10, 1676

While Indian men considered by the English to be guilty of war crimes were sold to overseas slave traders, others received lesser penalties depending on their identity and their condition. The following document illustrates how Massachusetts disposed of Indian children who lost their parents either to the war itself or to English justice thereafter. The children became indentured servants in English households, a condition from which they were not freed until reaching about twenty years of age. Note that two members of the committee assigned to carry out the sale, Daniel Gookin and Thomas Prentis, received child laborers through this process themselves.

August 10 1676. A memorandum of Indian Children put forth into service to the English Beeing of those indians that came in & submitted with John Sachem of Packachooge, with the names of the persons with whome they were placed & the names and age of the children & the names of their relations & the places they Did belong to, By Mr Daniel Gookin Senr, Thomas Prentis Capt' & Mr Edward Oakes, who were a comittee appointed by the Counsel to mannage that affayr. The termes & conditions upon which they are to serve is to be ordered by the General Court who are to provide that the children bee religiously educated & taught to read the English tounge

2 Boy A maid	To Samuel Simonds Esq. a boy named John his father named Alwitankus late of quantisit his father & mother p^rent both consenting the boys age about 12 years To him a girle named Hester her father & mother dead late of Nashaway her age ten years her onkel named John woosumpigin of Naticke
1 Boy	To Thomas Danforth esq a boy aged about 13 yeares his name John
1 Boy	To Leift Jonathan Danforth of [Billericay?] a boy aged twelve yeares, son to papamech alius David late of Warwick or Cowesit.
2 Boyes	To Mathew Bridge of CamBridge two Boyes the one named Jabez aged about ten yeares the other named Joseph aged six yeares their father named woompthe late of Packachooge one or both these boyes is away with his father 8 ber 17th 1676
3 A boy & two Girls	To Mr Jerimiah Shepard of Rowley a boy named Absolom his father of the same name late of Manehage aged about ten yeares. To him a girle sister to the Lad named Sarah aged eleven yeares. These [*illegible*] of Naticke. To him another girle aged about 8 yeares her named Jane her father & mother dead.

1 Mayd	To Mrs Mitchell of Cambridg widdow a maid named Margaret aged about twelve yeares, her father named Suhunnick of quantisit her mother dead.
1 Boy	To Thomas Jacob of Ipswich a boy aged ten yeares, one wennaputanan his guardian & one upacunt of quantisitt his grand mother was present. The Boy [*illegible*].
1 Boy	To on Goodman Read a Tanner of cambridge a Boy named John aged about thirteen yeares his father Dead.
1 Boy	To Mr Jacob Green of Charel Towne a boy aged about seaven yeares his parrents Dead Late of quantisit but his mother of Narraganset.
1 Boy	To Thomas Woolson of Wattertowne a boy aged about 14 yeares his name John his father dead who was of Cowesit or warwick, his mother p^rsent.
1 Boy	To Ciprian Steuens of Rumny Marsh but late of Lancaster a boy aged about six yeares son to nohanet of Chobnakonkonon. The Boy named Samuel.
1 Mayd	To Thomas Eliot of Boston a carpenter a maid aged about ten yeares her name Rebecka.
1 Boy	To Jacob Green Junior of Charles towne a Boy named Peter aged nine years his father dead his mother p^rsent named nannantum of quantisit.
1 Boy	To on Goodman Greenland a carpenter of Charles towne on misticke side a boy named Tom aged twelue yeares his father named santeshe of Pakachooge.
1 Girle	To Mr Edmund Batter of Salem a maid named Abigal aged sixteen her mother a widow named quanshishe late of Shookannet Beyond mendon.
2 a Boy A girle	To Daniel Gookin Senr A Boy named Joshua aged about eight yeares son to William wunuko late of magunkoog; his father dead. To him a girle aged about six yeares daughter to the widdow quinshiske late of Shookanet beyond mendon
1 Girle	To Andrew Bordman Tayler of cambridge a girle named Anne sister to ye Last named.
1 Boy	To Thomas Prentis Junior son to Capt Prentis of Cambridge village a boy named John son to William Wunnako late of magnkoy that was executed for Thomas Burney, aged thirteen.
1 Boy	To Benjamin Mills of Dedham a boy aged about six years is [named?] Joseph Spoonans late of Marlboro.

1 Boy	To Mr Edward Jackson a Boy named Joseph aged about 12 yeares Late of magalygook cosen to Pyambow of Naticke.
1 Mayd	To Widdow Jackson of Cambridge village a girle named Hope aged nine yeare her parents dead who wer of Narraganset.
1 Boy	To old Goodman Myles of Dedham a boy of [ ] yeares old. son to Annaweeken Decesed who was late of Hassanamesit his mother p^{r}sent.
1 Boy	To Capt. Thomas Prentis a Boy named Joseph son to Annaweken decesed Brother to the last named aged about 11 yeares this boy was after taken from Capt Prentice & sent up Mr Stoughton for [ ] Capt Prentis is to bee considered about it for hee has taken more care & paynes about those indians.
1 Boy	To John Smith of Dedham a boy aged about eight yeares his father dead late of Marlborow hee is Brother to James Printers wife
1 Mayd	To Mr John Flint [?] of Concord a mayd aged about [ ] yeares [*illegible*]
1 Boy	To Mr Jonathan Wade of mistick a Boy named Tom Aged about 11 yeares sonne to William Wunakhow of Magunkgog deceased
1 Mayd	To Mr Nathaniel Wade of mistick a maid aged about ten years daughter to Jame Natomet [?] late of Packachooge her father & mother dead

It is humbly proposed to the Honble Generall Court, to set the time these children shall serve; & if not less than till they come to 20 yeares of age. unto which those that had relations seemed willing. and also that the Court lay som penalty upon them if they runne away before the time expire & on their parents or kindred that shall entice or harborr & conceale them if they should runne away

Signed By the Comitee
Above named

DANIEL GOOKIN SEN^R
EDWARD OAKES.

Cambridge
   8 ber 28 1676

14

JOHN HULL

Excerpt from John Hull's Journal
August 24, 1676

John Hull was one of the wealthiest and most prominent of Boston's merchants in the late seventeenth century. With connections in England and Barbados, he epitomized the New England merchant whose ships carried commodities linking the far-flung outposts of England's emerging empire. Among his services to the Massachusetts Bay colony after Metacom's War, he occasionally presided over and recorded sales of Indian captives as slaves to English owners. While many of the natives referred to in this selection undoubtedly worked in New England households and farms, those included in the larger sales, such as those to Thomas Smith and Samuel Shrimpton, were clearly fated for sale abroad. Note the presence, one directly above the other, of the names of Daniel Henchman, a strong ally of Daniel Gookin's toleration of praying Indians, and Samuel Moseley, the most forceful opponent of such toleration. Whereas Henchman probably put the Indian woman and, eventually, her child to work in his Massachusetts home, Moseley's connections in the West Indies may have led him to transport his purchases there in hopes of profiting. Another purchaser for purposes of export was trader James Whitcomb, in whose house the Rowlandsons stayed after being reunited in Boston.

Captives Cr. By Sundry Acc'p^{ta} Viz.

	£. s. d.	£. s. d.
Isaac Waldron for a Boy		3 00 00
Ephraim Savage for 2 girles		04 10 00
Samuel Shrimpton,		
4 Squawes, 3 girls, 2 infants	.30 00 00	
1 old man, 3 squawes & 2 for one		41 12 00
returned by order	.09 00 00	
1 man	.02 12 00	

George Madison Bodge, *Soldiers in King Philip's War,* 2nd ed. (Leominster, Mass., 1896), 479–80.

Samuel Lynd for 1 maid 03 10 00
Thomas Smith,
    1 girl and 2 men . . . . 09 10 00 ⎫
    10 Squawes, 8 papooses, & 1 man . . . . 25 00 00 ⎪
    2 Lads, Viz. Pomham & Matoonas . . . . 07 00 00 ⎬ 47 02 00
    1 Woman, 4 little children . . . . . 05 12 00 ⎭
Samuel Symons, Esq.
    For 1 Boy and Girl 05 00 00
George Perkes
    For 2 Boyes 06 00 00
John Mors
    For 1 Girle . . . . 02 00 00 ⎫
    For 2 Girles . . . . 07 00 00 ⎬ 12 00 00
    For 1 Boy . . . . 03 00 00 ⎭
John Mann, for 1 Girle 03 00 00
Thomas Davis, for 1 Boy 03 00 00
Daniel Henchman, for 1 squawe & infant 02 10 00
Samuel Mosely,
    1 Boy & Girle . . . . 06 00 00 ⎫ 26 00 00
    13 Squawes & papooses wounded 1 sick . . 20 00 00 ⎭
Timothy Batt, for 1 squawe 02 15 00
———— Rawlings, 1 squawe 03 00 00

September 23, 1676.

Thomas Smith for 41 (captives) 82 00 00
Isaac Waldron for 1 . . . . 02 00 00
Richard Middlecott for 6 . . . . 10 00 00
James Meares   " 2 . . . . 03 10 00
Samuel Apleton " 3 . . . . 04 00 00
John Buttolph   " 1 . . . . 01 15 00
William Gilbert   " 1 . . . . 02 00 00
George Sphere   " 1 . . . . 02 00 00
William Needham " 1 . . . . 00 05 00
Thomas Grant   " 5 . . . . 08 01 00
David Waterhous " 1 . . . . 02 00 00
James Whitcomb " 13 . . . . 14 15 00
John Turner   " 1 . . . . 02 00 00
Ann Shepcutt   " 1 . . . . 01 15 00
Richard Wharton " 8 . . . . 08 00 00
———— Rawlins   " 3 . . . . 04 10 00
John Wait   " 4 . . . . 04 10 00
Josiah Flynt   " 2 . . . . 03 15 00

Samuel Leach	"	2	. . . .	02 00 00
Jarvis Ballard	"	2	. . . .	02 00 00
James Meares	"	2	. . . .	02 08 00
John Mason	"	1	. . . .	02 00 00
Benjamin Gibbs	"	8	. . . .	05 00 00

15

DANIEL GOOKIN

An Account of the Disposall of the Indians, Our Friends

November 10, 1676

With the war over, Massachusetts was determined to prevent future out-breaks by carefully supervising its native population, notwithstanding that most remaining Indians had not been hostile during the late war. Daniel Gookin was commissioned to conduct a report that constituted not only a census of native communities in the eastern part of the colony but also a notation of those English who lived near and watched over each community.

1676, *November* 10th — *An account of the disposall of the Indians, our friends (pro tempore),*[41] *presented to the Council (at their desire) by Daniel Gookin, sen.*

The Punkapog Indians are residing about Milton, Dorchester, and Braintree, among the English, who employ them (as I am informed) to cut cord wood, and do other labors. These are under the inspection of quarter-master Thomas Swift; their number, as I conjecture, may bee about one hundred and seventy-five; whereof   35 men: 140 women and children.

The Naticke Indians are disposed in four companies, as followes, viz.,

[41] For now, for the time being.

Daniel Gookin, "An Historical Account of the Doings and Sufferings of the Christian Indians in New England," *Transactions and Collections of the American Antiquarian Society* 2 (1836), 532–33.

one company, with James Rumny Marsh and his kindrd, live in Medfield, with the approbation and consent of the English; these are in number about twenty-five. 5:20.[42]

Another company live neare Natick, adjoyning to the garrison-house of Andrew Dewin and his sons, (who desire their neighbourhood,) and are under their inspection; the number of these may be about fifty souls. 10:40.

A third company of them, with Waban, live neare the falls of Charles river, neare to the house of Joseph Miller, and not farr from Capt. Prentce. The number of these may be about sixty souls; whereof are 12:50.

A fourth company dwell at Nonantum-hill, neare Leift. Trowbridge and John Coones, who permitts them to build their wigwams upon his ground. The number of this company, including some that live neare John White's, of Muddy river, and family or two neare Mr. Sparhake, and Daniel Champney, and Mr. Thomas Olivers, which are employed by the said persons to cut wood, and spin, and make stone walls; being but a small distance from the hill of Nonatum, where their meeting is to keepe Sabath. These may be about seventy-five souls. 15:60.

Among the Natick Indians are to bee reckoned such as are left, which came in with John of Pakchoog; which are not many, for sundry of that company are dead (since they came in); above thirty are put out to service to the English; three were executed about Tho. Eames his burning;[43] about twenty rann away; and, generally, such as remaine are of those Indians that formerly (before the war) lived under our government at Hassanamesit, Magunkog, Marlborough, and Wamesitt. The men belonging to these are not above fifteen, and they are abroad with the army at the eastward, under Capt. Hunting.[44]

The Nashobah or Concord Indians live at Concord, with the consent of the English there, and are employed by them; and are under the inspection of the comittee of militia and selectmen of that towne. Their number may be about fifty. 10:40.

The Indians that relate to Wannalancet,[45] are placed neare Mr. Jonathan Ting's, at Dunstable, with Mr. Tyng's consent and under his

---

[42]As in the preceding paragraph, the ratios here and at the ends of the following paragraphs express the proportion of adult males to women and children.

[43]That is, for burning the house of Thomas Eames, a settler, during the war.

[44]While fighting had stopped in southern New England, Anglo-Abenaki tensions plus the northward flow of anti-English refugees gave rise to warfare in what is now New Hampshire and Maine that continued until 1677. The Indian troops referred to here are among those employed by the English in this northern extension of Metacom's War.

[45]Wannalancet was the sachem of the Pawtucket people of Pennacook, in the lower Merrimack River valley.

inspection (when at home); and in Mr. Tyng's absence, the care of them is under one Robert Parris, Mr. Tyng's bayl.[46] The number of these may be about sixty, or more; some of their children are ordered to be put forth to English service, by the selectmen at Chelmsford and committee of militia there.   10:50.

There are about twenty-five live at or about Ipswich, under the government of authority there; som of their children were ordered to be put to service; there are about twenty-five.   8:17.

Besides these, there are some familys of them that live about Watertown and in Cambridge bounds, under English inspection and neare them; as at one Gate's, at Watertown, two families; at Justinias Holden, one family; at or neare Corprall Humand, two familys; at one Wilson, at Shawsin, one family. All these may be about forty souls.   7:33.

117 men, 450 women and children; and in all 567.

It must not be understood, that this computation of the number is exact; they may be a few more or a few less. Also of the men there are above thirty now abroad, under Capt. Hunting, at the eastward.

All these Indians meet together to worship God and keepe the Sabbath; and have their teachers at six places, viz.: Meadfield, Andrew Dewins, at Lower Falls, at Nonnanum, at Concord, at Dunstable.

[46]A bailor was someone who delivers goods in trust or, as in this case, assumes a responsibility in someone's absence.

JOSEPH ROWLANDSON'S FINAL SERMON

16

JOSEPH ROWLANDSON

"The Possibility of God's Forsaking a people, That have been visibly near & dear to him"

November 21, 1678

Joseph Rowlandson's fame derived primarily from his wife and the fact of her captivity. Indeed, the publication of his final sermon came not only five years after his death but also three years after Mary Rowlandson remarried. Yet the sermon warrants our attention because it was published with

Henry S. Nourse, ed., *The Narrative of the Captivity and Restoration of Mrs. Mary Rowlandson* (Lancaster, Mass., 1903), 125–45.

THE
Possibility of Gods For-
saking a people,

That have been visibly near & dear to him

TOGETHER,

with the Misery of a People thus forsaken,

Set forth in a

SERMON,

Preached at *Weathersfield*, Nov. 21. 1678.
Being a Day of FAST and HU-
MILIATION.

By Mr. *Joseph Rowlandson* Pastor of the
Church of Christ there. Being
also his last SERMON, *but
2 Days before he died. (Pref)*

2 Chron. 15. 2. *The Lord is with you, while ye be
with him, and if ye seek him, he will be found of
you : but if ye forsake him, he will forsake you.*
Hos. 9. 12. *Wo also to them, when I depart from them.*

BOSTON in *NEW-ENGLAND*
Printed for *John Ratcliffe*, & *John Griffin.*
1682.

her narrative and because it exemplifies the type of sermon known as the jeremiad, in which New England's sufferings were seen as caused by the spiritual laxness and complacency of God's followers. Thus while written in an entirely different way from Mary's narrative, it is thematically consistent with her account. Through references to scripture, the sermon explains how it was that New Englanders, a people near and dear to God, alienated him from them, bringing down his wrath in the form of the long, terrible war with the Indians and all its calamities. It is not difficult to see how Joseph Rowlandson and his sermons influenced the narrative even as Mary's experience shaped his subject matter and ways of thinking about it. The sermon is laid out in the careful outline form typical of Puritan ministers in the seventeenth and early eighteenth centuries. As such it lacks the greater vividness and complexity that Mary's real-life experience gives her narrative; but we must bear in mind that the sermon was intended not to be read but to be heard. If Joseph was a sufficiently powerful orator, his message of God's abandonment, along with the tantalizing possibility of redemption, may well have been as effective on his listeners as Mary's narrative on her readers.

Like Mary Rowlandson's narrative, the sermon begins with a preface by another author. Convention dictated a preface in both cases — for the narrative because it was by a woman, for the sermon because it was by someone no longer living.

To the Courteous READER, (especially the Inhabitants of the Town of Weathersfield, and Lancaster in New England.)
GODS forsaking of such as he hath been near to, is a thing of such weight, and solemnity, and hath such bitter effects, that it is a meet subject, (especially in a dark and mourning day) for Ministers to speak to, and for People to hear of; that the one may warn of the danger, and the other avoid the judgement. As God's presence is the greatest glory to a People on this side Heaven, so his absence is the greatest misery on this side hell; this therefore must needs be a concerning point, to such as will concern themselves in their concernments. The ensuing Sermon will appear a solemn word, if duely considered; the subject matter is very solemn and weighty, (Treating of God's being with, or forsaking a people) the time when it was delivered was a solemn time, (a day of Fast throughout the Colonies)[47] the Reverend Author that Composed, and Preached it, was one solemn and seri-

---

[47]The New England colonies proclaimed fast days, solemn occasions for collective spiritual contemplation and thanksgiving, with great frequency during and after King Philip's War.

ous above many others, and that which adds one great circumstance to its solemnity, is in that it was the last word he spake to the World, being but about two dayes before he left it. As it is solemn, so 'tis seasonable, and pertinent. It is a time wherein we have given God just cause to forsake us, a time wherein God is threatning to forsake us. A time wherein God hath in some measure forsaken us already, and what can be more seasonable, than to shew the evils that befall a forsaken People, that we may yet be awakened, and return, that the Lord do not forsake us utterly.

As for the Reverend Author, there needs nothing to be said in his commendation, he was known amongst the Churches in the Wilderness, and known to be a workman that needed not to be ashamed. That his Name (which was sometimes precious amongst those that knew him) may not be forgot, and that being dead, he may yet speak to a land that have in some measure forsook their God, and are in danger of being forsaken, it is the ground-work of the publishing this small part of his labours. It is commended especially to the perusal of the Inhabitants of Lancaster and Weathersfield; He was a Man well known to you, the one had his Life, and the other his death, and both his loss, you cannot easily forget his name, and 'tis desired that you may not forget the labour and travel, he hath had amongst you; the word which he Preached to you was acceptable whilst he was living, and it is presumed it will be accepted with the like candor now he is dead. Indeed had it been intended, and fitted by himself for the Press, you might have expected, and found it more large, and polished; but as it is, it is thought fit, not to be lost, and may be of great use, and benefit, to open to us the danger of forsaking God, to humble us for all our coolings, and declinings from God, to quicken us in our return to, and close walking with God, and that it may attain this end, is the hearts desire, and prayer of him, who abundantly wishes thy welfare, and prosperity in Christ Jesus.

B.W.[48]

The Last Sermon of Reverend Joseph Rowlandson

Jeremiah 23.33.

And when this People, or the Prophet, or a Priest, shall ask thee, saying, what is the burden of the Lord? thou shalt then say unto them, what burden? I will even forsake you; saieth the Lord.

[48]Probably Benjamin Woodbridge, minister in nearby Windsor, Connecticut; Kathryn Zabelle Derounian, "The Publication, Promotion, and Distribution of Mary Rowlandson's Indian Captivity Narrative in the Seventeenth Century," *Early American Literature* 23 (1988), 242.

In the Words, there lies before us, (First) A Question, supposed, to be propounded, wherein there is two things:

1. The Questionists, this People, or a Prophet, or a Priest.
2. The Question itself, or the matter of it, What is the burden of the Lord? (Secondly,) There is an Answer, and a solemn Answer too, which is put into his mouth by the Lord, and which he is to return as the Lord's Answer to the Question? thou shalt then say unto them, what burden? I will even forsake you, saith the Lord.

In which Answer there is three things.

1. An expression of Indignation, What burden?
2. An assertion by way of Answer to the question, I will forsake you.
3. A Seal of ratification, in the last words, Saith the Lord.

God having before dealt with the Pastors, that did destroy, and scatter the flock, as in the beginning of the Chapter,[49] Wo be to the Pastors that destroy and scatter the sheep of my pasture, & ver. 2. I will visit upon you the evil of your doings, saith the Lord, and also with the false Prophets, that prophesied lies in his Name, as ver. 9. My heart within me is broken because of the prophets, & ver. 32. Behold I am against them, that prophesie false dreams, saith the Lord, and do tell them, and cause my people to erre by their lies, and by their lightness; which sort of Prophets went without their Commission, as ver. 21. I have not sent these Prophets yet they ran. He proceeds from the head Rulers, to the people that were reduced by them; for by this means their hands were strengthened in sin, so as that they did not return from their wickedness, as ver. 14. It was a usual thing for the Prophets of the Lord, to begin their Sermons (the matter whereof was minatory, wherein the Lord threatened them with just judgements) with that Phrase, the burden of the Lord, as will easily appear if you consult Isai. 13. 1 & 15. 1 & 22. 1 & 30. 6. Now they do in the words of the Text, or are supposed in mockery to demand, what Burden he had from the Lord, for them. For the opening of the words, And; or moreover because he here enters upon new matter; this People, or the prophane sort of them, whom the false Prophets had seduced to which he joyns the Prophet, and the Priest, in that they were alike prophane, as ver. 11. for both Prophet and Priest are prophane, yea in my house, saith the Lord: and when Prophets are prophane there is

---

[49]Meaning chapter 23 of the Book of Jeremiah, the chapter from which Rowlandson drew the sermon's topical verse.

wont to be a pack of them, as Jer. 5.31. The Prophets prophesies falsly, and the Priests bear rule by their means, and my people love to have it so: shall ask thee, saying, viz. in a deriding way, not out of a holy end, or desire, What is the burden of the Lord? or from the Lord? so were the prophesies stiled, that contained in them, Threatnings, Judgements, and Plagues, 2 King. 9.25. as if they had said, what hast thou further mischief in thy head to declare? further Woes and Threatnings to pronounce? hast thou nothing else to prophesie, but Mischief and Calamity? What is the burden now? Thou shalt then say unto them, the Lord knew what they would say to him, and tells him what he should say, by way of reply, What burden? a retorting by way of holy indignation; ask ye indeed what burden? and that in a way of derision? are you of that strain, and spirit? I will even forsake you saith the Lord: a burden heavy enough, and you are like to feel it so ere long, heavy enough to break your Backs, to break your Church, and your Common wealth, and to sink your haughty Spirits, when this Burden shall come upon you, in its force and weight.

Doct. That the Lord may even forsake a People that have been near to him, and he hath been near to, though for the Lord thus to do, is as fearful and hideous a judgement as can be inflicted on any People.

The Doctrine is double, it hath two parts:

First, That the Lord may do thus.

Secondly, when he doth, it is a very sad and heavy burden. It may be prosecuted as two distinct points.

1. God may forsake a People that hath been near to him, and that he hath been near to. This may be spoken to in this order.
1. What is meant by God's forsaking a People.
2. How may it appear that God may forsake, even such a People as the point speaks of?
3. The Reasons.
4. The use.

1. What doth Gods forsaking mean? what is intended thereby?

Sol. It means Gods withdrawing himself, as the Prophet Hosea phraises it, Hos. 5.6. They shall go with their Flocks and their Herds to seek the Lord, but shall not find him, he hath withdrawn himself from them. They shall seek him, and not find him, and there is a good reason, he hath withdrawn himself, he is gone, in respect of his gracious presence. We must here distinguish betwixt God's general presence and his gracious presence. In respect of his general presence, he is not far from any one of us, for in him we live, and move, and have our being, Act. 17,

27, 28. We have not only our beginning from, but our being in him. As the beam hath its being in the sun. Of this general presence of God, we read, Psal. 149.7. There is no flying from it. Whither shall I go from the Spirit, or whither shall I flie from thy presence? In this sense God is every where, as it is ver. 8, & 9. If I ascend up into Heaven thou art there; if I make my bed in Hell, behold thou art there. He fills Heaven and Earth, and there is no hiding from him, Jer. 23, 24. Can any hide himself in secret places, that I shall not see him? saith the Lord; do not I fill Heaven and Earth? saith the Lord. He hath Heaven for his Throne, and the Earth for his Footstool, as it is, Isai. 66.1. This general presence of God, if believingly apprehended, and strongly believed, might be of great use.[50]

But it is not this general presence that is meant: but his especial presence, his favourable and gracious presence, the removing whereof, is that that is intended, by the forsaking that the Text and Point speaks of. God is said to forsake a People two wayes.

1. As to Affection.
2. As to Action.
1. As to Affection, when he discontinues his love to them, when he takes away his love from a people, then he takes his leave of a people. My mind is not toward this people, Jer. 15.1. a very heavy Judgement, and sad removal. Be instructed O Jerusalem, least my soul depart from thee.
2. As to Action, when God takes away the signs of his presence.
1. When he takes away merciful and gracious providences, when he carries not towards them as he was wont to do: but vexes them with all manner of adversity, Deut. 31.17. I will forsake them, and many evils and troubles shall befal them: when he ceases to protect them from evils, and enemies, as in times past, and provides not for them, as he was wont to do. When he takes away his Ordinances, and bereaves a people of the glorious things of his house; or takes away his spirit from accompanying them, whereby the glory ceases, and the ordinances are rendered ineffectual for the saving good of a people.
2. How may it appear that God may forsake such a People?

It may appear by what God hath threatned. What God hath threatned, to such as the point speaks of, may be inflicted on them: but God hath threatned such judgement to such a people. My anger shall be kindled

---

[50]Rowlandson here wants to make sure his listeners understand that there is a distinction between God being present, as he is always and everywhere, and God's bestowing or witholding his grace.

against them, and I will forsake them, as near as they are to me, and as dear as they have been to me, Deut. 31.17. Many such threatnings are found in the Scripture against Israel, who are stiled a people unto him.

In that such as have been near to God, and he near to them, have complained of their being forsaken by God. Thou hast forsaken us, is one of the bitter moans, on record, that the Church of God did often make unto him.

What God hath inflicted on such, may be inflicted on such again; what God hath done to some, he may do to others, in the same state, and relation: for he is unchangeable. Those that were once the only peculiar people of God, near to God, and had God near to them, yet what is their condition at this day? A forsaken condition, is the condition, of the Offspring of Abraham Gods Friend, a seed whom he had chosen, and hath been so, for above sixteen hundred years. God hath been angry with them, and forsaken them, as they were foretold long ago. How is it with the Churches of Asia, that were once famous golden Candlesticks? that had Epistles written to them. Are they not in a forsaken condition? not the face of a Church to be found amongst them.

In that they may do that, which may deserve a forsaking, therefore they may do that which may actually procure it. They may do that which may deserve a forsaking, they may through the corruption and unbelief of their hearts forsake God, and God may in just judgement retaliate, and thereupon forsake them. This is spoken to in the forequoted place, Deut. 31. 16, 17. They will forsake me, and break my Covenant which I have made with them: then my anger shall be kindled against them in that day, and I will forsake them, and hide my face from them. So again, 2 Chron. 15.2. But if you forsake him he will forsake you; the first is supposed, if you forsake him, the latter is imposed, he will forsake you:

But why doth the Lord forsake such a People? The Reasons:

1. To shew that he hath no need of any, he hath forsaken many, and may forsake many more, to shew that he hath no need of any. God would have all the world to take notice, (that though all men have need of him, yet) he hath no need of any man.
2. To testifie his Sanctity, and severity against sin. He will not spare them, that have been near him, if they will not spare their sin for him. He is a holy God, and if they will have their sins, and their lusts, and their wayes, and their lovers, he will vindicate his holiness, by inflicting this judgement on them.
3. To be a warning to all that enjoy his gracious presence. That they see that they make much of it, and that they take heed that they

do not sin against him) and forsake him, and provoke him to forsake them also.

Caut. The point is to be understood of a people that are visibly and externally near and dear to him, and these may be totally and finally forsaken of God: and yet here it must be noted, that God may exercise a deal of patience, and forbearance toward such as he is about to forsake, he did so with the old world, he did so with the Israelites of old, he did so with the seven Churches of Asia: he is not wont suddenly, and at once to forsake a people, that have been near and dear to him; but he is wont to give them warning, and in patience to bear a while with their forwardness, and wait to see if there be any returning to him, before he doth inflict this heavy and sharp judgement.

Use. It serves to admonish us, not to bear ourselves too high, upon the account of priviledges. It is a great priviledge to have the Lord near us, and to be near unto him: and some lean upon this though they abide in their sin, Micah 3.10, 11. They build up Sion with blood, and Jerusalem with iniquity, yet will they lean upon the Lord, and say, is not the Lord amongst us? But if our deportment be not according to our priviledges, if we do not carry it thereafter, by becoming an humble, fruitful, and holy people; the Lord will bring forth this heavy burden against us, we shall be rejected, and forsaken of the Lord, whatever our external priviledges be.

But the second part of the Doctrine; or the second Doctrine may now be spoken to, viz.

That it is the heaviest burden, or the forest of Judgements for the Lord to forsake a people.

There may be two things spoken to in the management of the Truth.

1. Arguments to evidence it.   2. The Uses of it.
1. If God hath threatned it as a very sore judgement, then sure it is so. Now when God hath been angry with a people, he hath manifested the same by menacing them with his forsaking them: when he hath been designed to do them a deep displeasure, upon the account of some high provocation he is wont to threaten them not by taking away this, or that outward comfort from them; but by taking away himself from them. And that is a woe indeed, a woe with a witness, Hos. 9.12. Yea, woe also to them, when I depart from them: this is the wofullest day that such a people are wont to meet with.
2. Gods forsaking a people is a sore judgement, in that it exposes them to all judgements. Sin is a great evil in that it exposes to all evil, this is a great evil of punishment, in that it exposes to all punishments.

If God be gone, our guard is gone, and we are as a City, in the midst of Enemies, whose walls are broken down. Our strength to make resistance, that's Gone, for God is our strength, as a carcase without life, is a prey, to beasts of prey; so are a people forsaken of their God, to all their devouring enemies, and to infernal, and cursed spirits: they are exposed to mischief, and the malice of all their malignant enemies. When the Lord had forsaken Jerusalem, the Romans quickly made a prey of it; when they were destitute of God, their habitation became desolate. There is not Protection to a People, whom the Lord forsakes; but they are perplexed on every side.

3. Because the evils that are on such, whom God hath forsaken, they are only evils. The Prophet Ezekiel sometime hath the expression, Ezek. 7.5. Thus saith the Lord God, an evil, an only evil behold is come. This is such an evil, an only evil to a people. An evil whilst God is present, may have much good in it, the Lord may sanctifie it for abundance of blessing: there is hopes of this whilst the Lord continues amongst them; but if he be gone, it is an only evil, and the evils that come upon them are such, they have nothing but evil in them.

4. Because no creature can then afford any help; for what can creatures do when God is departed, he makes the creatures useful and helpful, but without him they can do us no good, stand us in no stead: they may say to thee as the King of Israel, said to the woman, that cried Help O King, He answered, If the Lord dont help, whence shall I help thee? all creatures may say if God be departed, we cannot help: Nay the very Devil cannot help if God be gone: when God departed from Saul, he sought help from the Devil, I Sam. 28.15. Wherefore (saith the Devil) asketh thou of me? seeing the Lord is departed from thee.

5. It appears to be a sore judgement, by the anguish and distress, that such have been in, that have been sensible that God hath forsaken them. Sin hath flown in the face of such, and terified them: Oh the blessed God is gone, and if he is gone, mercy is gone; and Oh for such and such sins, that lie upon me! what shall I do? what a moan have Saints themselves made in such a case? as David, Psal. 22.1, 2. My God, my God, why hast thou forsaken me? why art thou so far from helping me? and from the words of my roaring? Oh my God, I cry in the day time, but thou hearest not, and in the night season, and am not silent. Oh how Saul roared out in his distress! and that on this account especially, that God was departed from him,

not so much that the Philistines were upon him, had not God been gone, he could have dealt well enough with them; but here was the misery, and the sting of the misery, God was departed from him.

6. It is a sore punishment, in that it is a great part of the punishment of Hell. The essential parts of that punishment, is pain of loss, and sense, and the former some reckon the greater.

Use 1. How foolish are sinners that do even bid God depart from them? as we read, Job 21.14. Therefore they say unto God, depart from us, for we desire not the knowledge of thy wayes. But do they know what they say? Oh sinners is this your wish? if it be granted it will prove your woe for ever. Happily Gods presence is now your trouble; but I tell you his absence would be your torment.

2. See here what an evil it is to forsake God, is it a judgement of judgements, to be forsaken of God? surely then it is the sin of sins to forsake him: the evil of punishment is in being left by God, and the evil of sin is in leaving God. What, forsake God, who is our only good? God who made us, and possest us from our beginning, God that hath been the guid of our Youth, that hath been good to us, and fed us all our dayes? Jer. 2.19. Know therefore and see, that it is an evil thing and bitter, that thou hast forsaken the Lord thy God. And there is an aggravation of it, ver. 17. Thou hast forsaken the Lord thy God, when he led thee by the way. As a guid to direct thee, as a staffe to support thee, as a convoy to guard thee, as a Father to provide for thee, that thou hast wanted nothing: well may it be said, how evil and bitter a thing is it, that thou hast forsaken the Lord? He adds in the 31. verse. Oh Generation! Generation of what? of what you will; God leaves a space that you may write, what you please, generation of Vipers, or Monsters, or any thing rather than generation of Gods people. See ye the word of the Lord, behold your face in that Glass. So your causless apostasies, have I been a wilderness unto Israel? Have you wanted any thing, Oh ye degenerating crooked, and wilful generation? God may say to such sinners, as Pharaoh to Hadad, when he would be gone, I King. 11.22. But what hast thou lacked with me, that thou seekest to be gone? what hast thou lacked sinner, that thou seekest to be gone from the Lord? The sinner must answer with him, nothing howbeit let me go in any wise. He came to him in his distress, and when his turn was answered, away he packs. They forsake because they will forsake.

3. Wonder not that Gods Saints have been so solicitous with him, not to forsake them. Thus David, Psal. 119.8. Oh forsake me not utterly. He might well be solicitous in this matter, for he understood what it was to be forsaken of the Lord. They press hard with the Lord whatever he doth he would not leave them, nor forsake them, Jer. 14.9. Leave us not. And no wonder, there are such moans, when the Lord may have seemed, to have forsaken them.

4. If Gods forsaking be so sore a judgement, it should make us more cautious, and wary least we pull down this judgement on our heads. Men should be afraid of this heaviest of judgements, more than the Child of whipping.

5. Let Gods dear ones take heed of concluding against themselves, that they are under this judgement. They are readiest to conclude against themselves, and yet really in the least danger. Thus we read, Isa. 49.14. But Zion said, the Lord hath forsaken me, and my Lord hath forgotten me. But why said Zion so? it was from diffidence: as Saints do not forsake God as others do, Psal. 18.21. I have not wickedly departed from my God; so God will not forsake them as he forsakes others, not utterly forsake them: His forsaking of his is but temporary, and partial.

But here a question may be moved what is the difference betwixt a sinner forsaken and a Saint forsaken? for the Lord doth not forsake both alike.

1. When God forsakes his own, yet they cry after him, he withdraws himself from them sometimes, yet so as that he draws their hearts after him as a mother may hide away from her Child, that it may seek and cry the more earnestly after her.

2. They retain good thoughts of him in his withdrawment, or absence. As the Spouse in the Canticles, she calls him her beloved still. As the faithful wife: she retains good thoughts of her husband, and keeps up her respect, though he be gone from home. But the wicked when the Lord forsakes them, harbour hard thoughts of him. Is this to serve the Lord, and walk in his wayes? what good have I got by all I have done? see how he hath served me.

3. They will seek him, till he return again, when the Lord forsakes others, they will seek after vanities, to make up the want of God's presence. The Adultress in her Husbands absence, will seek after other lovers. The true Saint will be satisfied in nothing else

but the Lord till he return. Moreover there is a difference in Gods forsaking the sinner and the Saint, when he forsakes the wicked they are left in darkness: but when he withdraws himself from his own he leaves some light, whereby they see which way he is gone; he leaves some glimmering light, by which they may follow after him, and find him.

And again, when he leaves his own, yet his bowels are towards them, Jer. 31.20. My bowels are troubled for him, I will surely have mercy upon him, saith the Lord. He hath an eye towards them for much good, in his forsaking them.

Use 2. Of Exhortation: 1. To thankfulness to God, for that he hath not yet forsaken us. Whatever he hath stript us of, he hath not yet stript us of himself, he hath not as yet forsaken us. He might have done it, and have done us no wrong; but he hath not yet done it.

2. To do our utmost that he may not forsake us. And here there may be added Motives and Means.

1. Consider God's lothness to forsake us. This is a thing that he is not desirous of, he doth not willingly afflict us with this sort of Affliction, or grieve us with this grievous stroak. God hath shewed himself loth to depart from those that have departed from him; but have warned them of his displeasure, that they might stay him. It goes near Gods heart to forsake a People that have been near to him. Methinks I hear him saying thus, How shall I give thee up, Oh New-England! thence speaking to warn us, of our forsakings of him, and to be instructed, why? least his Spirit depart from us, Jer. 6.8. Be thou instructed Oh Jerusalem, least my Soul depart from thee, least I make thee desolate, a land not inhabited. You may easily stay him, the matter is not so far gone, but you might yet stay him: were we but as loth he should forsake us, as he is to forsake us, he would never leave us. His gradual motions from a people argue his lothness, and unwillingness to leave them.

2. Consider what the Lord is to us, or what relation he stands in to us, while he is with us. He is our friend, we have found him to be so, and a special friend too: men in the World are not willing to forego a Friend, a good Friend: he is as faithful, skilful, powerful, and tender hearted a Friend as ever a people had, he stuck by us when also we had been in a woe case, Psal. 124.1. If it had not been

the Lord, who was on our side may Israel now say. And had not the Lord been on our side, may New-England now say. He is a Father, and a tender-hearted Father, Isai. 63.16, Doubtless thou art our Father. Can children be willing their Father should leave them? he is a Husband, Isai. 54.5. For thy Maker is thy Husband, a loving, careful, tender husband too; can the Wife be willing to part with her Husband? if the Lord forsake us, we are bereft of our friend, left friendless, he is all friends in one, none can be our friend, if he be not. If he leave us, we shall be as Orphans, for he is related as a Father, and how sad is the state of poor Orphans: and we shall be in a state of Widow-hood, a very solitary, and sorrowful state. He is our guide, and our pilot; what will become of the blind if their guid leave them? and what will become of the Ship if the Pilot desert it? thus the Lord is to his, and well may he say, as Mic. 6.3. Oh my People what have I done? or wherein have I wearied thee, or given thee any cause to be weary of me.

3. Consider there are shrewd signs of Gods intent to leave us, unless somewhat can be done. If you enquire what? I answer:

1. The sins for which God hath forsaken others are rife amongst us. The sins for which God forsook the Jews, are our sins.

1. Horrid Pride, Hos. 5.5. The Pride of Israel doth testifie to his face. Pride in Parts, and pride of Hearts, pride in Apparel, and Vestures, and Gestures, and in Looks, how lofty are their eyes! New-England is taken notice of abroad, for as proud a People, of a professing people, as the World affords. When a People are humble the Lord will stay with them. If our immunities, which are Gods mercies, puffe us up, God will empty us: he will blast that to us that we are proud of.

2. Deep and high Ingratitude. Do you thus requite the Lord? Deut. 32.6. So the Prophet Hosea taxes them, Hos. 2.8. God gave her Corn, and Wine, and Oyl, silver and Gold, but she consumed them on Baal. We have been blest but hath God had the glory of our blessings.

3. Oppression. Amos 8.4. Ye that swallow up the needy. These Jews were like the fishes, the greater did devour the less. Some are like wild Beasts, like Wolves that tear off the fleece, and eat the flesh of the flocks. There is more justice to be found in hell, then amongst some men on earth: for there is no innocent person oppressed there.

4. Weariness of Gods Ordinances. Amos 8.5. When will the Sabbath be done? They that are weary of the service of God, and the Ordi-

nances of God, they are weary of God. God indeed hath fed us to the full, as to Ordinances: and we are glutted, and surfeited, and have lost our esteem. When mens Commodities bare but little price in a place, they will remove the market! if Gospel Ordinances are but a cheap commodity, have lost their price, and men are weary of them: God will let out his Vineyard to another People. If our mercies become our burdens, God will ease us of them.

5. Cousenage in mens dealings, making the Ephah small, and the Shekel great, selling the refuse of Wheat, Amos 8.5, 6. They pick out the best Grain for themselves, and the refuse is to sell.

6. Idolatry, which is Spiritual Adultery, and is there nothing of this? chusing of new Gods.

7. Incorrigibleness, or opposition of a spirit of reformation. When God calls to a People to return, by repentance, but they will go on still in their sin: God calls to them by his judgments, and by his Rod; but they will not hear, as 'tis Jer. 5.3. Thou hast stricken them, but they have not grieved; thou hast consumed them, but they have refused to receive Correction: they have made their faces harder than a Rock, they have refused to return. When it is thus with a People, God will pluck up and be gone; so Jer. 7.13, 14. Because they would not hear, and would not answer the call of God, I will do to this house as I did to Shiloh, why? what did the Lord do to Shiloh? ver. 12. Go to Shiloh, and see what I did to it, for the wickedness of my People Israel. Go, and view it, and you will see what he did, he left tokens of his wrath upon them, and forsook them.

2. Another sign of his intent to forsake us, is, in that he is dealing with us as he is wont to deal with them that he is about to forsake, he takes away those that are mostly with him. He will take away his Moses's, those that stand in the Gap, and binds his hands with their Prayers, when he is designed to pour out wrath upon a People: he will remove the lights, when he is about to darken a land. Wise men send away their Plate, and Jewels, and choice things; it intimates their intention of removal.

3. Another sign is our Lukewarmness, and Indifferency in Religion: a usual forerunner of its removal. When a People care not for God, and the things of God, he hath left them in some measure, already; and if that Spirit abide he will not tarry long with them.

Use 1. Of Direction. 1. Examine and humble your selves, for all your departures from God, your forsakings of him; humble your selves for them, confessing with bitterness your evil therein, bemoaning yourselves before the Lord upon the account thereof. May the Lord hear his People, from Dan to Beersheba bemoaning themselves, Ephraim like, then the Lord will hear, and have mercy, and not leave us, for his Names sake.

2. Judge your selves worthy to be forsaken, because of your forsaking of him. If you judge your selves worthy to be forsaken, God will not judge you worthy to be forsaken, II Cor.11.31.

3. Pray the Lord not to forsake you, the Lord is sometimes staid with Prayers: Prayers have prevailed with his Majesty often, and may do again.

4. Forsake your sins, whereby you have forsaken him. Nothing less then this will prevent this mischief, coming upon us. If there be any, either Son or Daughter that will not leave their sins for God, God will leave such.

THE CAPTIVITY OF HANNAH DUSTIN

17

COTTON MATHER

Excerpt from Decennium Luctousum

1699

Prompted by Mary Rowlandson's literary success, ministers expanded their use of Indian captivity as a metaphor for the vulnerability of human beings before God. Among the most successful was Cotton Mather, son of Increase, who, like his father, was a preacher in Boston whose sermons and other works were widely published. Among Mather's best-known uses of captivity was his account of the next truly prominent New England captive after Rowlandson, Hannah Dustin. Dustin lived in the small town of Haverhill, Massachusetts, when it was attacked by Indians during the Anglo-French imperial conflict known as King William's

---

Charles H. Lincoln, ed., *Narratives of the Indian Wars, 1675–1689* (New York, 1913), 263–66.

War (1689–97). As Mather reveals, she led her fellow captives in a well-coordinated slaying and scalping of their captors before successfully escaping.

As indicated in the Introduction, the Rowlandson and Dustin captivities were linked by the fact that Dustin's captor had lived in the Rowlandson household. Nevertheless, there were several striking differences between the two captivities. In their religious orientation, Dustin's captors were fervent Catholics rather than either Puritans or strict adherents of native traditions. And Dustin traveled with a single family rather than with a far larger party such as the one that Rowlandson generally accompanied. Finally, Dustin actively engineered not only the captives' escape but also the murder and scalping of their captors, for which they knew they would receive a bounty. Compared with Dustin, Rowlandson conforms far more closely to the passive behavior associated with and prescribed for women in seventeenth-century Europe and its colonies. But Mather was able to draw on the biblical story of Jael to show that, under extreme circumstances, women could legitimately assume male roles — even to the point of murdering and dismembering enemies.

Mather was among those hailing Dustin on her visit to Boston. He first told her story in a sermon and later reworked it as an article (chapter) in Decennium Luctousum *(Sorrowful Decade), his account of the New England colonies' experience with Indian warfare during King William's War. In 1702, Mather incorporated* Decennium Luctousum *into a still larger work,* Magnalia Christi Americana, *his sprawling, multivolume history of the Puritan church in New England. During the nineteenth century, Dustin's exploits and Mather's account attracted the attention of such notable writers as Henry David Thoreau and Nathaniel Hawthorne.*

Article XXV

A Notable Exploit; wherein Dux Foemina Facti.[51]

On March 15, 1697, the Salvages made a descent upon the Skirts of Haverhill, Murdering and Captivating about Thirty-Nine Persons, Burning about Half a Dozen Houses. In this Broil, one Hannah Dustan, having lain in about a Week, attended with[52] her Nurse, Mary Neff, a Widow, a Body of Terrible Indians drew near unto the House, where she lay, with Designs to carry on their Bloody Devastations. Her Husband hastened from his Employments abroad, unto the Relief of his Distressed Family; and first bidding

---

[51]The Latin phrase translates as "a woman the leader in the achievement."
[52]By.

Seven of his Eight children (which were from Two to Seventeen years of Age) to get away as fast as they could, unto some Garrison in the Town, he went in, to inform his Wife of the horrible Distress come upon them. E'er she could get up, the fierce Indians were got so near, that utterly despairing to do her any Service, he ran out after his Children; Resolving that on the Horse which he had with him, he would Ride away with That which he should in this Extremity find his Affections to pitch most upon, and leave the Rest unto the care of the Divine Providence. He overtook his Children about Forty Rod from his Door; but then, such was the Agony of his Parental Affections, that he found it impossible for him to Distinguish any one of them from the rest; wherefore he took up a Courageous Resolution to Live and dy with them all. A party of Indians came up with him; and now, though they Fired at him, and he Fired at them, yet he manfully kept at the Reer of his Little Army of Unarmed Children, while they Marched off, with the pace of a Child of Five years old; until, by the Singular Providence of God, he arrived safe with them all, unto a place of Safety, about a Mile or two from his House. But his House must the mean Time have more dismal Tragedies acted at it. The Nurse trying to Escape, with the New-born Infant, fell into the Hands of the Formidable Salvages; and those furious Tawnies coming into the House, bid poor Dustan to Rise Immediately. Full of Astonishment, she did so; and sitting down in the Chimney with an Heart full of most fearful Expectation, she saw the Raging Dragons rifle all that they could carry away, and set the House on Fire. About Nineteen or Twenty Indians now led these away, with about Half a Score other English Captives; but e'er they had gone many Steps, they dash'd out the Brains of the Infant against a Tree; and several of the other Captives, as they began to Tire in the sad Journey, were soon sent unto their Long Home; the Salvages would presently bury their Hatchets in their Brains, and leave their Carcases on the Ground for Birds and Beasts to feed upon. However, Dustan (with her Nurse), notwithstanding her present Condition, Travelled that Night, about a Dozen Miles, and then kept up with their New Masters in a long Travel of an Hundred and Fifty Miles, more or less, within a few Days Ensuing, without any sensible Damage, in their Health, from the Hardships of their Travel, their lodging, their Diet, and their many other Difficulties.

These Two poor Women were now in the Hands of those, whose Tender Mercies are Cruelties; but in the Good God, who hath all Hearts in His own Hands, heard the Sighs of these Prisoners, and gave them to find unexpected Favour from the Master, who laid claim unto them. That Indian Family consisted of Twelve Persons; Two Stout men, Three Women, and Seven Children; and for the Shame of many an English Family, that has the Character of Prayerless upon it, I must now Publish what these poor Women assure me: 'Tis this; In Obedience to the Instructions which the French have given them, they would have Prayers in their Family, no less than Thrice Every Day; in the Morning, at Noon, and in the Evening; nor would they ordinarily let their Children Eat or Sleep, without first saying their Prayers. Indeed these Idolaters were like the rest of their whiter Brethren, Persecutors; and would not endure, that these poor Women should Retire to their English Prayers, if they could hinder them. Nevertheless, the poor Women had nothing but fervent Prayers, to make their Lives Comfortable, or Tolerable; and by being daily sent out, upon Business, they had Opportunities together and asunder, to do like another Hannah, in Pouring out their Souls before the Lord: Nor did their praying Friends among ourselves, forbear to Pour out Supplications for them. Now, they could not observe it without some wonder, that their Indian Master, sometimes when he saw them Dejected, would say unto them, "What need you Trouble your self? If your God will have you delivered, you shall be so!" And it seems, that our God would have it so to be. This Indian Family was now travelling with these Two Captive Women, (and an English Youth, taken from Worcester, a year and a half before,) unto a Rendezvous of Salvages, which they call, a Town, some where beyond Penacook; and they still told these poor Women, that when they came to this Town, they must be Stript, and Scourg'd and run the Gantlet through the whole Army of Indians. They said, this was the Fashion, when the Captives first came to a Town; and they derided some of the Fainthearted English, which they said, fainted and swoon'd away under the Torments of this Discipline. But on April 30, While they were yet, it may be about an Hundred and Fifty Miles from the Indian Town, a little before Break of Day, when the whole Crew was in a Dead Sleep; (Reader, see if it prove not So!) one of these Women took up a Resolution, to imitate the Action of Jael upon Sisera;[53] and being where she had not her own Life secured by any Law unto her, she thought she was not Forbidden by any Law to take away the Life of the Murderers, by whom her Child had been butchered. She heartened the Nurse, and the Youth, to assist her in this Enterprize; and all furnishing themselves with Hatchets for the purpose, they struck such Home Blows, upon the Heads of their Sleeping Oppressors, that e'er they could any of them Struggle into any Effectual Resistance, *at the Feet* of these poor Prisoners, *they bow'd, they fell, they lay down: at their feet they bowed, they fell; where they bowed, there they fell down Dead.*[54] Only one Squaw escaped sorely wounded from

[53]Judges 4.
[54]Judges 5:27.

them, in the Dark; and one Boy, whom they Reserved Asleep, intending to bring him away with them, suddenly wak'd, and skuttled away from this Desolation. But cutting off the Scalps of the Ten Wretches, they came off, and Received Fifty Pounds from the General Assembly of the Province, as a Recompence of their Action; besides which they Received many presents of Congratulation from their more private Friends; but none gave 'em a greater Tast of Bounty than Colonel Nicholson, the Governor of Maryland, who hearing of their Action, sent 'em a very generous Token of his Favor.

A Rowlandson Chronology

1602: Beginning of sustained Indian-European contacts in southern New England.

1616–19: Epidemic of unknown disease devastates coastal natives in New England.

1620: First European settlement in New England established at Plymouth.

1629–42: "Great Migration" of approximately twenty thousand English to southern New England.

1633–34: Smallpox sweeps through native societies in New England and elsewhere in northeastern North America.

ca. 1637: Mary White born in Somerset county, England.

1637: English colonies and their Indian allies wage war on the Pequot Indians. Antinomian Anne Hutchinson and many followers exiled from Massachusetts.

1639: White family emigrates to Wenham, Massachusetts.

1643: United Colonies of New England established by Massachusetts, Connecticut, Plymouth, and New Haven. English settlement begins at Nashaway.

1644: Massachusetts Bay extends its authority over Nashaway and other Indian communities located near its settlements. John Eliot begins missionary work among some subject natives.

1645: Nashaway sachem Shawanon deeds 80-square-mile tract to Nashaway settlers.

1653: English town of Nashaway renamed Lancaster. White and Rowlandson families move to Lancaster.

1654: Shawanon succeeded by Matthew as principal sachem at Nashaway.

ca. 1656: Mary White marries Joseph Rowlandson.

1660s: Fur trade declines in southern New England; settler demand for land escalates.

1662: Wampanoag sachem Wamsutta dies of mysterious causes; Wampanoags accuse the English of poisoning him. Succeeded by Metacom.

ca. 1673: Christian sachem Matthew dies and is succeeded by Shoshanim.

1673: Daniel Gookin tours Nipmuc villages, attempting to organize them into praying towns.

1675, March: John Sassamon murdered.

1675, June: Three Wampanoags executed for the death of Sassamon. Metacom's War begins with fighting between Wampanoags and Plymouth; Massachusetts troops aid Plymouth.

1675, July: Nipmucs divided, some attacking English, others supporting English, and still others trying to remain neutral. Trapped by English troops, Wampanoags evacuate homeland and seek refuge among friendly Nipmucs.

1675, August: Nashaway Nipmucs stage first attack on Lancaster.

1675, September: Indians in Connecticut Valley launch attacks on nearby English towns.

1675, December: English troops attack and burn the Great Swamp Fort, holding several hundred Narragansetts. Narragansetts join Nipmucs and Wampanogs in central Massachusetts.

1676, January: Metacom travels to Hoosic, New York, to seek broader native support for war; his forces routed by Mohawks. James Quanapohit informs English of planned attack on Lancaster.

1676, February: Four hundred Nipmucs, Narragansetts, and Wampanoags attack Lancaster; take Mary Rowlandson and twenty-two other captives to Menameset.

1676, March: Rowlandson's captors carry her north of Baquag (Miller's) River; rendezvous with Metacom.

1676, April: Narragansett sachem Canonchet dies in battle. Rowlandson returns to central Massachusetts. Battle of Sudbury.

1676, May: Rowlandson released from captivity. Anti-English Indians disperse, some surrendering to English.

1676, June: Rowlandson children reunited with parents in Boston.

1676, July: Most remaining anti-English Indians captured or surrender; many executed or enslaved.

1676, August: Metacom slain; Metacom's War ends.

1677: Rowlandsons move to Wethersfield, Connecticut.

1678: Joseph Rowlandson dies suddenly at the age of forty-seven.

1679: Mary Rowlandson marries Samuel Talcott. Lancaster resettled.

1682: Four editions of Mary Rowlandson's narrative published, with Joseph Rowlandson's final sermon attached.

1689:   War of the League of Augsburg (known in England and its colonies as King William's War) begins, pitting England against France. In North America, both empires use Indian allies. Indian allies of the French in northern New England, including refugees from southern New England colonies after Metacom's War, attack English towns in and near their original homelands.

1691:   Samuel Talcott dies.

1697:   Anti-English Indians attack Haverhill, Massachusetts; capture Hannah Dustin and her family; she leads successful effort to kill and scalp her attackers, and is given hero's welcome in Boston. War of the League of Augsburg ends.

1711:   Mary Rowlandson dies at about the age of 73.

Questions for Consideration

1. What were Rowlandson's reasons for writing a narrative of her captivity? Were some of these reasons more important than others?

2. How does Rowlandson view her own society after her experience as a captive?

3. Which factors does Rowlandson say were most important in enabling her to survive captivity—her religion, her skills as a housewife, pure luck, her treatment by the Indians? Which do you think were most important?

4. How does an understanding of Indian history during the seventeenth century affect your reading of Rowlandson's narrative?

5. For what audience was Rowlandson writing? How do you think her narrative affected their religious beliefs? Their attitudes toward Native Americans? Their attitudes toward their own society?

6. How did Rowlandson's life before her capture affect her experience as a captive?

7. What impact did the prior relationship between Lancaster and Nashaway have on their relations during Metacom's War?

8. Why does Rowlandson place so much emphasis on the praying Indians in her account?

9. In what ways does Rowlandson's narrative provide evidence about Native American experiences during Metacom's War?

10. What does Rowlandson's narrative tell you about New England Puritanism in the late seventeenth century?

11. What difference does Puritanism make in Rowlandson's narrative? How would a non-Puritan's account compare with hers?

12. Although it was not Rowlandson's intention to present them, can you uncover any Indian viewpoints on the English and on Metacom's War from her narrative?

13. How does Rowlandson's experience as a captive and author inform our understanding of women in seventeenth-century New England?

14. How did her experience as a captive affect Rowlandson's life thereafter?

15. How might one of Rowlandson's captors have answered her narrative?

Selected Bibliography

NATIVE AMERICANS
AND THEIR RELATIONS WITH EUROPEANS

Axtell, James. *The Indian and the European: Essays in the Ethnohistory of Colonial North America.* New York: Oxford University Press, 1981.

———. *The Invasion Within: The Contest of Cultures in Colonial North America.* New York: Oxford University Press, 1985.

Bragdon, Kathleen J. *Native People of Southern New England, 1500–1650.* Norman: University of Oklahoma Press, 1996.

Calloway, Colin G. *The Western Abenakis of Vermont, 1600–1800: War, Migration, and the Survival of an Indian People.* Norman: University of Oklahoma Press, 1990.

Cronon, William. *Changes in the Land: Indians, Colonists, and the Ecology of New England.* New York: Hill and Wang, 1983.

Drake, Samuel G. *Biography and History of the Indians of North America, from Its First Discovery.* 11th ed. Boston: Benjamin Mussey, 1851.

Grumet, Robert S., ed. *Northeast Indian Lives: 1632–1816.* Amherst: University of Massachusetts Press, 1996.

Jennings, Francis. *The Invasion of America: Indians, Colonialism, and the Cant of Conquest.* Chapel Hill: University of North Carolina Press, 1975.

Kawashima, Yasuhide. *Puritan Justice and the Indian: White Man's Law in Massachusetts, 1630–1763.* Middletown, Conn.: Wesleyan University Press, 1986.

Lauber, Almon Wheeler. *Indian Slavery in the Colonial Times within the Present Limits of the United States.* 1913; rpt. Williamstown, Mass.: Corner House, 1970.

Leach, Douglas Edward. *Flintlock and Tomahawk: New England in King Philip's War.* New York: Macmillan, 1958.

Lepore, Jill. "The Name of War: Waging, Writing, and Remembering King Philip's War." Ph.D. dissertation, Yale University, 1995.

Malone, Patrick M. *The Skulking Way of War: Technology and Tactics among the New England Indians.* Lanham, Md.: Madison Books, 1991.

Salisbury, Neal. *Manitou and Providence: Indians, Europeans, and the Making of New England, 1500–1643.* New York: Oxford University Press, 1982.

Simmons, William S. *Spirit of the New England Tribes: Indian History and Folklore, 1620–1984.* Hanover, N.H.: University Press of New England, 1986.

Strong, Pauline Turner. "Captivity in White and Red: Convergent Practice and Colonial Representation on the British-Amerindian Frontier, 1606–1736." In Daniel Segal, ed., *Crossing Cultures: Essays in the Displacement of Western Civilization,* edited by Daniel Segal. Tucson: University of Arizona Press, 1992.

Vaughan, Alden T. *New England Frontier: Puritans and Indians, 1620–1675.* 1965. 3rd ed., Norman: University of Oklahoma Press, 1995.

Vaughan, Alden T., and Richter, Daniel K. "Crossing the Cultural Divide: Indians and New Englanders, 1605–1763." *Proceedings of the American Antiquarian Society* 90 (1980), 23–99.

THE NEW ENGLAND COLONISTS

Anderson, Virginia DeJohn. *New England's Generation: The Great Migration and the Formation of Society and Culture in the Seventeenth Century.* Cambridge, Eng.: Cambridge University Press, 1991.

Bailyn, Bernard. *The New England Merchants in the Seventeenth Century.* Cambridge, Mass.: Harvard University Press, 1956.

Breen, T. H. *Puritans and Adventurers: Change and Persistence in Early America.* New York: Oxford University Press, 1980.

Canup, John. *Out of the Wilderness: The Emergence of an American Identity in Colonial New England.* Middletown, Conn.: Wesleyan University Press, 1990.

Cressy, David. *Going Over: Migration and Communication between England and New England in the Seventeenth Century.* Cambridge, Eng.: Cambridge University Press, 1987.

Demos, John. *Little Commonwealth: Family Life in Plymouth Colony.* New York: Oxford University Press, 1970.

———. *The Unredeemed Captive: A Family Story from Early America.* New York: Alfred A. Knopf, 1995.

Hall, David D. *The Faithful Shepard: A History of the New England Ministry in the Seventeenth Century.* Chapel Hill: University of North Carolina Press, 1972.

———. *Worlds of Wonder, Days of Judgment: Popular Religious Belief in Early New England.* New York: Alfred A. Knopf, 1989.

Hall, Michael G. *The Last American Puritan: The Life of Increase Mather, 1639–1723.* Middletown, Conn.: Wesleyan University Press, 1988.

Innes, Stephen. *Creating the Commonwealth: The Economic Culture of Puritan New England.* New York: W. W. Norton, 1995.

Martin, John. *Profits in the Wilderness: Entrepreneurship in the Founding of New England Towns in the Seventeenth Century.* Chapel Hill: University of North Carolina Press, 1991.

Miller, Perry. *Errand into the Wilderness.* Cambridge, Mass.: Harvard University Press, 1956.

Morgan, Edmund S. *The Puritan Family: Religion and Domestic Relations in Seventeenth-Century New England.* 1944; rev., New York: Harper and Row, 1966.

Norton, Mary Beth. *Founding Mothers and Fathers: Gendered Power and the Forming of American Society.* New York: Alfred A. Knopf, 1996.

Ulrich, Laurel Thatcher. *Good Wives: Image and Reality in the Lives of Women in Northern New England, 1650–1750.* New York: Alfred A. Knopf, 1980.

Vickers, Daniel. *Farmers and Fishermen: Two Centuries of Work in Essex County, Massachusetts, 1630–1850.* Chapel Hill: University of North Carolina Press, 1994.

EARLY AMERICAN LITERATURE
AND THE CAPTIVITY NARRATIVE

Breitweiser, Mitchell Robert. *American Puritanism and the Defense of Mourning: Religion, Grief, and Ethnology in Mary White Rowlandson's Captivity Narrative.* Madison: University of Wisconsin Press, 1990.

Castiglia, Christopher. *Bound and Determined: Captivity, Culture-Crossing, and White Womanhood from Mary Rowlandson to Patty Hearst.* Chicago: University of Chicago Press, 1996.

Derounian, Kathryn Zabelle. "Puritan Orthodoxy and the 'Survivor Syndrome' in Mary Rowlandson's Captivity Narrative." *Early American Literature* 22 (1987), 82–93.

Derounian-Stodola, Kathryn Zabelle, and Levernier, James A. *The Indian Captivity Narrative, 1550–1900.* New York: Twayne Publishers, 1993.

Ebersole, Gary L. *Captured by Texts: Puritan to Postmodern Images of Indian Captivity.* Charlottesville: University Press of Virginia, 1995.

Fitzpatrick, Tara. "The Figure of Captivity: The Cultural Work of the Puritan Captivity Narrative." *American Literary History* 3 (1991), 1–26.

Kolodny, Annette. *The Land Before Her: Fantasy and Experience of the American Frontiers, 1630–1860.* Chapel Hill: University of North Carolina Press, 1984.

Minter, David L. "By Dens of Lions: Notes on Stylization in Early Puritan Captivity Narratives." *American Literature* 45 (1973), 335–47.

Namias, June. *White Captives: Gender and Ethnicity on the American Frontier.* Chapel Hill: University of North Carolina Press, 1993.

Pearce, Roy Harvey. *Savagism and Civilization: A Study of the Indian and the American Mind.* 1953; rev., Baltimore: Johns Hopkins University Press, 1965.

———. "The Significances of the Captivity Narrative." *American Literature* 19 (1947), 1–20.

Seelye, John. *Prophetic Waters: The River in Early American Life and Literature.* New York: Oxford University Press, 1977.

Slotkin, Richard. *Regeneration through Violence: The Mythology of the American Frontier, 1600–1800.* Middletown, Conn.: Wesleyan University Press, 1973.

Toulouse, Teresa A. " 'My Own Credit': Strategies of (E)valuation in Mary Rowlandson's Captivity Narrative." *American Literature* 64 (1992), 655–76.

Index